Reading the Song of Songs with St. Thomas Aquinas

THOMISTIC RESSOURCEMENT SERIES

Volume 22

Reading the Song of Songs with St. Thomas Aquinas

SERGE-THOMAS BONINO, OP

TRANSLATED BY ANDREW LEVERING
WITH MATTHEW LEVERING

The Catholic University of America Press
Washington, D.C.

Originally published as *Saint Thomas d'Aquin, lecteur du Cantique des Cantiques*

The paper used in this publication meets the minimum requirements of American National Standards for Information Science—Permanence of Paper for Printed Library Materials, ANSI Z39.48–1984.
∞

Cataloging-in Publication Data is available from the Library of Congress
Hardcover ISBN 9780813235981
eBook ISBN 9780813235998

To Rev. Fr. Jean-Pierre Torrell, OP,

"spiritual master"

Contents

Preface

It is difficult to imagine Immanuel Kant giving himself to the study of Ovid's *The Art of Love.* Similarly, we might be surprised at the improbable meeting between a scholastic master such as Thomas Aquinas (who, moreover, is a saint) and a work of erotic love like the Song of Songs. This surprise would be a mistake, for two reasons. The first is that the Song of Songs is not a masterpiece of erotic literature which has snuck its way into the corpus of the sacred texts of Judaism and Christianity. Without ever underestimating the human value of the passionate love of man and woman, which the poem celebrates, the Jewish and Christian traditions have above all seen in the Song of Songs a "mystical" celebration of the overwhelming love that unites God to His people, the Bridegroom Christ to the Bride Church—and in the Church, to every believer.

The second reason is that friar Thomas Aquinas never lets himself be easily reduced to the conventional figure of the purely speculative philosopher (to which a certain neo-Thomism long succeeded in confining him). He is and claims to be, above all, *Magister in sacra pagina,* master of sacred Scripture. He never rests from lovingly and meticulously scrutinizing Scripture, in the light of Tradition, because Scripture contains and communicates to men and women the wisdom that comes from God and that introduces believers in Christ, Wisdom incarnate, to blessed communion in the Trinitarian mystery. The study we intend to conduct here on the presence of the

Song of Songs in Thomas's corpus will give more attention to this dimension of the teaching of Saint Thomas, as theologian, exegete, and spiritual master. We will come back to this in the conclusion.

This little book still retains traces of its origin: a scholarly search on Saint Thomas's use of citations from the Song. It would have found a place in some erudite journal meant for medievalists or for theologians, but it appeared to me along the way that this investigation was fundamentally appealing to a broader audience than that of scholarly journals, and could maintain its technicality while being presented in an accessible fashion. The present work offers a taste of many beautiful fruits of medieval exegesis, which are always apt, despite (or because of?) their exotic side, to nourish the meditation of today's believer. What is more, this book introduces the tangible meditation on the Word of God that is at the heart of the interior life of this exceptional believer: Saint Thomas Aquinas.

Abbreviations

CCCM	Corpus Christianorum Continuatio Medievalis. Turnhout: Brepols.
CCSL	Corpus Christianorum Series Latina. Turnhout: Brepols.
CSEL	Corpus Scriptorum Ecclesiasticorum Latinorum. Vienna: F. Tempsky; Berlin: De Gruyter.
PG	Patrologia Cursus Completus: Series Graeca. Edited by J.-P. Migne. Paris.
PL	Patrologia Cursus Completus: Series Latina. Edited by J.-P. Migne. Paris.
SC	Sources Chretiennes. Paris: Cerf.

ABBREVIATED TITLES OF WORKS BY ST. THOMAS AQUINAS

Comp. theol.	*Compendium theologiae*
Contra impugnantes	*Liber contra impugnantes Dei cultum et religionem*
In Boet. de Trin.	Super Boetium De Trinitate
In de div. nom.	*Super Librum Dionysii De divinis nominibus*
In Ier.	*Super Ieremiam*
In Ioan.	*Lectura super Iohannem*
In Iob	*Expositio super Iob ad litteram*

In Is.	*Expositio super Isaiam ad litteram*
In Matth.	*Lectura super Matthaeum*
In Ps.	*Postilla super Psalmos*
In Sent.	*Scriptum super Libros Sententiarum*
In Thren.	*In Threnos*
Q. de virt.	*Quaestiones disputatae de virtutibus*
SCG	*Summa contra Gentiles*
ST	*Summa theologiae*

Lectura super S. Pauli epistolas:

In ad Ro.	*Lectura super epistolam ad Romanos*
In 1 ad Co.	*Lectura super I epistolam ad Corinthios*
In 2 ad Co.	*Lectura super II epistolam ad Corinthios*
In ad Ga.	*Lectura super epistolam ad Galatas*
In ad Ep.	*Lectura super epistolam ad Ephesios*
In ad Ph.	*Lectura super epistolam ad Philipenses*
In ad Col.	*Lectura super epistolam ad Colossenses*
In 1 ad Th.	*Lectura super I epistolam ad Thessalonicenses*
In 1 ad Tim.	*Lectura super I epistolam ad Timotheum*
In ad Tit.	*Lectura super epistolam ad Titum*
In ad Philem.	*Lectura super epistolam ad Philemonem*
In ad He.	*Lectura super epistolam ad Hebraeos*

Introduction

William of Tocco, the first biographer of Saint Thomas Aquinas, reports in his *Ystoria* (1323) that some Cistercian monks of Fossanova, who charitably received and cared for the Dominican friar (fallen sick in the middle of his last trip to Lyon), asked of him a "memento of his science." "He then briefly expounded on the Song of Songs." And Tocco comments on it:

"It is suitable that our doctor, at the point of leaving the prison of his body, finished his study of wisdom with the Song of love between the bridegroom and the bride: even as he applied his study to God, he reached to embrace the Lover."[1]

Friar Thomas Aquinas thus concluded his terrestrial existence meditating on this love song, which, according to a well-established tradition, is the expression of the spiritual life of the "perfect"—that is, the spiritual life of those who, after embarking resolutely on the way of "beginners," and having passed through the austere path of "progressors," have attained to the spiritual maturity of charity: they already taste, on earth, some of the joy of the heavenly union of the soul with the Holy Trinity.

The story is beautiful, and it will later be even more beautifully told, in a manner that highlights the humility of the holy Doc-

1. Guillaume de Tocco, *Ystoria sancti Thome de Aquino,* ed. C. Le Brun–Gouanvic (Toronto: Pontifical Institute of Mediaeval Studies, 1996), 196. [Courtesy translation provided by Andrew and Matthew Levering. All translations not otherwise attributed are our own.]

tor.[2] But in fact it has little chance of being authentic: none of the Cistercian monks who testified in 1318 at Naples during his trial for canonization mentioned it. Admittedly, the ancient catalogues of the works of Aquinas, including those that Bartholomew of Capua inserted in his deposition at the trial for canonization,[3] attribute to him a commentary *Super Cantica*; and it is not unlikely that, over the course of his teaching, Saint Thomas had commented on the biblical poem. It would have been nothing exceptional.[4] If this is the case, however, the text is lost. Neither of the two commentaries that have reached us under his name, and that have been reproduced in the editions of his complete works, is his.[5] The first (*Salomon inspiratus divino spiritu*), which according to Sixtus of Siena is the commentary that contains the last testaments of Aquinas at Fossanova, later completed by some scholar (*studiosus*), is found in the *Piana* edition of 1570[6] and is today attributed to Haimo of Auxerre (ninth century).[7] The other (*Sonet vox tua*) is today attributed to Giles of Rome.[8]

2. See Francis de Sales, *Treatise on the Love of God*, trans. Henry Benedict Mackey, OSB (Rockford, Ill.: TAN Books, 1997), 457: "S. Thomas Aquinas, that great star of theology, being sick of the disease of which he died, at the Monastery of Fossanuova, of the order of Citeaux, the religious besought him to make them a short exposition of the Canticle of Canticles in imitation of S. Bernard, and he answered them: My dear fathers, give me S. Bernard's spirit and I will interpret this divine Canticle like S. Bernard." The anecdote comes from Sixtus of Siena (†1569), who identifies the commentary *in extremis* to *Salomon inspiratus*, see Sixtus Senensis, 1. IV, t. 1, in *Bibliotheca sancta ex praecipuis Catholicae Ecclesiae auctoribus* (Naples: Ex Typographia Mutiana, 1742), 484.

3. See Marie-Hyacinth Laurent, ed., *Fontes vitae S. Thomae Aquinatis, fasc. IV. Processus canonizationis S. Thomae Neapoli* (Saint-Maximin: Revue Thomiste, 1937), 388.

4. Many Dominican masters of the thirteenth century (Guerric of Saint-Quentin, William of Alton, Peter of Tarentaise, and others) commented on the Song. See Helmut Riedlinger, *Die Makellosogkeit der Kirche in den lateinischen Hohelied-kommentaren des Mittelsalters* (Münster: Aschendorff, 1958), 268–311.

5. See Thomas Aquinas, "Praefatio," p. 1* n. 2, in *Expositio super Iob ad litteram*, Leonine edition, vol. 26 (Rome: Ad Sanctae Sabinae, 1965); Wilhelm Vrede, *Die beiden dem hl. Thomas von Aquin zugeschrieben Kommentare zum Hohen Liede* (Berlin: Germania, 1903).

6. *Tomus tertiusdecimus divi Thomae Aquinatis doctoris angelici complectens Expositionem in Iob, In primam Davidis quinquagenam, In Cantica canticorum, In Esaiam, In Ieremiam et in Threnos* (Rome: Apud Iulium Accoltum, 1570), fol. 70v–80r.

7. See Raffaele Savigni, "Il commentario di Aimone di Auxerre al Cantico dei cantici e le sue fonti," in *Il Cantico dei cantici nel Medioevo*, ed. Rossana E. Guglielmetti (Florence: Sismel, 2008), 189–225.

8. Thomas Aquinas, *In Canticum canticorum exposition altera*, in *Sancti Thomae*

Yet, even if Thomas Aquinas probably never commented on the Song of Songs, he meditated on it, prayed on it (in the liturgy as in personal prayer), and absorbed it, so that the words of the Song are for him familiar and come spontaneously to his lips or his pen.[9] Admittedly, Saint Thomas is not Saint Bernard, who had so assimilated the language of the Scriptures that it became his habitual mode of expression. Nevertheless, we find in the Angelic Doctor's work numerous explicit citations of the biblical poem, not counting the implicit borrowings of vocabulary and images from the Song.[10] I have noted, in addition to two references to the Song in general,[11] 312 citations of the Song in the whole of Thomas's corpus, to which can be added those that are included in citations that Saint Thomas

Aquinatis doctoris angelici Ordinis Praedicatorum opera omnia, vol. 14 (Parma: Typis P. Fiaccadori, 1863), 387–426. *Sonet vox tua* is attributed to Saint Thomas by Sixtus of Siena (*Bibliotheca sancta*, 1. IV, t. I, 484). Francesco Del Punta, Silvia Donati, and Concetta Luna, the authors of the article "Egidio Romano" in *Dizionario biografico degli Italiani*, vol. 42 (Rome: Istituto dell'Enciclopedia Italiana, 1993), 319–41, at 331, place the *Super Cantica* of Giles of Rome in the first period of his teaching, before 1277–1278.

9. See Jean-Pierre Torrell, OP, "Quand saint Thomas méditait sur le prophète Isaïe," *Recherches thomasiennes* (Paris: J. Vrin, 2000), 242–81, at 249: "This shows at least that he is familiar with the *Song*: we already know that it is one of the most quoted books after the Psalms in his *collationes*.... If Saint Thomas had not commented on the *Song* in his last days, the story of Tocco would still contain at least a part of truth since it underlines his predilection for this biblical book."

10. For example, in Sermon 18 (collation) [no. 120'] [the numbers in between square brackets refer to the numbering of quotations in appendix 1], when Saint Thomas says regarding the wood of the Cross that it is like the litter of Solomon (*ferculum Salomonis*), the reference to Song 3:9 is clear but implicit. Likewise in Thomas Aquinas, *Lectura super Iohannem* [*In Ioan.*], c. 19, lect. 6 (n° 2468) [no. 152'] Saint Thomas observes: "Christ was arrested in a garden, underwent his agony in a garden, and was buried in a garden. This indicates to us that by the power of Christ's passion we are freed from the sin which Adam committed in the Garden of delights, and that through Christ the Church is made holy, the Church, which itself is like a garden enclosed." *Commentary on the Gospel of John: Chapters 13–21*, trans. Fabian Larcher, OP, and James A. Weisheipl, OP, ed. Daniel A. Keating and Matthew Levering (Washington, D.C.: The Catholic University of America Press, 2010), 251. The description of the Church as a "garden enclosed" refers implicitly to Song 4:12.

11. See Thomas Aquinas, *Principium "Hic est liber mandatorum Dei"* (n° 1207) [no. 313] (trans. Ralph McInerny under the title "Commendation of and Division of Sacred Scripture," in *Thomas Aquinas: Selected Writings*, ed. Ralph McInerny [London: Penguin, 1998], 5–12); *Expositio super Isaiam ad litteram* [*In Is.*], *In Prol. S. Iheronimi* (p. 5) [no. 314].

makes of other authors, especially in the *Catena aurea*.[12] The full list, as well as the Latin texts with their contexts, is in the first appendix of the present book. The great majority of these 312 citations (251, approximately 80 percent) are found in his scriptural commentaries. His commentaries on Old Testament books contain 111 citations of the Song: *Expositio super Isaiam ad litteram* (62, with 8 in the *collaciones* studied by J.-P. Torrell[13]); *Postilla super Psalmos* (36); *Super Ieremiam* (10); *In Threnos* (2)[14]; and *Expositio super Iob ad litteram* (1). His commentaries on the New Testament books contain 140 citations of the Song: *Lectura super S. Pauli epistolas* (64); *Lectura super Iohannem* (42); and *Lectura super Matthaeum* (34). The various *Sermons*, including those recently edited by the Leonine Commission, contain 25 citations of the Song (8 percent of the total). As for the theological syntheses, they struggle to collect 25 citations (14 in the *Summa theologiae*, 7 in the *Scriptum*, only 2 in the *Summa contra Gentiles*, and 2 in the *Compendium theologiae*). Finally, there are a few scattered citations in Q. 2 (*De caritate*) of *Quaestiones disputatae de virtutibus* (4), in the commentary on *Divine Names* by Dionysius (2), in *Contra impugnantes Dei cultum* (2), in *De perfectione vitae spiritualis* (1), and in the Office of the Blessed Sacrament (1).[15]

12. I counted twenty-two "included" citations, of which eighteen are in the *Catena aurea* (eleven in the *Catena in Matthaeum*). The others are found in the citations of Saint Bernard or of Saint Jerome.

13. See Torrell, "Quand saint Thomas méditait sur le prophète Isaïe."

14. According to Jean-Pierre Torrell, OP, *Initiation à saint Thomas d'Aquin*, vol. 1: *Sa personne et son œuvre* (Paris: Cerf, 2015), 446 [*Saint Thomas Aquinas*, vol. 1, *The Person and His Work*, 3rd ed., trans. R. Royal and M. Minerd (Washington, D.C.: The Catholic University of America Press, 2022), 398], this commentary on Lamentations "is probably not authentic."

15. The absence of a critical edition for most of Saint Thomas's works in which are concentrated the quotations of the Song, especially the commentaries on the New Testament, unfortunately affects our research with a certain coefficient of imprecision. We also know that Saint Thomas, like his contemporaries, quoted only the first words of the biblical text to which he referred, leaving to his listeners or readers, familiar with the biblical text, the task of completing them. Sometimes even the key word that justifies the quote is not transcribed. See *In Is.*, c. 53 [no. 95]: "Now he did indeed have beauty: *you are beautiful above the sons of men* (Ps 44:3), but it lay concealed, on account of his assumed infirmity. He [also] had beauty: *strength and beauty are in her clothing* (Prov 31:25),

The use of citations of the Bible in Thomas's corpus needs to be understood correctly. In the works of theological synthesis, such as the *Summa theologiae*, a scriptural citation is not simply a literary ornament.[16] No matter in which part of the article it appears, it plays a role in the argumentative process: it allows a doctrine to be established or even confirmed. For example, in the *sed contra* of *Summa theologiae* [*ST*] III, q. 27, a. 3, Song 4:7 (where a Marian interpretation is presupposed) serves as a major premise for a short syllogism that allows Thomas, by leaning on the authority of Scripture, to exclude from the Virgin Mary the existence of the fomes of sin (*fomes peccati*), that is, the disorder of faculties resulting from original sin:

> On the contrary, it is written (Song 4:7): *Thou art all fair, O my love, and there is not a spot in thee!* But the fomes implies a blemish, at any rate in the flesh. Therefore the fomes was not in the Blessed Virgin.[17]

Most of the time, however, the citation of the Song comes primarily to confirm a doctrine established by other means. For example, in *ST* I-II, q. 68, a. l, regarding the distinction between the virtues and the gifts of the Holy Spirit, Saint Thomas rejects the idea that the existence of the gifts is justified by the specific need to repel the temptations contrary to the virtues. He makes the point that the virtues, especially charity, are capable by themselves of opposing their contraries, and he supports this claim with Song 8:7:

---

but it lay concealed, on account of the poverty he assumed. Hence: *let your voice sound in my ears* (Song 2:14)." All translations of *In Is.* are taken from Joshua Madden, "Saint Thomas Aquinas's *Expositio super Isaiam*: Introduction, Translation, and Notes" (PhD diss., Ave Maria University, 2017). The meaning of the reference to the Song stays enigmatic until we complete the quotation of Song 2:14 with the words that immediately follow, particularly: "and thy face comely [*Facies tua decora*]." The majority of modern editions believe it best to complete the quotations, or to insert in the edited text the exact reference according to the standards of their times.

16. See Wilhelmus G. B. M. Valkenberg, *Words of the Living God: Place and Function of Holy Scripture in the Theology of St Thomas Aquinas* (Leuven: Peeters, 2000). See also Matthew Levering, *Paul in the "Summa Theologiae"* (Washington, D.C.: The Catholic University of America Press, 2014).

17. Thomas Aquinas, *Summa Theologica* [*ST*], trans. Fathers of the English Dominican Province (Westminster, Md.: Christian Classics, 1981), III, q. 27, a. 3, s.c. [no. 136].

Because the virtues also resist those temptations which lead to the sins that are contrary to the virtues; for everything naturally resists its contrary: which is especially clear with regard to charity, of which it is written (Song 8:7): *Many waters cannot quench charity.*[18]

In the biblical commentaries, which contain the great majority of the citations of the Song, their purpose is different.[19] Most of the time, the citation is invited by an association of words: the same word appears in the passage commented upon (or in the theme developed) and in the text of the Song, which is quoted as support. Often, the citation of the Song is simply juxtaposed, without any explanation, with the passage or the theme under consideration. What is the purpose of such a citation, which could appear artificial? Sometimes it acts to clarify the *littera* or meaning of the passage by offering, through the text of the Song, a lexicographical, topographical, historical, ethnographic, or cultural explanation.[20] For example, the words of the Song about feminine finery can allow for better understanding of other passages of Scripture, including the diatribe of Isaiah against the provoking luxury of the women of Zion (Is 3:16–24),[21] or the references of Saint Paul to the care a person takes in clothing the members of the body.[22]

18. *ST* I-II, q. 68, a. 1 [no. 290].

19. See Gilbert Dahan, "Introduction: Exégèse et théologie dans le commentaire de Thomas d'Aquin sur la Seconde Épître aux Corinthiens," in Thomas Aquinas, *Commentaire de la Deuxième* Épître *aux Corinthiens*, trans. J.-É. Stroobant de Saint-Éloy, OSB (Paris: Cerf, 2005), i–xli, at xvii–xxiii ("Fonctions des citations scriptuaires"); Piotr Roszak, "The Place and Function of Biblical Citations in Thomas Aquinas's Exegesis," in *Reading Sacred Scripture with Thomas Aquinas: Hermeneutical Tools, Theological Questions and New Perspectives*, ed. Piotr Roszak and Jörgen Vijgen (Turnhout: Brepols, 2015), 115–39.

20. See, on the definition of the watches of the night, Thomas Aquinas, *In Threnos* [*In Thren.*], c. 2, 19 [no. 114]; on the fortifications of Jerusalem, *In Is.*, c. 22 [no. 132].

21. Saint Thomas explains the meaning of the word *murenulae* (chain, little necklace) that Isaiah uses to describe the luxurious finery of the women of Jerusalem in referring to the Song 1:10, which uses the same term. See *In Is.*, c. 3 [no. 44]: "a certain kind of chain of silver rods and inlaid with gold in the fashion of a necklace, which is placed around the neck: *we will make you chains of gold, inlaid with silver* (Song 1:10)." See also *In Is.*, c. 3 [no. 241]; *In Is.*, c. 3 [no. 22].

22. See Thomas Aquinas, *Lectura super I epistolam ad Corinthios* [*In 1 ad Co.*], c. 12, lect. 3 (n° 748) [no. 240]. All translations of *In 1 ad Co.* are taken from *Commentary on*

Yet, there is much more in these associations of biblical verses, even if this may confuse those who think Aquinas's thought can be reduced to the chains of univocal reasons of which modern rationalism is fond. Saint Thomas has a fundamental conviction that sacred Scripture is one, and that by virtue of the principle of the unity of its inspiration, God being the *auctor principalis*, "the Bible makes up a homogenous whole in which the parts answer, clarify, and explain each other."[23] The typological reading of the Old Testament in light of the mystery of Christ manifested in the New Testament is only one realization, though an exemplary one, of this principle of unity. Thus, according to Piotr Roszak, the goal of these textual associations "is to deploy the hermeneutical context that reveals all the dimensions of the theme under consideration."[24] A biblical text, as a fragment of a whole, does not give up its full meaning except in the context of the whole Bible, which is the expression of the divine Wisdom and its designs. The citations therefore have the purpose of bringing the text into resonance with this ensemble and of placing the text into relation with the entirety of the "Mystery." Is this not, moreover, the meaning of the interpretation called "mystical"? Through the interplay of citations and internal references, the reader is placed "in the broad context of the history of salvation"[25] that permits him or her to perceive the fullness of meaning and theological density of the text. Given that the Song of Songs is the celebration of the union of love between Christ and the Church, Saint Thomas, by returning us to the Song through the use of citations, implicitly places the particular text on which he is commenting within the "mystical" horizon of the wedding of the Lamb, which governs the entire economy of salvation.

the Letters of Saint Paul to the Corinthians, trans. F. R. Larcher, OP (Lander, Wyo.: The Aquinas Institute for the Study of Sacred Doctrine, 2012). See also, regarding hair and the veil, *In 1 ad Co.*, c. 11, lect. 3 (n° 619) [no. 127].

23. Dahan, "Introduction," xvii.

24. Roszak, "The Place and Function of Biblical Citations in Thomas Aquinas's Exegesis," 120.

25. Roszak, "The Place and Function of Biblical Citations in Thomas Aquinas's Exegesis," 135.

Because Saint Thomas reads the Song in a tradition that precedes and upholds him, the use that he makes of citations of the Song is sometimes suggested to him by the sources from which he draws. Among these, Saint Thomas many times makes reference to a "gloss."[26] This is usually the *Glossa ordinaria in Canticum*, whose editor, Mary Dove, attributes it to the school of Laon at the beginning of the twelfth century, particularly to Anselm of Laon and to his brother Ralph.[27] The *Glossa Ordinaria* establishes an important interpretive background for Thomas's use of citations of the Song. It puts Aquinas into direct contact with the commentaries of Origen, Bede the Venerable,[28] and some others. In addition, Saint Thomas has also read the *Sermons on the Song of Songs* by Saint Bernard of Clairvaux, from which he quotes often in his work.[29] In a sermon on the Virgin Mary, for instance, he takes a passage from Bernard's sermon for the nativity of Mary titled "The Aqueduct," itself immersed in words from the Song.[30] Similarly, when commenting on Isaiah, Thomas refers explicitly to Bernard's interpretation of the "clefts in the rock" where the dove nestles (Song 2:14): these clefts signify the wounds of Christ, where the believer finds refuge.[31] This interpretation is found elsewhere in the *Glossa Ordinaria*,[32] and, as Saint Ber-

26. See [no. 59]; [no. 62]; [no. 69]; [no. 104]; [no. 125]; [no. 225]; [no. 310]. On the notion of "gloss," see Dahan, *L'Exégèse chrétienne de la Bible en Occident médiéval: XII*e–*XIV*e *siècle* (Paris: Cerf, 1999), 123–29.

27. *The Glossa Ordinaria on the Song of Songs*, trans. Mary Dove (Kalamazoo, Mich.: Medieval Institute Publications, 2004). We can identify, in addition to the explicit references to the *Glossa ordinaria*, mentioned in the previous note, the implicit references, see [no. 107]. On the *Glossa ordinaria*, see Jenny Swanson, "The *Glossa Ordinaria*," in *The Medieval Theologians: An Introduction to Theology in the Medieval Period*, ed. G. R. Evans (Oxford: Blackwell, 2001), chap. 10; Lesley Smith, *The "Glossa ordinaria": The Making of a Medieval Bible Commentary* (Boston: Brill, 2009).

28. Bede the Venerable, *In Cantica canticorum*, in Bede, *Opera exegetica* 2B, ed. J. E. Hudson and D. Hurst, Corpus Christianorum Series Latina [CCSL] 119B (Turnhout: Brepols, 1983), 166–375.

29. See Thomas Aquinas, *Scriptum super Libros Sententiarum* II [*In* II *Sent.*], d. 43, q. 1, a. 5, obj. 1 (p. 1107); *In* IV *Sent.*, d. 50, q. 2, a. 1, qlc. 2, obj. 1 (p. 1252); *ST* I, q. 51, a. 1, obj. 1; *Quaetiones de spiritualibus creaturis*, a. 5, obj. 3.

30. See Thomas Aquinas, *The Academic Sermons*, trans. Mark-Robin Hoogland, CP (Washington, D.C.: The Catholic University of America Press, 2010), 244–45 [no. 152"].

31. *In Is.*, c. 2 (p. 23) [no. 93].

32. See *The Glossa ordinaria on the Song of Songs*, II, 132 (p. 56).

nard himself indicates, it comes from an "other," in this case one of the first Latin commentators of the Song, Apponius (first half of the fifth century), whom Saint Bernard knew through Saint Bede.[33]

Origen, the great commentator on the Song who influenced the entire Christian tradition of its interpretation, is mentioned many times by Saint Thomas in connection with a citation of the Song, in the *Catena aurea* as well as in other scriptural commentaries. Yet, Saint Thomas draws Origen's interpretations of the Song from Origen's commentary on the Gospel of Saint Matthew, rather than directly from his commentary on the Song.[34]

The indispensable task of identifying the sources should not lead us astray. This is analogous to the free act of a human person. Once an act is done, it is always possible and even very useful to reconstruct its development and identify the factors that influenced it and that explain it in part. But a free act is in itself irreducible to its conditionings. It is a kind of creation. It introduces something new. In the same way, Saint Thomas's placing of a verse of the Song into relation with other biblical texts or with a given theological doctrine sometimes has antecedents (as one would expect), but very often it is original and resists archeological reduction. Saint Thomas does not

33. See Bernard of Clairvaux, "Sermon 61," in *On the Song of Songs III*, trans. Kilian Walsh, OCSO, and Irene M. Edmonds (Kalamazoo, Mich.: Cistercian Publications, 1979), 142. Also Apponius, *Commentaire sur le Cantique des cantiques*, vol. 2, *Books IV–VIII*, Sources Chrétiennes [SC] 421 (Paris: Cerf, 1997), 50–57. The reference to 1 Cor 10:4—"the rock was Christ"—is already found in Apponius's work.

34. Regarding Mt 21:46, on the chief priests and the Pharisees who seek to lay hands on Jesus to arrest him, Origen distinguishes two manners of seizing Jesus, that of his enemies and that of the beloved of the Song (Song 3:4 and 7:8). This use of the Song is found in the *Catena in Matthaeum*, c. 21, 7 [no. 118'] and [no. 248'] and Saint Thomas is inspired by it twice in his commentary of John: *In Ioan.*, c. 7, lect. 3 (n° 1067) [no. 247]; c. 7, lect. 5 (n° 1104) [no. 248]. Another use of Origen's commentary on Matthew, connected with the Song (but, here, by Saint Thomas and not by Origen), is found in *Lectura super Matthaeum* [*In Matth.*], c. 25, 1 (n° 2017) [no. 8], regarding the parable of the ten virgins: "According to Origen, the oil signifies holy teaching; *your name is as oil poured out* (Song 1:2). The oil of justice signifies right teaching; *your words have I hidden in my heart* (Ps 118:11). Hence those are called virgins who preserve continence, who show mercy, who seek interior joy, who take up right teaching." All translations of *In Matth.* are taken from Thomas Aquinas, *Commentary on the Gospel of Matthew*, trans. J. Holmes and B. Mortenson (Lander, Wyo.: The Aquinas Institute for the Study of Sacred Doctrine, 2013).

content himself with mechanically applying an already-established corpus of interpretations of the Song to theological or exegetical use. His own faith-filled meditation on Scripture and on the Fathers, his immersion in the liturgy of the Church, and his deeply personal intellectual and spiritual history constitute a "living milieu" from which arises the flash of understanding. Consequently, the ever-incomplete cataloguing of sources that could have inspired Thomas's use of citations from the Song does not aim to dissect a corpse or to reduce it to its simple components, but rather aims better to understand a living person.

Lastly, we note the polyvalence of images and associations of ideas in the scriptural commentaries. A text's depths of meaning do not run dry in one single and univocal application. For instance, the "thousand bucklers hung from the tower of David" (Song 4:4) evoke the arguments, authorities, and examples with which the Fathers defend the Church's faith—and, equally well, the always available aid procured by the Virgin Mary.[35] Even more, one same image can take on opposite meanings according to the context of its application. The winds invoked by the beloved—the north wind and south wind that blow on her garden (Song 4:16)—sometimes signify the Holy Spirit, because of the heat (love) that the south wind diffuses that makes the garden fruitful, and sometimes signify the devil, because of the violence of the north wind that impedes the garden's fruitfulness.[36]

When serving as an argument from authority in the synthetic works or as a gateway to the global meaning of Scripture in the biblical commentaries, the citation of the Song also constitutes—particularly in Saint Thomas's sermons—a foundation for moral and spiritual exhortation. This happens when, according to the tropological or moral sense, the biblical text indicates the manner in which

35. See *In Sent.*, Prol., div. text. (p. 335) [no. 129]; Thomas Aquinas, *Super Ieremiam* [*In Ier.*], c. 1, 5 [no. 130]; *Collaciones in salutationem angelicam* (n° 1118) [no. 133].

36. See *In Ier.*, c. 1 [no. 156]; *In Ier.*, c. 13, 2 (p. 612) [no. 157]; *In Matth.*, c. 12, lect. 3 (n° 1058) [no. 156]; *In Ier.*, c. 13, 2 [no. 157]; *In Matth.*, c. 12, lect. 3 (n° 1058) [no. 158].

the believer should integrate himself or herself into the mystery of Christ.[37]

The immediate and specific objective of this book is to study Saint Thomas Aquinas's use of certain themes and images from the Song of Songs. In order to do this, we will begin by exploring the general tradition of interpretation of the Song to which Saint Thomas belongs and which he makes explicit through scattered indications in his work. He sees in the Song a prophetic celebration of the wedding of Christ and the Church, from which emerges a spiritual teaching addressed first and foremost to the "perfect" (chap. 1). We will then focus our attention on each of the two principal protagonists of the drama of the Song: the lover and the beloved. The lover is the figure of Jesus Christ (chap. 2). Regarding the beloved, her figure lends itself to a triple identification. She is firstly and fundamentally the Church, the Spouse of Christ, without stain or wrinkle, one in her diversity (chap. 3). Within this first identification, she can also signify the blessed Virgin Mary (chap. 4) and, ultimately, every faithful soul who strives for the perfection of the love of God (chap. 5).

37. See for example, Thomas Aquinas, "*Exiit Qui Seminat*," in *The Academic Sermons*, 120 [no. 107]; idem, "*Beatus Vir*," in *The Academic Sermons*, 323–24 [no. 119].

1

The General Meaning of the *Song of Songs*

Saint Thomas reads the Song of Songs in an ecclesial tradition of interpretation already firmly established in his day.[1] Exegetes will long debate the original meaning of this poem (or collection of poems): was it a "profane" exaltation of human love or, from the beginning, a symbolic celebration of the love of God for his people? In any case, the Synagogue, if only by integrating the Song into the biblical "canon," had already oriented in a decisive way the reading of the Song as a celebration of the love between God and his people Israel—the human love of man and woman lending itself comfortably to this analogy, as stands out in the teaching of the prophets, beginning with that of Hosea.[2]

1. On the history of interpretation of the Song, see, among others, Anne-Marie Pelletier, *Lectures du Cantique des cantiques: De l'énigme du sens aux figures du lecteur* (Rome: Gregorian University Press, 1989); Henri Crouzel, SJ, introduction to Origen's *Commentaire sur le Cantique des Cantiques*, trans. L. Brésard and H. Crouzel with M. Borret (Paris: Cerf, 1991); Roland E. Murphy, O.Carm., "History of Interpretation," in *The Song of Songs: A Commentary of the Book of Canticles or the Song of Songs* (Minneapolis, Minn.: Fortress, 1990), 11–14; Anne-Marie Pelletier, "Petit bilan herméneutique de l'histoire du Cantique," in *Regards croises sur le Cantique des cantiques*, ed. J.-M. Auwers (Brussels: Lessius, 2005), 130–47.

2. On the current state of exegetical research on the Song, see, for example, Association catholique française pour l'étude de la Bible, *Les nouvelles voies de l'exégèse: En lisant le Cantique des cantiques* (Paris: Cerf, 2002); Anselm C. Hagedorn, ed., *Perspectives on the Song of Songs* (New York: De Gruyter, 2005); Jean-Marie Auwers, ed., *Regards croisés sur le Cantique des cantiques* (Brussels: Lessius, 2005); Ludger Schwienhorst-Schönberger, "Das

The Fathers of the Church take up this interpretation in Christianizing it. The Song celebrates the "marriage of the Lamb" (Rev 19:7); it announces the nuptial union of Jesus Christ and the Church, a central theme of the New Testament, in which Jesus repeatedly presents himself or is presented as the Bridegroom, and in which the union of man and woman becomes the sacrament par excellence of the indissoluble union of Christ and the Church.[3] The commentary of Origen, around 240 A.D., defines for all posterity the key features of this Christian interpretation of the Song.[4] Tracing the effects of Origen's ideas in the medieval Latin tradition, Henri de Lubac writes:

> It is, moreover, Origen's commentary on the Song of Songs that established the mystical interpretation of this book once and for all. By "mystical" here is meant the double meaning of the word, both exegetical and spiritual. This was the interpretation that was so profoundly incorporated into the tradition of the Church.[5]

Several principles stated in the Prologue of Origen's commentary are taken up again in the *Prothemata* of the *Glossa ordinaria on the Song*, and, later, in the Prologue of the *Postilla on the Song* by the Do-

Hohelied," in *Einleitung in das Alte Testament*, 8th ed., ed. Erich Zenger (Stuttgart: W. Kohlhammer GmbH, 2011), 474–83.

3. See Mt 9:15; 25:6; Jn 3:29; 2 Cor 11:2; Eph 5:21–33. George Sabra (*Thomas Aquinas' Vision of the Church: Fundamentals of an Ecumenical Ecclesiology* [Mainz: Matthias-Grünewald-Verlag, 1987], 34–35), who mentions the designation of the Church as Spouse in the works of Saint Thomas, nevertheless maintains that the symbol does not play a true role in the "scientific" ecclesiology of Saint Thomas. The matter deserves to be reexamined.

4. Origen, *The Song of Songs: Commentary and Homilies*, trans. R. P. Lawson (New York: Paulist Press, 1988). Nothing indicates a direct reading of the commentary of Origen by Saint Thomas, but the principal themes of Origen's commentary have reached him through multiple channels, including the *Glossa ordinaria* on the Song.

5. Henri de Lubac, SJ, *Medieval Exegesis: The Four Senses of Scripture*, vol. 1, trans. Mark Sebanc (Grand Rapids, Mich.: Eerdmans, 1998), 170–71. Pages 142–59 are devoted to the principles of Origen's exegesis and to their posterity, and pages 161–224 to "The Reading of Origen in the Middle Ages." Starting from Saint Gregory of Elvira (fourth century), Origenian exegesis of the Song spread in the Latin West (see 156) and Origen is read "particularly on the Hexateuch and on the Song of Songs, with the same tractable diligence as Ambrose on the life of the Patriarchs and David, as Augustine on the Psalms, and as Gregory on Ezekiel and the Book of Job" (159).

minican Hugh of Saint-Cher (†1263).[6] The latter text, which owes much to the *Glossa ordinaria*, reflects the state of Dominican exegesis of the Song at the time when Saint Thomas began his work. It will serve us as a reference or guide to the background of Thomas's interpretation of the Song.[7]

THE PROLOGUE OF THE *POSTILLA* OF HUGH OF SAINT-CHER

The Prologue of Hugh's *Postilla on the Song* combines the literary genre of a prologue based on a scriptural theme with the genre of a prologue of the form *accessus*, which is a systematic introduction.[8] It

6. See Hugo de Sancto Charo [Hugh of Saint-Cher], *Postillae in Bibliam*, vol. 3, *In libros Proverbiorum, Ecclesiastae, Canticorum, Sapientiae, Ecclesiastici* (Venice: Pezzana, 1703). The Latin text of the Prologue to the Postilla on the Song is transcribed in appendix 2 of the present book. On Hugh of Saint-Cher, see above all L.-J Bataillon, OP, G. Dahan, and P.-M. Gy, OP, eds., *Hugues de Saint-Cher (1263), bibliste et théologien* (Turnhout: Brepols, 2004).

7. On the exegesis of the Song of Songs in the Middle Ages, see E. Ann Matter, *The Voice of My Beloved: The Song of Songs in Western Medieval Christianity* (Philadelphia: University of Pennsylvania Press, 1990); R. A. Norris, Jr., ed., *The Song of Songs: Interpreted by Early Christian and Medieval Commentators*, trans. R. A. Norris, Jr. (Grand Rapids, Mich.: Eerdmans, 2003); Guy Lobrichon, "Espaces de lecture du Cantique des cantiques dans l'Occident médiéval (IXe–XVe siècle)," in Association catholique française pour l'étude de la Bible, *Les nouvelles voies de l'exégèse*, 197–216; Rossana E. Guglielmetti, ed., *Il Cantico dei cantici nel Medioevo* (Florence: Sismel, 2008); Hannah W. Matis, *The Song of Songs in the Early Middle Ages* (Leiden: Brill, 2019). The studies on the Song in the Middle Ages focus on the period from the sixth to the twelfth century, which marks a kind of peak. See Carlo Dezzuto, "Il Cantico dei cantici nel XII secolo: Una presenza davvero significativa," *Studia monastica* 48 (2006): 59–99; Rossana E. Guglielmetti, *La tradizione manoscritta dei commenti latini al Cantico dei cantici (origini–XII secolo): Repertorio dei codici contenenti testi inediti o editi solo nella "patrologia latina"* (Florence: Sismel, 2006); David N. Bell, "Twelfth-Century Commentaries on the Song of Songs and the Nature of Monastic Spirituality: A Reassessment," in Guglielmetti, *Il Cantico dei cantici nel Medioevo*, 371–96; Suzanne LaVere, *Out of the Cloister: Monastic Exegesis of the Song of Songs 1100–1250* (Leiden: Brill, 2016). The place of the Song in the religious literature of the thirteenth century is more neglected. See nevertheless H. Riedlinger, *Die Makellosogkeit der Kirche*, 237–334; Gilbert Dahan, "Recherches sur l'exégèse du Cantique au XIIIe siècle," in Guglielmetti, *Il Cantico dei cantici nel Medioevo*, 493–536.

8. On the literary genre of the Prologue, see Gilbert Dahan, "l'exégèse de Hughes: Méthode et herméneutique," in Bataillon, Dahan, and Gy, *Hugues de Saint-Cher*, 65–99, at 70–73: "Les prologues."

opens with a short quotation of Psalm 47:4, drawn from a liturgical reading, which evokes a gradation in the knowledge of God. This allows Hugh of Saint-Cher to introduce a central theme of Origen's exegesis: the Song of Songs takes its place in the ensemble of the biblical books attributed to Solomon (Proverbs, Ecclesiastes, and the Song) and it constitutes, in this context, the completion of the spiritual itinerary outlined by these three books, which correspond to the three ages of the spiritual life:

"God shall be known in his degrees" (Ps 47:4). So it says in another version, where ours reads: "God shall be known in his houses." Now the degrees are three: initial wisdom, advanced wisdom, and perfected wisdom. By this threefold wisdom, as by three degrees, one ascends to the knowledge of God. In the first degree are the beginners; in the second, the proficient; in the third, the perfect. The first degree of Wisdom teaches one to use the world in a good and licet fashion. The second, to despise the world, and to trample it underfoot in a good and useful way. The third, to be delighted only by the embraces and kisses of the Bridegroom. We ascend to the first degree in Proverbs and to the second degree in Ecclesiastes; and this book [= the Song] teaches us to ascend to the third. So Solomon wrote these three books according to the three degrees of wisdom. The Proverbs, where he teaches and instructs children and beginners how they should live peacefully in the world and abstain from evil. For this reason, it says there, "Wisdom cries without: 'How long, O children, will you love childhood, and fools desire that which is harmful to them: and the imprudent hate knowledge? Turn at my reproach, etc.'" In Ecclesiastes, he instructs the advanced, and those who are nigh well grown, about despising the world. For this reason he begins: "Vanity of vanity, etc." In the Song of Songs he instructs the mature and perfect concerning the one love, wherefore, beginning from the kiss, which is the sign of love, he says: "*Let him kiss me with the kisses of his mouth.*"[9]

The Song is then the book of the "perfect," for whom perfection essentially consists in love. Later in the Prologue, while discussing the meaning of the title of the book, Hugh revisits the logic that

9. Hugh of Saint-Cher, *Postilla super Cantica canticorum*, Prologue (fol. 105v) (unpublished English translation by Benjamin Martin). The reading "Deus in gradibus" comes, according to Dahan, from the Roman Psalter. See Dahan, "Recherches sur l'exégèse du Cantique," 505n36.

TABLE 1.1

	The book is addressed to . . .	God is . . .	Solomon speaks as a . . .
Proverbs	Actives	Loved as a Father	Moralist
Ecclesiastes	Those who pass from action to contemplation	Honored as a Physician	Physician
Song of Songs	Contemplatives	Desired as a Spouse	Theologian

governs the succession of the books of Solomon, and he establishes a system of correspondences that can be illustrated as in table 1.

Most of these themes and correspondences are already conveyed in the *Glossa ordinaria* and come from chapter 3 of Origen's Prologue. This chapter begins with the division of philosophy (common among the Greeks) into ethics (*moralis*), physics (*naturalis*), and epoptics (*inspectiva*), which consists in the intellectual contemplation of divine realities.[10] In line with the well-known topos of the "theft of the Greeks," Origen suggests that this division of philosophy was borrowed from the wise Solomon and, through him, from God himself.[11] In any case, Origen establishes a correspondence between the three sections of philosophy and the three books of Solomon:

[5] Wishing, therefore, to distinguish one from another those three branches of learning, which we called general just now—that is, the moral, the natural, and the inspective, and to differentiate between them, Solomon issued them in three books, arranged in their proper order. [6] First, in Proverbs he taught the moral science, putting rules for living into the form of short and pithy maxims, as was fitting. Secondly, he covered the science known as natural in Ecclesiastes; in this, by discussing at length the things of nature, and by distinguishing the useless and vain from the profitable and essential, he counsels us to forsake vanity and cultivate

10. See Sandro Leanza, "La classificazione dei libri salomonici e i suoi riflessi sulla questione dei rapporti tra Bibbia e scienze profane, da Origene agli scrittori medievali," *Augustinianum* 14, no. 3 (1974): 651–66.

11. See Origen, Prol. 3, in *The Song of Songs: Commentary and Homilies*, 40: "It seems to me, then, that all the sages of the Greeks borrowed these ideas from Solomon, who had learnt them by the Spirit of God at an age and time long before their own."

things useful and upright. [7] The inspective science likewise he has propounded in this little book that we have now in hand—that is, the Song of Songs. In this he instills into the soul the love of things divine and heavenly, using for his purpose the figure of the Bride and Bridegroom, and teaches us that communion with God must be attained by the paths of charity and love.[12]

For Origen, the three books are not simply juxtaposed, but rather they constitute the three stages of a spiritual journey, with the Song representing the final stage:

This book comes last that a man may come to it when his manner of life has been purified, and he has learnt to know the difference between things corruptible and things incorruptible; so that nothing in the metaphors used to describe and represent the love of the Bride for her celestial Bridegroom—that is, of the perfect soul for the Word of God—may cause him to stumble. For, when the soul has completed these studies, by means of which it is cleansed in all its actions and habits and is led to discriminate between natural things, it is competent to proceed to dogmatic and mystical matters, and in this way advances to the contemplation of the Godhead with pure and spiritual love.[13]

The rest of the Prologue of Hugh's Postilla systematically addresses the questions that an *accessus* must treat: *Auctor, intentio, materia, finis, modus agendi, titulus, cui parti philosophiae supponatur* (author, intention, subject matter, end or purpose, literary style, title, and relevant parts of philosophy). With regard to the author, in accordance with the *Glossa ordinaria* and also with Saint Jerome, Hugh links each degree of the spiritual ascension to one of the three names attributed by the Bible to Solomon: as the author of Proverbs, the book that teaches one how to live in peace in this world, Solomon is the Peaceful (*Pacificus*); as the author of Ecclesiastes, he is the Preacher-Convener (*Concionator*) who works for reconciliation among men; as the author of the Song, in which "are expressed

12. Origen, Prol. 3, in *The Song of Songs: Commentary and Homilies,* 41.

13. Origen, Prol. 3, in *The Song of Songs: Commentary and Homilies,* 44. See Gregory the Great, *On the Song of Songs,* trans. Mark DelCogliano (Collegeville, Minn.: Liturgical Press, 2012), 115–16.

in an alternating manner the affections, desires, and other manifestations of love, as well as the mutual meetings of lovers," he receives the name "Edida" (*Idida*), which means "loved by the Lord" according to 2 Samuel 12:25.[14]

The intention of Solomon in the Song, according to Hugh, is "to exhort the Bride, that is, the Church, in anticipation of the embraces and the kisses of the Bridegroom, who is the sign of perfect love"—a point that leads the commentator to describe the different forms of love. He continues: "The subject matter is the bridegroom and bride, that is, Christ and the Church."[15] Inspired again by the *Glossa ordinaria* and ultimately by Origen, the future Dominican cardinal explains that, in the Song, there are four characters or groups of characters: the Bridegroom, who is Christ; the friends of the Bridegroom, who are the angels and prophets who invite the Bride to love only the Bridegroom; the Bride, who is the Church or else the faithful soul; and the young girls (*adolescentulae*), who are the imperfect souls, that is, the *incipientes*, who try to imitate the Bride.[16] The beloved, therefore, is identified with the Church, or indeed with every faithful soul. This double identification, ecclesiological and personal, was already explained and systematically implemented by Origen,[17] and

14. "Prefaces, 5," in *The Glossa ordinaria on the Song of Songs*, 2–3; Jerome, *Commentary on Ecclesiastes*, trans. Richard Goodrich and David J. D. Miller (New York: Paulist Press, 2012), I, 1, pp. 33–35.

15. See "Prefaces, 6," in *The Glossa ordinaria on the Song of Songs*, 3: "The subject matter is the bridegroom and bride, that is, the church and its head."

16. See "Prefaces, 2," in *The Glossa ordinaria on the Song of Songs*, 1–2. See, regarding the wedding at Cana, *In Ioan.*, c. 2, lect. 1 (n° 343): "In its mystical meaning, the mother of Jesus, the Blessed Virgin, is present in spiritual marriages as the one who arranges the marriage, because it is through her intercession that one is joined to Christ through grace: 'in me is every hope of life and of strength' (Sir 24:25). Christ is present as the true groom of the soul, as is said: 'he who has the bride is the bridegroom' (John 3:29). The disciples are the groomsmen uniting the Church to Christ, the one of whom it is said: 'I betrothed you to one husband, to present you as a chaste virgin to Christ' (2 Cor 11:2)." Thomas Aquinas, *Commentary on the Gospel of John*, trans. Larcher and Weisheipl, 135.

17. See Origen, I, 1, in *The Song of Songs: Commentary and Homilies*: "The spiritual interpretation is equally in line with that which we pointed out in our prologue; the appellations of Bride and Bridegroom denote either the Church in her relation to Christ, or the soul in her union with the Word of God."

it finds its climax in the twelfth century with Saint Bernard's *Sermons on the Song*. Following above all the commentary of Rupert of Deutz (†1129), the Marian interpretation comes naturally to be inserted into this schema. Stephen Langton (†1228) could therefore write: "There is the general bride, the Church; the special bride, the faithful soul; and the very special bride, the Virgin Mary."[18]

The end or purpose of the Song, continues Hugh, "is the love of God, which Solomon invites."[19] He characterizes the literary style of the book (*modus agendi*) as one of few words but a rich content. He proposes several explanations of the title,[20] before affirming that, among the parts of philosophy, it is to theology that the Song is related "totally." Thus, in the milieu of the thirteenth century, at the time when Thomas is immersed in it, the Song appears as the summit of the spiritual journey of the believer: it is addressed to the "perfect," to contemplatives, and it celebrates their union of love with Christ.

SAINT THOMAS: AN EPITHALAMIUM FOR THE USE OF THE PERFECT

Saint Thomas's use of citations of the Song enters into this general interpretive frame, whose broad strokes are outlined by the Prologue of the *Postilla* of Hugh of Saint-Cher. But Saint Thomas himself makes direct reference to the general meaning of the Song of Songs in two particularly illuminating texts.

The first is his inaugural lecture (*principium*) *Hic est liber mandatorum Dei*, in which Jean-Pierre Torrell, following James Weisheipl,

18. Quoted by Dahan, "Recherches sur l'exégèse du Cantique," 509n58.

19. See "Prefaces, 6," in *The Glossa ordinaria on the Song of Songs*, 4: "The end [is] love of God."

20. Hugh of Saint-Cher connects the Song of Songs with two other great songs of the Old Testament. The triad that they form corresponds analogically to the spiritual progression associated with the three Solomonian books. Indeed, Exodus 15 concerns "the exit out of vices" (*de egressu vitiorum*); Deuteronomy 32, "progress in virtue and good works" (*in progressu virtutum, et bonorum operum*); and the Song of Songs, "the accomplishment of virtues" (*in consummatione virtutum*). See Origen, Prol, 4, in *The Song of Songs: Commentary and Homilies*, 46–50.

sees the fruit of the second phase of the *inceptio* or inaugural lecture of Saint Thomas as *Magister in sacra pagina*, extending the *principium Rigans montes* (1256).[21] In *Rigans montes*, the young Master delivers a *commendatio*, which is an erudite praise of Holy Scripture, and proposes a general overview of the Bible, considered not as a library of diverse and varied works but ultimately as the one work of a single author, who is God. The purpose of the Bible is to communicate to men the wisdom of God, and so lead them to eternal life. The Bible does this in the Old Testament by teaching the commandments that lead to life, and in the New Testament by depicting the aid of Christ's grace, which is necessary for obeying the commandments. Saint Thomas distinguishes, within the Old Testament, the books of the Law, the books of the prophets, and the books of the hagiographers. The books of the hagiographers paternally exhort the reader to observe the commandments, either by proposing models or by directly instructing. The three works attributed to Solomon enter into this last category. Saint Thomas reclaims the traditional doctrine that sees in them the three degrees or stages of a spiritual journey that concludes, with the Song, at the fullness of the virtuous life:

Wisdom is commended to us, and this in the book of *Wisdom*, or the precepts of wisdom are proposed, and this in the three books of Solomon, which indeed differ according to the three grades of virtue that Plotinus, in *Enneads* 1.1.2.2–7, distinguishes, since the precepts of wisdom ought to concern only the acts of virtue. In the first grade, according to him, are political virtues, whereby a man moderately uses the things of this world and lives among men, and this in the *Proverbs*. In the second grade are the purgative virtues, whereby a man regards the world with contempt, and this in *Ecclesiastes*, which aims at contempt of the world, as is clear from Jerome's prologue.[22] In the third grade are the virtues of the purged soul,

21. See Torrell, *Initiation à saint Thomas d'Aquin*, 84–85 [*Saint Thomas Aquinas: The Person and His Work*, 66–67]; Inos Biffi, "Presenza e divenire nel Mistero di Cristo nel *Principum* 'Hic est liber mandatorum Dei'," in *I Misteri di Cristo in Tommaso d'Aquino: La Costruzione della teologia*, vol. 1 (Milan: Jaca Book, 1994), 39–49; Stéphane Loiseau, *De l'écoute à la parole: La lecture biblique dans la doctrine sacrée selon Thomas d'Aquin* (Paris: Cerf, 2017), 69–72 and 275–76.

22. See Jerome, I, 1, in *Commentary on Ecclesiastes*, 34: "In Ecclesiastes he is educating

whereby a man, wholly cleansed of worldly cares, delights in the contemplation of wisdom alone, and this is found in the *Song of Songs*. In the fourth grade are the exemplar virtues existing in God, concerning which precepts of wisdom are not given but are rather derived from them.[23]

Saint Thomas establishes a link between the spiritual itinerary outlined by the three books of Solomon and the Plotinian doctrine of the virtues. In *ST* I-II, q. 61, after having presented in an essential, formal, and "static" perspective the four cardinal virtues that structure the entirety of the virtuous life, Saint Thomas adds by manner of complement a final article that, through Macrobius, reclaims the Plotinian division of virtues and highlights the "dynamic" aspect of the spiritual life as a journey of the soul to God.[24] We are "in a perspective where morality is underpinned by mysticism."[25] In any case, in *Hic est liber mandatorum Dei*, the Song is clearly recognized as the "book of the perfected" that, at the end of the spiritual journey, describes the joy procured by the contemplation of wisdom.

This wisdom, the Incarnate Word, appears under the traits of the Bridegroom. For this reason, the Song takes the form of an epithalamium, that is, a song that celebrates a wedding. The second of Thomas's texts that engages the general meaning of the Song—the commentary on Psalm 44—says it clearly. Indeed, according to Saint Thomas, Psalm 44's "subject" is exactly the same as the Song's:

This psalm is called epithalamic. For it was the custom in nuptial celebrations that certain songs be sung in praise of the bride and groom, and these songs are called epithalamic.[26] The theme of this psalm, therefore,

---

a man of a mature age not to believe that anything among the affairs of the world is perpetual. To the contrary, he asserts, everything that we see is transitory and brief."

23. Thomas Aquinas, *Principium Hic est liber mandatorum Dei*, trans. McInerny, 5–12.

24. See *ST* I-II, q. 61, a. 5. The doctrine of Plotinus reaches Saint Thomas through Macrobius. See Macrobius, *Commentaria in Somnium Scipionis*, 1. I, c. 8, ed. F. Eyssenhardt (Leipzig: Teubner, 1868), 505–9; Henri van Lieshout, *La Théorie plotinienne de la vertu: Essai sur la genèse d'un article de la Somme théologique de Saint Thomas* (Fribourg: Studia Friburgensia, 1926).

25. Marie-Michel Labourdette, OP, *Cours de théologie morale: Les principes des actes humains (Ia-IIae, q. 49–70); Habitus et vertus* (Toulouse: Parole et Silence, 2017), 151.

26. The characterization of the Song as an "epithalamium" is entirely traditional. It already opens the Prologue of Origen's commentary. Origen, Prol., 1, in *The Song of Songs*

is the marriage of Christ and his Church, which was first entered in upon when Christ united human nature to himself in the womb of the Virgin. Psa. 18: "And he like a bridegroom coming forth from his chamber." For this reason the material dealt with in this psalm is the same as that spoken of in the book called the Song of Songs.[27]

However, for Aquinas, the human epithalamium is only the background subject of Psalm 44, as well as of the Song of Songs. The immediate subject of each text is the wedding of Christ and the Church. Thus, the loves of Christ and the Church are not an allegorical meaning that has been superimposed on the text. Instead, they truly form the literal meaning of the Song, the meaning that its author (and through him, the Holy Spirit) prophetically intended. Certainly, the poem borrows its images and its symbols from "pro-

Commentary and Homilies: "It seems to me that this little book is an epithalamium, that is to say, a marriage-song, which Solomon wrote in the form of a drama." It is found several times under the pen of Saint Augustine. See Augustine, Sermon 147A, in *Sermons*, vol. 4, *94A–147A, on the New Testament*, trans. Edmund Hill, OP, ed. John E. Rotelle, OSA (Brooklyn, N.Y.: New City Press, 1992), 451–56, at 452: "Listen to it in the holy book which is called the Song of Songs. Holy love songs are to be read there, the bridegroom and the bride, Christ and the Church. And that whole book is a kind of wedding song, such as they call an epithalamium, but one sung at a holy, a chaste bridal chamber." See also *Sermo 138*, IX, 9, in *Sancti Aurelii Augustini Hipponensis Episcopi Opera Omnia ...*, vol. 5, *Sermonum classes quator, necnon sermones dubii*, Patrologiae Cursus Completus: Series Latina [PL] 38, ed. J.-P. Migne (Paris, 1841) col. 768; *Homilies on the Gospel of John*, LXV, 3, trans. John Gibb and James Innes, in *Augustin: Homilies on the Gospel of John, Homilies on the First Epistle of John, Soliloquies*, ed. Philip Schaff, Nicene and Post-Nicene Fathers [NPNF] (1st series) 7 (Peabody, Mass.: Hendrickson, 1995), 7–452, at 318–19. Augustine also qualifies Psalm 44 as an epithalamium: see Ps 44, 3, in *Expositions on the Book of Psalms*, trans. J. E. Tweed et al., ed. A. Cleveland Coxe, NPNF (1st ser.) 8 (Peabody, Mass.: Hendrickson, 1995), 146: "Let the Psalm then now sound of Him, let us rejoice in the marriage-feast, and we shall be with those of whom the marriage is made, who are invited to the marriage; and the very persons invited are the Bride herself. For the Church is 'the Bride,' Christ the Bridegroom. There are commonly spoken by balladists certain verses to Bridegrooms and Brides, called *Epithalamia*." See Anne-Marie La Bonnardière, "Le Cantique des cantiques dans l'œuvre de saint Augustin," *Revue d'Études augustiniennes et patristiques* 1 (1955): 225–37. La Bonnardière highlights how much Augustine's use of quotations of the Song "is in close relation with the mystery and the liturgy of baptism," especially in the context of the controversy against the Donatists. It is not surprising that the theme of the epithalamium is found in "Prefaces, 2," in *The Glossa ordinaria on the Song of Songs*, 2.

27. Thomas Aquinas, *Postilla super Psalmos* [*In Ps.*] 44, 1 (p. 319) (unpublished English translation by Benjamin Martin).

fane" human love, but this has the intention of signifying the union of Christ and the Church. A similar case is found in the Gospels' parables of Christ, regarding which Aquinas says:

The parabolical sense is contained in the literal, for by words things are signified properly and figuratively. Nor is the figure itself, but that which is figured, the literal sense. When Scripture speaks of God's arm, the literal sense is not that God has such a member, but only what is signified by this member, namely operative power.[28]

The symbols drawn from human love as they are used in the Song are, *mutatis mutandis*, comparable to the agricultural images used by Jesus Christ in the parable of the sower (Mt 13). The literal meaning is not the (fairly rudimentary) agricultural lesson that we can draw from the parable, but rather the teaching on the manner of receiving the Word of God. It is the same for the Song of Songs: the literal meaning is the union of Christ with the Church or the faithful soul, not the workings of human love. Even more, Saint Thomas is convinced that the literal meaning of certain texts of the Old Testament is directly Christological. Their application to Christ is not, as Theodore of Mopsuestia believed, an artificial procedure.[29] This is the case with the Psalms or with the passages of Isaiah—such as

28. *ST* I, q. 1, a. 10, ad 3. See *Lectura super epistolam ad Galatas* [*In ad Ga.*], c. 4, lect. 7 (nº 254): "There are two ways in which something can be signified by the literal sense: either according to the usual construction, as when I say, 'the man smiles'; or according to a likeness or metaphor, as when I say, 'the meadow smiles.' Both of these are used in Sacred Scripture; as when we say, according to the first, that Jesus ascended, and when we say according to the second, that he sits at the right hand of God. Therefore, under the literal sense is included the parabolic or metaphorical." All translations of *In ad Ga.* are taken from Aquinas, *Commentary on the Letters of Saint Paul to the Galatians and Ephesians*, trans. Fabian R. Larcher, OP (Lander, Wyo.: The Aquinas Institute for the Study of Sacred Doctrine, 2012).

29. See *In Ioan.*, c. 12, lect. 7 (nº 1705): "Theodore of Mopsuestia ... said that all the prophecies of the Old Testament bore on some current event, but the apostles and evangelists appropriated them to the life of Christ, like things said about one event can be appropriated to another event." Given that the theory of Theodore was condemned at the Second Council of Constantinople (558), Saint Thomas takes it to be heretical: see *In Ps.*, pr. (p. 149); *In Ps.* 21, 1 (p. 217). See Paul Gondreau, *The Passions of Christ's Soul in the Theology of St. Thomas Aquinas* (Münster: Aschendorff, 2002), 39–44; Martin Morard, "Thomas d'Aquin, lecteur des conciles," in *Archivum franciscanum historicum* 98 (2005): 211–365, at 300–302; Timothy F. Bellamah, OP, "The Interpretation of a Contemplative:

the Servant songs—that cannot be applied adequately to persons or events of the Old Testament and that therefore speak directly of Jesus Christ.[30]

Thomas' Commentary *Super Iohannem*," in Roszak and Vijgen, *Reading Sacred Scripture with Thomas Aquinas*, 229–55, at 248–49.

30. One example among so many others: Thomas Aquinas, *Lectura super epistolam ad Hebraeos* [*In ad He.*], c. 1, lect. 3 (n° 51): "in the Old Testament some things are said of what is a figure, not insofar as it is a certain thing, but insofar as it is a figure; and then they do not apply to that thing except insofar as it is referred to the thing prefigured. For example, in Psalm 72, certain things are said of David or of Solomon only inasmuch as they prefigured Christ; but other things are said of them inasmuch as they are men. Such things can be applied to them and also to Christ. Thus, 'give to the king your judgment, O God' (Ps 72:1) can be applied to Solomon. But those things that are said of them insofar as they are figures can never be applied to them. Thus, 'and he will rule from sea to sea' (Ps 72:8) can never be verified of Solomon." All translations of *In ad He.* are taken from Aquinas, *Commentary on the Letter of Saint Paul to the Hebrews*, trans. Fabian R. Larcher, OP (Lander, Wyo.: The Aquinas Institute for the Study of Sacred Doctrine, 2012). See also *In Thren.*, c. 4, 20 (p. 683) [n° 73], where the author [Saint Thomas?], while considering the application to King Josiah or to Zedekiah of Lam 4:20 to be correct ("The breath of our mouth, Christ the Lord, is taken in our sins: to whom we said: Under thy shadow we shall live among the Gentiles," Douay-Rheims), holds that it is better to hear in this verse Christ Jesus, to whom Song 2:3 applies: "I sat under his shadow, whom I desired." For further discussion see Matthew Levering, "Mystagogy and Aquinas's *Commentary on Isaiah*: Initiating God's People into Christ," in *Initiation and Mystagogy in Thomas Aquinas: Scriptural, Systematic, Sacramental and Moral, and Pastoral Perspectives*, ed. Henk Schoot, Jacco Verburgt, and Jörgen Vijgen (Leuven: Peeters, 2019), 17–40.

2

Christ and His Beauty

The wedding of Jesus Christ and the Church is, then, the principal subject of the Song. As is appropriate for an epithalamium, the Song often takes the form of an alternating praise: the lover contemplated by the loving eyes of the beloved, and the beloved whose perfections are surveyed by the passionate eyes of the lover. Saint Thomas uses the verses of the Song that describe the lover to highlight the physical and spiritual perfections of Jesus Christ. The actions and behaviors of the lover are also a prophecy of the mysteries of the life of Jesus Christ.

"BEAUTIFUL ABOVE THE SONS OF MEN" (PS 44:3)

"Behold, you are beautiful, my love" (Song 1:15). In his commentary on chapter 4 of Dionysius's *Divine Names,* Saint Thomas mentions the admiring exclamation of the beloved to justify the attribution (which is, in Thomas's work, rather rare) of beauty to God himself, considered in his essence.[1] But the admiration of the be-

1. See Thomas Aquinas, *Super Librum Dionysii De divinis nominibus* [*In de div. nom.*], c. 4, lect. 5 (n° 334) [no. 50]. See also *In de div. nom.*, c. 4, lect. 11 (n° 443) [no. 11]. On the attribution of beauty to God by Saint Thomas, see Serge-Thomas Bonino, *Dieu, "Celui qui est"* (Paris: Parole et Silence, 2016), 337–43.

loved is firstly addressed to the perfect beauty, physical and spiritual, of Jesus, the Word in his humanity. Commenting on Psalm 44, Saint Thomas sees in verses 3–10 a "praise of Christ according to his humanity"; the first motive of such praise, developed in the third verse ("Thou art beautiful above the sons of men, grace is poured abroad in thy lips; therefore hath God blessed thee for ever"), comes from the attraction (*gratiositas*) that Jesus Christ exercises on human sensibility:

Note that two senses flourish in man principally, namely vision and hearing: hence, by way of these two senses a person appears pleasing; through beauty to the sight, and through a gracious word to the hearing. Hence, these two qualities were chiefly in Christ: hence it says in Cant. 2: "*Show me your face, let your voice sound in my ears; for your voice is sweet and your face pleasant.*" For he himself was beautiful and eloquent in those things which became his eloquence.[2]

The beauty of Christ is, then, firstly visual: he charms the eye. Is the beautiful not *id quod visum placet* (that which pleases upon being seen)? The commentary on Psalm 44, which distinguishes several aspects of the beauty of Christ, returns to the Song for corporeal beauty: "The fourth [form of beauty] is corporeal beauty: and this also was present in Christ. *'Behold, you are beautiful, my beloved'* (Song 1:15)."[3] Yet, the affirmation of Christ's physical beauty immediately raises a *quaestio* because it seems to be contradicted, on one hand (first objection) by the fact that Christ in his Passion had "no form or comeliness that we should look at him, and no beauty that we should desire him," as Isaiah had prophesied (Is 53:2), and, on the other hand (second objection), by the fact that physical beauty, like material riches, seems to be one of those goods that Christ willed to renounce in the spirit of poverty in order to teach us to despise them.[4] In the determination of this small *quaestio,* Saint Thomas defines what type of beauty is suited to Christ. Like health,

2. *In Ps.* 44, 2 (p. 320) [no. 94] (trans. Benjamin Martin).
3. *In Ps.* 44, 2 (p. 320) [no. 48] (trans. Benjamin Martin).
4. *In Ps.* 44, 2 (p. 320).

beauty is a quality relative to each subject because it comes from an immanent equilibrium or proportion that is specific to each species and even to each individual:

It is to be said, that beauty, health, and qualities of this kind, are spoken of, in a certain sense, with regard to some thing. For a certain co-mingling of the humors makes for health in a boy, but not in an old man; for there is a certain sort of health that pertains to a lion, which would be death to a human. Wherefore, health is the due proportion of humors in relation to a given nature. And likewise, beauty consists in a due proportion of the members and colors. And therefore, the beauty of one is quite different from the beauty of another: and just so, Christ had that beauty which accorded with his state, and the reverence due his condition. It is not therefore to be understood, that Christ had blond hair, or that he was ruddy, because this would not have become him; but rather that he had that corporeal beauty in the highest degree which pertained to his status, reverence and graciousness of appearance; such that some divine quality shown from his face, because of which everyone revered him, as Augustine says.[5]

The responses that Saint Thomas offers to the two objections are rather superficial: the disfiguration of Christ in his passion is simply reported, without his theological reasons being further explained in this commentary on the Psalm.[6] However, in his commentary on Isaiah 53, which includes a citation of Song 2:14, Saint Thomas suggests that this temporary eclipse of the beauty of Christ was accepted by him for reasons that are "economic." It could be because of the weakness he assumed (*propter infirmitatem assumptam*) or to maintain poverty (*propter paupertatem servatam*). In any case, it is for the purpose of our salvation and the restoration of our lost beauty.[7]

In addition to its visual aspect, the beauty of Christ is also "auditive"; and citations from the Song repeatedly serve to illustrate the

5. *In Ps.* 44, 2 (p. 320). The reference to Saint Augustine is not identified.

6. See *In Ps.* 44, 2 (p. 320) (trans. Benjamin Martin): "With regards to the first, it is to be said that the prophet wished to express the contempt of Christ in his passion, in which the form of his body was deformed by the multitude of his afflictions. To the second, it is to be said that those riches and beauties are to be spurned which we would use wrongly."

7. See *In Is.*, c. 53 (p. 214) [no. 95].

allure and great sweetness that emanate from the teaching of Christ, in its manner as well as in its content: "Let thy voice sound in my ears: for thy voice is sweet, and thy face comely" (Song 2:14).[8]

The beauty of Christ obviously does not stop at what charms the senses. It is also, first and foremost, moral and spiritual. In the above-quoted commentary on Psalm 44, Saint Thomas, in addition to the corporeal beauty of Christ, also mentions the beauty that flows from his divinity, the beauty of justice and of truth, and the moral beauty of his behavior (*conversatio honesta*).[9] A similar enumeration is found in the Commentary on Isaiah, but there the moral beauty, resulting from the diversity of virtues, is illustrated by a verse of the Song, Song 5:10:

> Concerning that phrase, "this beautiful one," it should be noted that Christ is beautiful first as glowing with the splendor of divinity: "being the splendor of his glory, and the figure of his substance" (Heb 1:3); second, as formed with the conformity of union: "you are beautiful beyond the sons of men" (Ps 44:3); third, as distinct by the various shades of virtue: "*my beloved is white and ruddy*" (Song 5:10); fourth, as clothed with an honest way of life: "[clothe yourself with nobility, and set yourself up on high,] be glorious, and put on beautiful garments" (Job 40:5).[10]

The presentation of the lover as a flower and as a lily—"I am the flower of the field, and the lily of the valleys" (Song 2:1)—fits with the identification of Jesus as the messianic flower arising from the root of Jesse (Is 11:1), and also with the supposed etymology of "Nazarene" (Mt 2:23):

> Nazarene is interpreted as 'blooming', and this is found in Isaiah: "and there will come forth a rod out of the root of Jesse, and a flower will rise up out of his root" (Isa 11:1). And what it said in Song of Songs fits with him, "*I am the flower of the field, and the lily of the valleys*" (Song 2:1).[11]

8. See *In Ioan.*, c. 7, lect. 5, (n° 1108) [no. 99]; *In Ioan.*, c. 10, lect. 1 (n° 1376) [no. 101]; *In Is.*, c. 55 (p. 222) [no. 96].

9. See *In Ps.* 44, 2 (p. 320).

10. *In Is.*, c. 63 (p. 245) [no. 201].

11. See *In Matth.*, c. 2, 4 (n° 204) [no. 57]. See also *In Is.*, c. 11 (p. 78) [no. 54]; ibid. (p. 78–79) [nos. 47 and 49]; *In Ioan.*, c. 19, lect. 4 (n° 2420) [no. 58].

The image well expresses the physical and spiritual perfection of the most beautiful of the children of men. It is used in two collations in the commentary on Isaiah. Entirely shaped by texts from the Song, they present Christ as the model and source of the beauty of the saints:

The saints are compared to lilies

on account of the height of their stem, whereby they are constant in adversity: "*as the lily among thorns*" (Song 2:2);

...

on account of their adherence, whereby is the charity of the saints: "*your belly is like [a heap of wheat, set about by lilies]*" (Song 7:2).[12]

And immediately after:

These lilies, Christ

clothes them by the gifts of the virtues: "consider the lilies of the field, [how they grow: they do not labor, nor do they spin]" (Mt 6:28)

gathers them in view of everlasting rewards: "*my beloved has gone down into his garden, [to the bed of aromatic spices, to feed in the gardens, and to gather lilies]*" (Song 6:1).

rests in them through tranquil delight: "*my beloved is mine, and I am his, [who feeds among the lilies]*" (Song 2:16).

and this is why he is himself, a lily: "*I am the flower of the field, [and the lily of the valley]*" (Song 2:1).[13]

CHRIST IN HIS MYSTERIES

The Kiss of the Incarnation

A venerable tradition of interpretation of the Song attempts to discern links between the actions of the protagonists of the poem and the moments of sacred history, whether it be the history of the people of Israel or the history of the Church.[14] This tradition finds

12. *In Is.*, c. 35 (p. 154) [no. 61].

13. *In Is.*, c. 35 (p. 154) [no. 56]. See Torrell, "Quand saint Thomas méditait sur le prophète Isaïe," 248–50.

14. The commentary of Apponius is a model of this kind of reading. As explained by its editors in their introduction: "The feat accomplished by Apponius, seduced by the mystery of the wedding of Christ and the Church, is to have known how to discover,

little echo in the use that Saint Thomas makes of citations of the Song.[15] Nevertheless, Aquinas sees in many words of the beloved the expression of humanity's ardent desire for the Incarnation. Indeed, from the outset of the Song, the beloved shows her eager expectation of the kiss of the beloved—"Let him kiss me with the kiss of his mouth" (Song 1:1)—which the exegetical tradition understood as the yearning of humanity for an unmediated contact with God, which only the incarnation of the Son could accomplish. In this vein, the *Glossa ordinaria* comments:

The voice of those heralding the coming of Christ, who pray to the father of the bridegroom. Let him touch me with the sweetness of his presence, which I have often heard promised by the prophets, and as if bringing a kiss let him also receive the touch of my mouth, that is, questioning me concerning the way of salvation let him hear and instruct and bring the kiss of peace, making two people one.[16]

Saint Thomas does not use the theme of the kiss as such, but three verses of the Song, according to Thomas, express the intense awaiting of the Incarnation by the patriarchs and the prophets, who so greatly desired to see the Day of Christ (Jn 8:56). He refers to Song 2:14: "Let thy voice sound in my ears," Song 5:1: "Let my beloved come into his garden," and Song 8:1: "Who shall give thee to me for my brother."

"Let my beloved come into his garden." Thomas's Sermon II, *Lauda et laetare,* preached for Advent, opens rather significantly with a

---

throughout the dialogues of the Lover and the Beloved, all the proceedings of their wedding across history. The *Song* becomes for him a vast historical saga where are revealed the different chapters of the incarnation of Christ in the world of men, that is, the progressive establishment of the Church on earth until the last day." Apponius, *Commentaire sur le Cantique des cantiques,* vol. 1, *Books I-III,* ed. and trans. B. De Vregille and L. Neyrand, SC 420 (Paris: Cerf, 1997), 77.

15. The one application of the Song to the history of the Church seems to be when Saint Thomas connects Song 2:13 ("The fig tree has put forth her green figs") with the manifestation, at the end of time, of the power of Christ and the saints that will come to help the Church. See *In Matth.,* c. 24, 3 (n° 1977) [no. 92].

16. "I, 2–3," in *The Glossa ordinaria on the Song of Songs,* 7 (from Bede the Venerable). See Gregory the Great, 12, in *On the Song of Songs,* 117–18.

text in which Saint Bernard, in view of Song 1:1, meditates upon the ardent desire of the ancients for the Incarnation.[17] In his sermon, Saint Thomas explains in the following way the "behold I come" of Zechariah 2:10:

"I come," as if he says: "I do not send an angel, not a spirit, not a deputy, but I myself come in person," in which the greatest love (*maxima caritas*) is shown [cf. Jn 3:16]. I interpret "I come" as meaning "invited by the holy fathers." For it is he whom all the holy people had invited from the beginning of the world, although their person was brought forth by the spouse. It says in Song of Songs 2: "*My beloved (dilectus) will come into his place*." And in the last chapter of Revelation [22:20]: "Come, Lord Jesus." And likewise Isaiah, Jeremiah, and the rest of the prophets have spoken.[18]

"*Let thy voice sound in my ears*" (*Song 2:14*). The desire to hear the voice of Christ himself, and not only his distant echo in the voice of the prophets that heralded him, evokes the newness that represents the immediacy in which the Word of God is given in Jesus Christ, the Incarnate Word. This is a central theme, for example, in the letter to the Hebrews:

"If you shall hear his voice," because we hear his voice, which was not true of the Old Testament, in which the words of the prophets were heard: God "spoke in times past to the fathers in the prophets, last of all, in these days, has spoken to us by his Son" (Heb 1:1–2); "therefore, my people shall know my name in that day, because it was I myself that spoke, behold, I am here" (Isa 52:6); "*let your voice sound on my ears*" (Song 2:14).[19]

The imperfect character of the Old Testament, which is set in relief by the immediate and perfect revelation of the New Testament, does not, however, invalidate the Old Testament. Against the Man-

17. See Bernard of Clairvaux, "Sermon 2," in *On the Song of Songs I*, trans. Kilian Walsh (Kalamazoo, Mich.: Cistercian Publications, 1971), 8: "During my frequent ponderings on the burning desire with which the patriarchs longed for the incarnation of Christ, I am stung with sorrow and shame. . . . All the more therefore do I pray that the intense longing of those men of old, their heartfelt expectation, may be enkindled in me by these words: 'Let him kiss me with the kiss of his mouth.'"

18. Thomas Aquinas, "*Lauda et laetare*," in *The Academic Sermons*, 41.

19. *In ad He.*, c. 3, lect. 2 (n° 174) [no. 97]. See also *In Ps.* 45, 5 (p. 328) [no. 98].

ichaeans, Saint Thomas recalls the necessity of both Testaments through the evocation of the "fruits new and old" (*nova et vetera*) (Song 7:13) that the lover offers to the beloved, which echo the new and old (*nova et vetera*) that every scribe instructed in the Kingdom of Heaven knows how to bring forth out of his treasure (Mt 13:52).[20] The legal precepts, like all the figures contained in the Old Testament, are like the wall (Song 2:9; Eph 2:14) that at the same time veils and unveils the presence of the lover.[21]

"Who shall give thee to me for my brother" (Song 8:1). Finally, the desire of the beloved that the lover be a brother to her makes it possible to emphasize a central aspect of the Incarnation: the consubstantiality of the Incarnate Word with humanity, which has, among other effects, that of making redemption possible:[22]

Concerning that phrase, "His name shall be called Immanuel," i.e. "God with us," it should be noted that Christ is with us in many ways. First, as a brother, through a participation of nature: "*Who would give you to me, my brother, nursing at the breasts of my mother, that I may find you without, and kiss you?*"[23]

The *Acta et Passa Christi*

In addition to the passages that evoke the fundamental mystery of the redemptive Incarnation, Saint Thomas discerns in certain

20. See Thomas Aquinas, *Principium biblicum* (Marietti, nº 1203) [no. 254]; *In Matth.*, c. 13, lect. 4 (nº 1205) [no. 255]. See "VII, 109–112," in *The Glossa ordinaria on the Song of Songs*, 156: "*all apples*, all patterns and witnesses, *new*, of the new apostles, *old*, of the old patriarchs and prophets, *I have served up to you*, to be expounded at that time."

21. See Thomas Aquinas, *Lectura super epistolam ad Ephesios* [*In ad Ep.*], c. 2, lect. 5 (no. 112) [nº 90]; Thomas Aquinas, "*Germinet Terra*," in *The Academic Sermons*, 277–79 [no. 154].

22. See *In Ps.* 48, 3 (p. 336) [no. 257]. Regarding the consubstantiality (in the sense of co-essentiality) of the Incarnate Word with humanity, see the traditional formula of the Creed of Chalcedon.

23. *In Is.*, c. 7 (p. 59) [no. 258]. See also *In ad Ep.*, c. 1, lect. 8 (nº 69) [no. 147]: "With respect to a conformity of nature, Christ is not the head of the angels, *for surely he did not take angels to himself, but he took the line of Abraham* (Heb 2:16); but in this respect he is the head of men only. *You have wounded my heart, my sister*, through nature, *and my spouse*, through grace (Song 4:9)"; *In Is.*, c. 9 (p. 69) [no. 259].

verses of the Song a prophecy of this or that mystery of the life of Christ. For example, Song 2:8 is used to illustrate the "ontological" primacy of nature that John the Baptist recognizes in Jesus in comparison to himself: "a man, who is preferred before me: because he was before me" (Jn 1:30):

As if to say: Although he comes to preach after me, yet he "ranks ahead of me" in dignity. "*See, he comes, leaping upon the mountains, skipping over the hills*" (Song 2:8). One such hill was John the Baptist, who was passed over by Christ, as is said, "he must increase, but I must decrease" (John 3:30).[24]

Regarding Jesus's public ministry, Saint Thomas insists repeatedly on the powerful attraction that Jesus's person and teaching exercised on the crowds, arousing their love in return. Indeed, creatures never have the initiative in the relationship of love with God: their love for God is always a response to the call and to the divine attraction that manifests itself particularly in and through Christ. Saint Thomas often supports this doctrine with Song 1:3—"Draw me: we will run after thee"—which he pairs with John 6:44: "No man can come to me, except the Father, who hath sent me, draw him."[25] This divine attraction, considered in its objective-moral dimension, that is, as an invitation addressed to free will,[26] can come through the mediation of a salutary trial:

Sometimes we sin and don't even look for God. Then God draws us to himself by sickness or something similar (Hos 2:6): "Therefore I will hedge her way with thorns." Paul was also treated this way (Ps 118:176): "I wandered like a lost sheep. Look for your servant, Lord." And (Song 1:3): "*Draw me after you.*"[27]

24. *In Ioan.*, c. 1, lect. 14 (n° 261) [no. 89].

25. See *In Ioan.*, c. 15, lect. 5 (n° 2055) [no. 19]: "no one can come to Christ by faith unless he is drawn: *no man can come to me, unless the Father, who has sent me, draws him* (John 6:44). So the spouse says: *draw me after you, we will run to the odor of your ointments* (Song 1:3)."

26. The divine attraction does not in the least reduce to this objective-moral attraction, but it also consists in the efficient motion that, alone, allows the will to consent freely but invincibly to this attraction.

27. Thomas Aquinas, *De decem preceptis*, X [no. 13], translated in *The Catechetical Instructions of St. Thomas*, trans. Joseph Burns Collins (New York: J. F. Wagner, 1939).

But this attraction is exercised in a privileged fashion through the manifestation of the sweetness and captivating goodness of Jesus Christ,[28] who reveals himself to be the object of all true desires that arise in the heart of man:

For if, as Augustine says, "each of us is drawn by his own pleasure," how much more strongly ought we to be drawn to Christ if we find our pleasure in truth, happiness, justice, eternal life: all of which Christ is? Therefore, if we would be drawn by him, let us be drawn through love for the truth, according to: "take delight in the Lord, and he will give you the desires of your heart" (Ps 36:4). And so the bride says: "*draw me after you, and we will run to the fragrance of your perfume*" (Song 1:4).[29]

The manifestation of the love of God in Jesus Christ, which provokes in return human love for God, attains its maximum intensity in the humiliations of the Passion. There, the divine mercy reveals itself fully and consequently deploys all its power of attraction:

And so thus lifted up "I will draw all things to myself," through love; "I have loved you with an everlasting love, therefore have I drawn you, taking pity on you" (Jer 31:3). Furthermore, the love of God for men appears most clearly in the fact that he condescended to die for them: "God shows his love for us in that while we were yet sinners Christ died for us" (Rom 5:8). By doing this he fulfilled the request of the bride: "*draw me after you, and we will run to the aroma of your perfume*" (Song 1:3).[30]

28. On the attraction exercised by the sweetness of Christ, see Thomas Aquinas, *Lectura super epistolam ad Philipenses* [*In ad Ph.*], c. 2, lect. 2 (n° 52) [no. 21].

29. *In Ioan.*, c. 6, lect. 5, (n° 935) [no. 16]. See Augustine, "Homily 26," 4–5 in *Homilies on the Gospel of John 1–40*, trans. Edmund Hill, OP (Hyde Park, N.Y.: New City Press, 2009), 452–54, which already quotes Song 1:3 in this context.

30. *In Ioan.*, c. 12, lect. 5 (n° 1673) [no. 17]. On the Passion of Christ as manifestation of the saving love of the Beloved, see also *In ad He.*, c. 9, lect. 4 (n° 357) [no. 202]. In *In Ioan.*, c. 1, lect. 15 (n° 285) [no. 9], Saint Thomas uses an idea of Saint John Chrysostom in his *In Ioan.* (*Homelia XVIII in Ioannem*, 1; Patrologiae Cursus Completus: Series Graeca, ed. J.-P. Migne, Paris [PG], 59, col. 115) to explain that the first disciples began to follow Christ not when John the Baptist revealed Christ's greatness but when he announced Christ's lowering himself: "because we are more moved by Christ's humility and the sufferings he endured for us. So it is said: *your name is like oil poured out*, i.e., mercy, by which you have obtained salvation for all; and the text immediately follows with, *young maidens have greatly loved you* (Song 1:2)."

Several words of the Song are linked with the Passion of Christ. The perfume of the anointing at Bethany (Jn 12:3)—an advance announcement of the death of Christ—echoes the perfumes of the lover that draw the young girls to follow him (Song 1:3).[31] We have already highlighted how, in commenting on Isaiah, Saint Thomas adopts Bernard's interpretation of the holes in the rock (*foramina petrae*) as signifying the wounds of Christ in which the soul must find refuge.[32] Similarly, with the image of the press (which traditionally refers to the Passion), Saint Thomas associates, through the motif of wine, a verse in which the lover is compared to "a cluster of cypress in the vineyards of Engaddi" (Song 1:13).[33] The verses of the Song that mention myrrh, which is a bitter perfume and is used in the rites of burial, are spontaneously connected with the Passion of Christ and with the penitence or mortification of the flesh by which believers participate in his Passion.[34] It is understood that the seal the beloved is invited to place on her heart (Song 8:6) is precisely the memory of the Passion and, more specifically, the memory of

31. See *In Ioan*, c. 12, lect. 1 (n° 1596) [no. 25].

32. See *In Is.*, c. 2 [no. 93].

33. See *In Is.*, c. 63 [no. 46]. In "I, 163" in The *Glossa ordinaria on the Song of Songs*, the "cluster of cypress in the vineyards of Engaddi" was mostly associated with the Resurrection, particularly as in the Song it comes after the evocation of the bundle of myrrh (Song 1:12), clearly linked with the Passion.

34. See *In Ps.* 44, 6 (p. 323) [no. 193] (trans. Benjamin Martin): "Myrrh has bitterness; and thus, if it is referred to the body of Christ, it symbolizes the bitterness of his passion. Cant. 5: 'his fingers' fixed to the wood 'are full of purest myrrh.' But if they are referred to the saints, it symbolizes repentance: Eccl. 24: 'As choice myrrh I have given forth the sweetness of my fragrance.'" *In Ioan.*, c. 19, lect. 6 (n° 2466) [no. 192] (with regard to John 19:39 where Nicodemus brings myrrh and aloes for burying Jesus): "As for the mystical sense, we understand from this that we should bury the crucified Christ in our hearts, with the sadness of contrition and compassion: 'My hands dripped with myrrh' (Sg 5:5)" (*Commentary on the Gospel of John: Chapters 13–21*, 251). The mortification of the flesh is also evoked through the celebrated verse "I am very dark, but comely" (*Nigra sum sed formosa*) (Song 1:5 [1:4 in the Vulgate]), of which there is only a single occurrence, quite marginal, in Saint Thomas. See *In Ier.*, c. 38, 1 (p. 662) [no. 39]: "[Ebed-Melech is] *Ethiopian*, because of his mortification of the flesh. 'Ethiopia shall stretch out her hand to God' (Ps 67:32). 'I am black, but beautiful' (Song 1:4)" (trans. Benjamin Martin [his translation of Aquinas's *Commentary on Jeremiah* is forthcoming from The Aquinas Institute for the Study of Sacred Doctrine]).

Christ's love "until the end": "In Christ's passion, one ought first to reflect upon the love, in order to return love: *set me as a seal upon your heart* (Song 8:6)."[35] The sign of the cross, a "seal" received in baptism and actualized daily, is an effective reminder of the Passion.[36]

As for the Resurrection of Christ, in which "flesh hath flourished again" (Ps 27:7), it is evoked through the springtime image of the lovers' bed that is covered in flowers (Song 1:15).[37] Through the Ascension, finally, Christ attracts the saints to himself, just as the lover attracts the beloved and her companions to himself: "Though the saints ascend to heaven, they do not do so as Christ did, because Christ ascended by His own power, whereas the saints are drawn up by Christ: 'Draw me after thee' (Song 1:3)."[38] It is thus that the Church Militant arrives at the eschatological fullness of the celestial Church.

35. *In Is.*, c. 57 [no. 264]. See *a contrario* the reproach of Saint Paul to the Galatians who are ignorant of Christ Crucified and consequently neglect to place him as a sign on the heart, *In ad Ga.*, c. 3, lect. 1, (nº 118) [no. 267].

36. See *In Ps.* 4, 5 [no. 265].

37. See *In Ps.* 27, 7 [no. 52].

38. See Thomas Aquinas, *Collaciones in Symbolum apostolorum*, 6 (nº 946) [no. 12]. The translation is taken from Thomas Aquinas, *The Three Greatest Prayers: Commentaries on the Lord's Prayer, the Hail Mary, and the Apostles' Creed*, trans. Laurence Shapcote, OP (Manchester, N.H.: Sophia Institute Press, 1990). See *In Ioan.*, c. 14, lect. 1 (nº 1859) [no. 18].

3

The Church, Spouse without Stain or Wrinkle

The lover's enthusiastic praise of the physical perfections of his beloved primarily reflects, in Thomas's exegesis, the description of the beauties, perfections and properties of the Church, Spouse of Christ.[1] Four features of the Church are more specifically illustrated by verses from the Song: the Church maintains a constitutive bond to Christ and to the Spirit; the Church is one; this unity is an organic unity (the Church is composed of an ordered diversity of members); in the Church, the good and the bad coexist until the end of time.

CHRIST'S GARDEN WHERE THE SPIRIT BLOWS

Aquinas uses several verses of the Song, which present the beloved as a garden with fragrant flowerbeds, to underline the Church's

1. See E. Ann Matter, "The Song of Songs as Changing Portrait of the Church," chap. 4 in *The Voice of My Beloved*. Saint Thomas evokes the beauty of the Church through that of the cities here below, like Capernaum, which "is interpreted as 'most beautiful village', and signifies the Church; '*you are beautiful, O my love*' (Song 6:3)" (*In Matth.*, c. 4, lect. 2 (n° 254) [no. 220]); or again like the city that the beloved of the Song traverses to search for her beloved. See *In Ps.* 47, 6 (p. 334) [no. 113] (trans. Benjamin Martin): "He says, therefore, go round about, namely the Church militant, or triumphant with the eye of contemplation: Cant. 3: '*I shall arise and go round about*,' etc. Some surround the Church with an evil eye looking to attack her, but we gather round about her to love her."

relationship to Christ and to the Holy Spirit. The Church is the garden where Christ never ceases to come spiritually, through his invisible missions, to make his home there and take pleasure in it:

"I will come again, and will take you to myself," can be understood as that spiritual coming with which Christ always visits the Church of the faithful and vivifies each of the faithful at death. Then the meaning is: "I will come again," to the Church, spiritually and continuously, "and will take you to myself," that is, I will strengthen you in faith and love for me: "*my beloved has gone down to his garden, to the beds of spices*," that is, to the community of the saints, "*to feed in the garden*," that is, to delight in their virtues, "*and to gather lilies*," to draw pure souls to himself when he gives life to the saints at death (Song 6:1).[2]

The beloved's appeal to the winds, that they blow on her garden and spread her garden's fragrance far and wide—"Arise, north wind, and come, O south wind, blow through my garden, and let the aromatical spices thereof flow" (Song 4:16)—allows Saint Thomas to mention in passing the bond between the Church and the Spirit, who causes the most beautiful fruits to germinate in the Church.[3] The description of the beloved as a dove (Song 6:8) suggests also, as we will see, the intimate presence of the Spirit of love, the "soul" of the Church, who, through the love that he spreads in hearts, ensures the unity and strength of the Church.[4]

2. *In Ioan.*, c. 14, lect. 1 (n° 1861) [no. 218]. The attachment of the Church to Christ, whom she wants to attract to her, is also signified by Song 3:4: "'*I held him, and I will not let him go, till I bring him into my mother's house, and into the chamber of she that bore me*.'" See *In Is.*, c. 4 [n° 260], where Saint Thomas connects this verse of the Song with Isaiah 4, which describes how the women of Jerusalem snatch up the rare men who survived the disaster of the war.

3. See *In Ier.*, c. 13, 2 [n° 157] (trans. Benjamin Martin): "The Holy Spirit is called South because of his heat.... Because of the fruiting of the trees. '*Come south wind, blow upon my garden, and its fragrances will spread abroad*' (Song 4:16)"; *In Matth.*, c. 12, lect. 3 (n° 1058) [no. 158]. However, Song 4:16 receives an opposite interpretation elsewhere, since the wind (specifically the north wind) is there presented as the demon that disperses and prevents fruition. See *In Ier.*, c. 1 (p. 582) [no. 156]. This negative interpretation of the effects of the winds on the garden is that of the Gloss. See "IV, 146–155," in *The Glossa ordinaria on the Song of Songs*, 100–101.

4. See *In Ps.* 47, 6 [no. 270] (trans. Benjamin Martin): "And this is the power of the

"ONE IS MY DOVE, MY PERFECT ONE" (SONG 6:8)

There are no fewer than nine quotations of Song 6:8 in the whole of Thomas's corpus. Each of them, unsurprisingly, is associated with the idea of the unity of the Church, which brings to perfection the unity of the elect people of the Old Testament.[5] These nine quotations can be grouped into four thematic sets. First, two of them refer to the different entities that come together in the unity of the Church. In accordance with a theme dear to Saint Augustine, angels and humans form one and the same City, the single Church of Christ.[6] The same is true with regard to the Jews and Gentiles. When Saint Thomas asks why the two women who come to the tomb on Easter morning (Mt 28:1) are both named Mary, he responds:

> But it was not without mystery that two women of the same name came.... Also, of the same name, because this signifies the unity of the Church: for one was a gentile and the other a Jew, but now all are one Church; "*one is my dove*" (Song 6:8).[7]

Holy Spirit, who protects this city: Luke 24: 'remain in the city until you shall be clothed with power.' This power is love. Cant. 8: '*Love is as strong as death.*'"

5. Saint Thomas connects Song 6:8 to the privileged, "unique," election of the Jewish people. See *In ad Ep.*, c. 3, lect. 1 (n° 142) [no. 232]. Anti-Judaism seems absent in Saint Thomas's use of the Song. He uses several verses of the Song to denounce only the hostility of Jesus's Jewish contemporaries toward him. See *In Ioan.*, c. 10, lect. 5 (n° 1435) [no. 91]: "'it was winter.' There is also a mystical reason for mentioning the time. As Gregory says in *II Morals*, the Evangelist took care to mention the season as winter in order to indicate the chill of evil in the hearts of those listening.... we read of this winter: '*the winter is past, the rain is over and gone*' (Song 2:11)." See Gregory the Great, *Moral Reflections on the Book of Job* (Collegeville, Minn.: Liturgical Press, 2014), 1:118. The reference to Song 2:11 is not found in Saint Gregory's work in this context. *The Glossa ordinaria on the Song of Songs*, however, already connected the winter of Song 2:11 to the disbelief that preceded the Incarnation (II, 103–104 [p. 173]). In other texts, the Jews, sons of the Synagogue, just like Jesus or Paul, play to the latter the hostile role that is that of the brothers of the beloved in the Song: "'*the sons of my mother have fought against me*'" (Song 1:5). See *In ad Ga.*, c. 1, lect. 4 (n° 41) [no. 41]; *In Matth.*, c. 12, 4 (n° 1070) [no. 123].

6. See *In* IV *Sent.*, d. 49, q. 4, a. 4, obj. 1 [no. 225]. See Augustine, XII, IX, 2, in *The City of God*, trans. Marcus Dods (New York: Modern Library, 1993), 389–90.

7. *In Matth.*, c. 28 (n° 2421) [no. 230].

Second, in order to emphasize the unity of the Church, two other quotations use the comparison of the beloved to a dove by connecting it to the Gospels' episode of the baptism of Christ, in which the Holy Spirit reveals himself in the form of a dove (Mt 3:16 and par.). The dove is presented by Saint Thomas as a sociable and loving animal. Now, love is the first principle, the very soul, of unity. It is not surprising, then, that the Church in the mystery of her unity would be called "dove":

The Holy Ghost appeared over our Lord at His baptism in the form of a dove, in order to designate the common effect of baptism—namely, the building up of the unity of the Church. Hence it is written (Eph 5:25–27): "Christ delivered Himself up … that He might present … to Himself a glorious Church, not having spot or wrinkle, or any such thing … cleansing it by the laver of water in the word of life." Therefore it was fitting that the Holy Ghost should appear at the baptism under the form of a dove, which is a creature both loving and gregarious. Wherefore also it is said of the Church (Song 6:8): "*One is my dove.*"[8]

Third, two other quotations of the Song help to present unity as the mark or criterion that allows the true Church to be distinguished from the proliferation of sects that never cease dividing in themselves:

Granting that various heretics have devised various sects, they nevertheless do not belong to the Church, because they have been divided into parts, but the Church is one. Cant. 6:8, "*One is my dove, my perfect one.*"[9]

Fourth and finally, two quotations of Song 6:8 appear in the context of the theology of marriage. Marriage is the sacrament that ex-

8. *ST* III, q. 39, a. 6 [no. 227]. See also *In Ioan.*, c. 1, lect. 14 (n° 272) [nos. 207 and 231]: The Spirit appears in the form of a dove "because of the unity of charity; for the dove is much aglow with love: '*one is my dove*' (Song 6:9). So, in order to show the unity of the Church, the Holy Spirit appears in the form of a dove"; *In Matth.*, c. 3, lect. 2 (n° 300) [no. 187].

9. See Thomas Aquinas, *Collaciones in Symbolum apostolorum*, 9 (n° 973) [no. 228] (trans. Benjamin Martin); *In Ps.* 21, 14 [no. 229] (trans. Benjamin Martin): "Now, by the garment which is not divided is signified the unity of the Church, which anyone might believe he possesses; but which only one possesses, because the unity of the Church is unique: Cant. 6: '*You are one my dove, my perfect one.*'"

plains the mystery of the union of Christ and the Church. The two quotes highlight, against the sin of polygamy, the necessary uniqueness of the spouse:

Since, then, the union of husband and wife gives a sign of the union of Christ and the Church, that which makes the sign must correspond to that whose sign it is. Now, the union of Christ and the Church is a union of one to one to be held forever. For there is one Church, as the Canticle (6:8) says: "One is My dove, My perfect one." And Christ will never be separated from his Church.[10]

"MANY MEMBERS, ONE BODY" (1 COR 12:20)

In the garden of the Church, there are all kinds of plants:

"I will water my garden of plants" (Sir 24:42). For this garden is the Church, concerning which Cant. 4:12 says, "*An enclosed garden is my sister, my bride:*" in which there are various plantings, according to the various orders, all of which the hand of the Almighty has planted. This garden is watered by Christ with the rivers of his sacraments, which flowed from his side.[11]

There is nothing uniform and monolithic about the unity of the Church. She is an organic unity that integrates a variety of components: the different categories (*ordines*) of faithful, the different functions, charisms, missions, and so on. Paul's image of the Church as the Body of Christ comprising different members resonates with

10. Aquinas, *Summa contra Gentiles* [SCG] IV, c. 78 (n° 4123) [no. 226]. The translation is from *Summa contra Gentiles: Book Four: Salvation*, trans. Charles J. O'Neil (Notre Dame, Ind.: University of Notre Dame Press, 1975). See *Lectura super I epistolam ad Timotheum* [*In 1 ad Tim.*], c. 3, lect. 1 (n° 96) [no. 233]: "But what is the reason for such a law [the episcopal should be the husband of a single woman]? Would it not be a greater impediment to have a number of concubines? I answer that this is interdicted not only by reason of the incontinence involved, but also by reason of what marriage represents, namely, the union between Christ and the Church: There is one spouse, Christ, and one Church: '*one is my dove*' (Song 6:8)." Translation from Aquinas, *Commentary on the Letters of Saint Paul to the Philippians, Colossians, Thessalonians, Timothy, Titus, and Philemon*, trans. Fabian R. Larcher, OP (Lander, Wyo.: The Aquinas Institute for the Study of Sacred Doctrine, 2012).

11. Aquinas, *In* I *Sent.*, Prol. [no. 152] (trans. Benjamin Martin).

the exegetical interpretation that sees, in the descriptions of the bodies of the two lovers of the Song, a description of the Church in its organic diversity.[12] Origen had already connected 1 Corinthians 12–13 with the beloved's description in the Song:

The Bride of Christ, who is the Church, is also His Body and His members. If, then, you hear mention of the members of the Bridegroom, you must understand by it the members of His Church. Among these, just as there are some who are called eyes, doubtless because they have the light of understanding and knowledge, and other ears, to hear the word of teaching, and others hands to do good works and to discharge the functions of religion: so also are there some who may be called His cheeks. But they are called the cheeks of the face, when integrity and modesty of soul appear in them.[13]

In the same vein, in his *Postilla* on the Song, Hugh of Saint-Cher copiously exploited, with an abundance of allegorical ingenuity, the parallel between the members of the body of the lover or of the beloved and the different "parts" of the Church (preachers, doctors, prelates, simple faithful, and so on). It is not surprising, then, that the commentary of Saint Thomas on 1 Corinthians 12–13 includes several quotations of Song 5:10–16, the passage in which the beloved describes the perfections of the body of her lover. Saint Thomas looks for there (and finds) connections between the different members of the human body and the different categories of the faithful who form the one Church. He distinguishes the faithful vowed to the active life, who correspond to the members of the body that are used for movement, from the faithful vowed to the contemplative life, who correspond to the members of the body that are used for understanding:

By the members involved in motion are designated in the Church men given to the active life, in such a way that the feet are subjects. About these it is said: "their legs were straight" (Ezek 1:7); by the hands are denoted

12. The Church is figured just as well by the body of the beloved as by that of the lover, because the Church is both the Spouse of Christ and the Body of Christ.

13. See Origen, II, 7, in *The Song of Songs: Commentary and Homilies*, 145.

prelates, through whom others are disposed; hence it is said: "*his hands are rounded gold, filled with hyacinth*" (Song 5:14). In the Church not only the hands, i.e., prelates, but also the feet are necessary, i.e., subjects.[14]

Among the contemplatives, the access to the truth passes through a hierarchical path: the teachers, as in Origen, are compared to eyes, in direct contact with the truth, while their disciples are signified by ears:

By the members which serve knowledge are designated in the Church those who apply themselves to the contemplative life among whom there are, as eyes, teachers who investigate truth. Hence it is said: "*his eyes are like doves beside springs of water, which live near the fullest waters*" (Song 5:12). By ears are signified disciples who receive the truth by hearing their masters.[15]

For understandable reasons, many verses of the Song are applied by Saint Thomas to his own "professional category," that of the teachers. "The writings of the teachers who are imbued with wisdom" are the precious offspring produced by the garden of delights (Song 4:13).[16] Their writings will earn the teachers, according to the *Glossa*, a special reward, a choice aureole.[17] Saint Thomas delivers to his confreres a professional piece of advice (a warning?): their lips will be "a dropping honeycomb" (Song 4:11) . . . if they know to convey "many and profound thoughts in a few short words"![18]

The same procedure, which consists of connecting the internal structures of the Church with the bodies of the lovers, leads Aquinas to apply to the apostles—pillars of the Church (Gal 2:9)—the verse of Song 5:15: "his legs as pillars of marble, that are set upon bas-

14. See *In 1 ad Co.*, c. 12, lect. 3 (n° 738) [no. 209].

15. See *In 1 ad Co.*, c. 12, lect. 3 (n° 739) [no. 208]. Saint Thomas compares to the sense of smell those who, while they cannot directly understand the words of wisdom, perceive several signs of wisdom and "*run after the odor of your anointing oils*" (Song 1:3). See *In 1 ad Co.*, c. 12, lect. 3 (n° 741) [no. 26].

16. See Thomas Aquinas, "*Germinet Terra*," in *The Academic Sermons*, 279 [no. 154].

17. See *In* IV *Sent.*, d. 49, q. 5, a. 3, qlc 3, s.c. 2 [no. 310]. See "VIII, 107," in *The Glossa ordinaria on the Song of Songs*, 169, which is inspired by the commentary of Bede the Venerable.

18. See *In ad Ep.*, c. 3, lect. 1 (n° 138) [no. 148].

es of gold";[19] and also to see in them the eyes of the Church, alike to doves (Song 4:1; 5:12), "on account of their purity of conscience."[20]

Thus the Church, like the perfect body of the beautiful Shulamite, appears as "an army set in array" (Song 6:9), formed of "companies of camps" (Song 7:1). These two verses underline the militant aspect of the Church, terrible to its enemies and a refuge against the demons for the faithful,[21] but, more fundamentally, they accentuate its perfect internal ordering, its unity in diversity:

If all the Church were of one state and grade, it would destroy the perfection and beauty of the Church, which is described as "adorned with many-colored robes" (Ps 45:14). [The Apostle] asserts the contrary truth, saying: "but now there are many members indeed, yet one body," which is made complete by all the parts. Thus, the Church is composed of diverse orders: "*terrible as an army with banners*" (Song 6:10).[22]

THE COHABITATION OF GOOD AND BAD PEOPLE IN THE CHURCH

Perfect as the ecclesial body is, it nonetheless contains in itself, until the last Judgment, bad people mixed with the good. With fourteen quotations, Song 2:2—"As a lily among thorns, so is my love among the daughters"—is one of the verses of the Song that is most often quoted in Thomas's corpus. One of the reasons for this is that the *Glossa ordinaria*, employing a text of Saint Gregory the Great,

19. See *In ad Ga.*, c. 2, lect. 2 (n° 74) [no. 211].

20. See *In Is.*, c. 60 [nos. 126 and 205].

21. See *In 1 ad Co.*, c. 5, lect. 1 (n° 237) [no. 222]: the excommunicated person "is cut off from the community of believers and from partaking of the sacraments and is deprived of the blessings of the Church, by which a man is defended against the attacks of Satan. Hence it is said of the Church: '*terrible as an army set in array*' (Song 6:10), i.e., to the devils"; *In Ioan.*, c. 21, lect. 2 (n° 2595) [no. 221].

22. *In 1 ad Co.*, c. 12, lect. 3 (n° 743) [no. 223]. See Thomas Aquinas, *Lectura supra epistolam ad Colossenses* [*In ad Col.*], prol (n° 2) [no. 224]: the Church is a camp that "should have a good relationship with its leader and in itself: '*what shalt thou see in the Sulamitess but the companies of camps?*' (Song 7:1); 'this is the camp of God' (Gen 32:21). It should also be a threat to the enemy: '*terrible as an army with banners*' (Song 6:10)"; *In Ioan.*, c. 21, lect. 2 (n° 2595) [no. 221].

had made of this verse the biblical confirmation of a fundamental Christian doctrine: the coexistence until the last Day of good and bad people in the Church,[23] with its moral consequence: the necessity for the good to bear with the bad with great patience.[24] These Gospel subjects—think of the parable of the chaff mixed with the wheat[25]—had received much attention in the controversy of Saint Augustine against the Donatists, who advocated a Church composed only of the pure:

The Donatists say that we must depart bodily from an evil society. But this is not true. Hence, the Apostle's words must be understood of a spiritual separation and are explained in this way: "go out" spiritually by not following their life. "*As a lily among brambles*" (Song 2:2), and this in order to avoid the very occasions of sin given by them.[26]

According to the Common Doctor, this verse first illustrates the general truth that "there is hardly ever a large congregation without someone evil."[27] Saint Thomas quotes Song 2:2, for example, regarding the difficulties of the first community of Corinth reported

23. The coexistence of the good and the evil in the Church is one of the motifs that explain the comparison of the Church-Spouse to the moon, which is at the same time bright (by the saints) and dark (by the sinners). See Aquinas, *In Ps.* 10, 1 [no. 234] (trans. Benjamin Martin): "The moon is the Church: Cant. 6: '*Fair as the moon,*' because of her brightness, and because of her darkening. The brightness of the moon is from the sun, just so the brightness of the Church is from Christ: John 1: "He was the true light which shines," etc. Also half the circle of the moon is bright, and half dark; thus in the Church there are some who are bright, and some dark. Now, the moon is obscured, according to the gloss, sometimes on account of its own orbit, and at such times it becomes dark; at other times because of an eclipse, in which case it is turned into blood, at other times when a cloud passes in front of it, and then it becomes black."

24. See "II, 7," in *The Glossa ordinaria on the Song of Songs*, 36: "In the church there cannot be bad people without good people or good people without bad people; there has been no good man who has not been able to tolerate wicked men"; Gregory the Great, *Moralia in Iob*, XX, xxxix, 74–75 (CCSL 143A) (Turnhout: Brepols, 2005), 1058–59, with a reference to Song 2:2. See *ST* II-II, q. 108, a. 1, obj. 2 [no. 59]; *In Matth.*, c. 9, 2 (n° 762) [no. 62]; *In 1 ad Co.*, c. 5, lect. 2 (n° 241) [no. 69].

25. See Matthew 13:24–30 and 13:36–43; Aquinas, *In Matth.*, c. 13, 2 (n° 1156) [no. 64]: "However long that time lasts, the evil are with the good, the weed with the wheat, the '*lily among the thorns,*' as it is said (Song 2:2)"; *In Matth.*, c. 13, 4 (n° 1199) [no. 65].

26. *In 2 ad Co.*, c. 6, lect. 3 (n° 243) [no. 71].

27. *In Matth.*, c. 10, 1 (n° 812) [n° 63]. See *In ad Ga.*, c. 4, lect. 9 (n° 275) [no. 72].

by Saint Paul.[28] The presence of Judas in the apostolic college has archetypal value here, and Saint Thomas often brings it up:

Our Lord chose Judas, whom he knew would become an evil person, so that we could realize that there would be no human society which does not have some evil members: "*as a lily among brambles, so is my love among maidens*" (Song 2:2).[29]

For the fact that certain men among religious commit crimes is no reason for defaming the whole religious body. Otherwise, the treachery of Judas ought to have been attributed to the whole College of the apostles on account of the words, "Have not I chosen you twelve, and one of you is a devil?" (John 6:71). St. Gregory, commenting on the words of Song of Songs 2:2: "*As a lily among brambles, so is my love among maidens*," says: "There cannot be bad men without good, nor good without bad."[30]

If the Church tolerates sinners within herself, the fact remains that her deep nature as the Spouse of Christ makes itself manifest essentially in her most holy members. Her nuptial sanctity finds in the Immaculate Virgin its model and highest realization.

28. Cf. *In 1 ad Co.*, c. 11, lect. 4 (nº 625) [no. 70].

29. *In Ioan.*, c. 13, lect. 3 (nº 1791) [no. 68].

30. Thomas Aquinas, *Contra impugnantes*, c. 20 [no. 60]. The translation is taken from Thomas Aquinas, *Liber contra impugnantes Dei cultum et religionem*, trans. John Procter, OP (London: Sands & Co., 1902). See also *In Ioan.*, c. 12, lect. 1 (nº 1605) [no. 67]: Why did Jesus entrust Judas with the money box, since he knew he was a thief? "According to Augustine, Christ did this so that his Church would be patient when it was robbed; for one is not good if he cannot endure those who are evil. Thus we read: '*as a lily among brambles, so is my love among maidens*' (Song 2:2)."

4

The Virgin Mary, All Beautiful and Spotless

The Virgin Mary is simultaneously the most excellent member of and the icon that synoptically recapitulates all the perfections of the Church. Consequently, it is not surprising that some commentators have seen in the beloved of the Song a figure of the Virgin Mary.[1] In the medieval Latin tradition, the Marian interpretation of the Song takes flight with Rupert of Deutz at the beginning of the twelfth century and becomes from then on an important aspect of any reading of the Song.[2] Entering into this perspective, Saint

1. See E. Ann Matter, "The Woman Who Is the All: The Virgin Mary and the Song of Songs," chap. 6 in *The Voice of My Beloved*; Riedlinger, *Die Makellosogkeit der Kirche*, 202–33 and 320–34.

2. See Rupert of Deutz, *Commentaria in Canticum canticorum*, Corpus Christianorum Continuatio Medievalis [CCCM] 26 (Turnhout: Brepols, 1974). See Benedict XVI, General Audience on Rupert of Deutz (Wednesday, December 9, 2009), http://w2.vatican.va/content/benedict-xvi/en/audiences/2009/documents/hf_ben-xvi_aud_20091209.html: "In the interpretation of the Bible, Rupert did not limit himself to repeating the teaching of the Fathers, but shows an originality of his own. For example, he is the first writer to have identified the bride in the Song of Songs with Mary Most Holy. His commentary on this book of Scripture has thus turned out to be a sort of Mariological *summa*, in which he presents Mary's privileges and excellent virtues. In one of the most inspired passages of his commentary Rupert writes: 'O most beloved among the beloved, Virgin of virgins, what does your beloved Son so praise in you that the whole choir of angels exalts? What they praise is your simplicity, purity, innocence, doctrine, modesty, humility, integrity of mind and body, that is, your incorrupt virginity'

Thomas attributes a Marian meaning to several verses of the Song.[3]

The principal Marian verse of the Song is clearly Song 4:7: "Thou art all fair, O my love, and there is not a spot in thee."[4] Saint Thomas quotes all or part of this verse thirteen times, and, with one exception,[5] he always explicitly applies it to the Virgin Mary. Sometimes Song 4:7 serves him solely to highlight some general perfection of the Virgin Mary in the order of grace.[6] But most of the time, this verse serves to support his teaching on the unique character of the sanctity of the Mother of Christ, in particular her separation from all sin. Mary, all beautiful and without sin, is "the stainless road" taken by Christ.[7] In the *Tertia pars* of the *Summa theologiae*, Song 4:7 is quoted three times in question 27 alone, which is devoted to the sanctification of the Virgin Mary as part of the group of questions that deal with the entrance of Christ into this world.[8] In article 4, Song 4:7 appears as the conclusion of the *respondeo*, in which the Angelic Doctor has established by three arguments that there was

(*In Canticum canticorum* 4, 1–6, *CCL* 26, pp. 69–70). The Marian interpretation of Rupert's *Canticum* is a felicitous example of harmony between liturgy and theology. In fact, various passages of this Book of the Bible were already used in liturgical celebrations on Marian feasts."

3. The Marian meaning and the ecclesial meaning are in no way mutually exclusive. On the contrary, they call for each other. For example, the same verse, Song 6:9, that compares the beauty of the beloved to that of the moon, is applied to the Church when Saint Thomas comments on Ps 10 [no. 234] and to the Virgin Mary when he comments on 1 Corinthians 15 on the different types of luminosity of celestial bodies. See *In 1 ad Co.*, c. 15, lect. 6 (n° 978) [no. 235]: "By the sun can be understood Christ: 'but for you who fear my name the sun of righteousness shall rise' (Mal 4:2); by the moon, the Blessed Virgin: "*fair as the moon*" (Song 6:10); by the stars mutually situated, the other saints: "the stars from their courses" (Judg 5:20)."

4. See also, with the same meaning, Song 1:14, quoted to exalt "Mary's purity" in *In Is.*, c. 11, (p. 78–79) [no. 47].

5. See *In Is.*, c. 40 (p. 172) [no. 140]. The verse is applied to the beauty of the virtuous life of the saints.

6. In *In Is.*, c. 16 (p. 97) [no. 139], Song 4:7 illustrates the unique character of the firmness of grace in Mary, who is the "rock of the desert" (Is 16:1) from which comes Christ, the Lamb of God.

7. See *In Ps.* 17, 18 (p. 203) [no. 141].

8. On *ST* III, q. 27, essential to the Marian theology of Saint Thomas, see Jean-Pierre Torrell, OP, *Encyclopédie Jésus le Christ chez saint Thomas* (Paris: Cerf, 2008), 481–92.

in the Virgin Mary, Mother of Christ, no actual sin, neither mortal nor venial:

> We must therefore confess simply that the Blessed Virgin committed no actual sin, neither mortal nor venial; so that what is written (Song 4:7) is fulfilled: "*Thou art all fair, O my love, and there is not a spot in thee.*"[9]

The third argument of this *respondeo*, which is taken from the unique way in which Wisdom Incarnate made his home in Mary, is already associated with Song 4:7 in the parallel text of the *Scriptum*:

> In Wisdom 1:4 it is said that "wisdom will not enter into an evil soul, nor will it dwell in a body given over to sin." But the wisdom of God does not only enter into the soul of the virgin, as it is also said concerning other matters in Wisdom 7:27: "she passes into holy souls," but he also dwelt within her body, taking flesh from her. Therefore, there was no sin in her, which may be gathered from what is said in Cant. 4:7, "*You are entirely beautiful, my beloved, and there is no stain in you.*"[10]

The absence in the Virgin Mary of all venial sin is already sufficient to distinguish her from all other saints:

> And there is one kind of sanctification which pertains to the Blessed Virgin, and another which belongs to the saints: for some had been sanctified because they had never sinned mortally, although they had venially, as it says in I John 1: "If we say that we have not sin," etc. But the Blessed Virgin never sinned either mortally, or venially: Cant. 4: "*You are entirely beautiful, my friend,*" etc. And therefore he says, she shall not be moved, even by venial sin.[11]

9. *ST* III, q. 27, a. 4 [no. 137].

10. *In* III *Sent.*, d. 3, q. 1, a. 2, qla 2, s.c. 2 [no. 134] (trans. Benjamin Martin). See also *In Ps.* 18, 3 [no. 142], where the Virgin is presented as the sun, wholly light, "without the darkness of sin," in which Christ made his home (Ps 18:6); *In Matth.*, c. 12, 4 (n° 1073) [no. 144], where Saint Thomas connects the Song with the famous assertion of Saint Augustine in *On Nature and Grace*, XXXVI, 42: "in whose case, out of respect for the Lord, I wish to raise no question at all when the discussion concerns sins." Translation taken from Augustine, *Four Anti-Pelagian Writings: On Nature and Grace, On the Proceedings of Pelagius, On the Predestination of Saints, On the Gift of Perseverance, trans.* John A. Mourant and William J. Collinge (Washington, D.C.: The Catholic University of America Press, 1992), 53–54. See also *Collaciones in salutationem angelicam* (n° 1115) [no. 145].

11. See *In Ps.* 45, 4 [no. 143] (trans. Benjamin Martin).

However, the preceding article of the *Tertia pars* (article 3 of q. 27) had also used Song 4:7 as a *sed contra* argument from authority to clarify the unique situation of the Virgin Mary with respect to the fomes of sin (*fomes peccati*), that is, the disorder of powers resulting from original sin. In her, the fomes was at first "tied," made ineffective, by virtue of a special action of Providence, and then it was totally removed when she conceived the Son of God according to the flesh. In her, the *fomes* would have constituted a "stain."[12] The neutralization of the *fomes peccati* also implies that Mary never knew the so-called sins of first movement, when an objectively disordered movement of the sensible appetite, contrary to right reason, occurs before reason has time to react.[13]

That said, Saint Thomas does not ignore that some could invoke Song 4:7 to support the immaculist thesis of a total exemption of original sin for the Virgin Mary, which Saint Thomas himself always refused to accept. He quotes Song 4:7 in an objection of article 2, where he examines—in order to dismiss—the possibility of a sanctification of the Virgin before her animation in the maternal womb:

Further, as Anselm says (*De Concep. Virg.* xviii), "it was fitting that this Virgin should shine with such a purity that under God none greater can be imagined": wherefore it is written (Song 4:7): "*Thou art all fair, O my love, and there is not a spot in thee.*" But the purity of the Blessed Virgin would

12. See *ST* III, q. 27, a. 3, s.c. [no. 136].

13. See Thomas Aquinas, *Sermo* XXIV [no. 146]. See Thomas Aquinas, *Compendium theologiae* [*Comp. theol.*], I, c. 224: "Moreover venial sin sometimes creeps up on us unawares, owing to the fact that an inordinate motion of concupiscence or of some other passion arises prior to the advertence of the mind, yet in such a way that the first motions are called sins. Hence we conclude that the Blessed Virgin Mary never committed a venial sin, for she did not experience such inordinate motions of passion. Inordinate motions of this kind arise because the sensitive appetite, which is the subject of these passions, is not so obedient to reason as not sometimes to move toward an object outside the order of reason, or even, occasionally, against reason; and this is what engenders the sinful impulse. In the Blessed Virgin, accordingly, the sensitive appetite was rendered so subject to reason by the power of the grace which sanctified it, that it was never aroused against reason, but was always in conformity with the order of reason. Nevertheless she could experience some spontaneous movements not ordered by reason." All translations of *Comp. theol.* are taken from Thomas Aquinas, *Light of Faith: The Compendium of Theology*, trans. Cyril Vollert, SJ (Manchester, N.H.: Sophia Institute Press, 1993).

have been greater, if she had never been stained by the contagion of original sin. Therefore it was granted to her to be sanctified before her flesh was animated.[14]

Certainly, Saint Thomas holds that the Virgin Mary was purified from original sin in an absolutely unique manner, "by a special privilege" that distinguishes her from all other saints:

And so we are to believe that she was free from every stain of actual sin—not only of mortal sin but of venial sin. Such freedom from sin can pertain to none of the saints after Christ, as we know from 1 John 1:8: "If we say that we have no sin we deceive ourselves, and the truth is not in us." But what is said in the Song of Solomon 4:7, "*You are all fair, my love, and there is no spot in you,*" can well be understood of the Blessed Virgin, Mother of God.[15]

But the Dominican theologian firmly excludes the idea that the Virgin would have been exempted from contracting original sin itself.

According to Saint Thomas, some other verses of the Song have a Marian meaning. Given the principle of the diffusion of perfection, Mary's fullness of grace makes her a source of grace for all others, as Saint Bernard had earlier explained with the same words of the Song in his famous sermon on the aqueduct:

Light is the gracious mother of colors. In the same way the Blessed Virgin is the mother of virtues.... Hence Bernard says: "If we have any virtue, if we have any salvation and grace, we know that we are completely satiated by her who overflows with delights. For here is that enclosed garden through which the Auster, the divine wind, blows, and the odors of it flow into the spiritual gifts of the graces [cf. Song 4.12–16]."[16]

In his *collatio* on the angelic salutation, Saint Thomas explains that the fullness of grace of the one who is "all beautiful and spotless" makes her a universal mediatrix of grace, always ready to of-

14. *ST* III, q. 27, a. 2, obj. 2 [no. 135].

15. *Comp. theol.*, I, c. 224, lines 12–13 [no. 138].

16. *Thomas* Aquinas, "*Lux Orta,*" in *The Academic Sermons,* 250 [no. 152]. See Bernard of Clairvaux, "Sermo De nativitate beatae Mariae," Sermones II, in *Opera omnia,* vol. 5 (Rome: 1968), 278–79.

fer her help. He links this theme with the protective bucklers of Song 4:4:

It is a great thing in a Saint when he has grace to bring about the salvation of many, but it is exceedingly wonderful when grace is of such abundance as to be sufficient for the salvation of all men in the world, and this is true of Christ and of the Blessed Virgin. Thus, "*a thousand bucklers,*" that is, remedies against dangers, "*hang therefrom*" [Sg 4:4].[17]

17. Thomas Aquinas, *Collaciones in salutationem angelicam* (nº 1118) [no. 133].

5

The Faithful Soul

The reader of the Song can identify himself with Christ, the Lover, given that according to the moral or tropological meaning of Scripture, it is up to him to reproduce in himself, under the motion of the Holy Spirit, the perfections and the mysteries of Christ. However, at least from Origen on, it is the beloved with whom the faithful soul identifies in a privileged way.[1] This identification not only does not compete with the ecclesial interpretation of the figure of the beloved—*Ecclesia vel anima* (the Church or the soul), as Saint Thomas occasionally says[2]—but rather supposes it. It is indeed by and in the Church, the unique Spouse of Christ, that each faithful person is the object of the prevenient love of Christ and adopts in return the sentiments of the Bride for the Bridegroom.[3] We will have confirmation of this when we consider the place of the doctrine of faith and the sacraments of the Church in the sanctification of the faithful soul. But it is already significant that in several passages of

1. E. Ann Matter, "The Marriage of the Soul," chap. 5 in *The Voice of My Beloved.*

2. See *In Ier.*, c. 1, 5 (p. 582) [no. 130].

3. See de Lubac, *Medieval Exegesis,* vol. 1, 146: "[In Origen's commentary on the Song of Songs], the individual soul always makes its appearance here within the Church. Its union with the Word is shown here as being a consequence of the union of Christ with his Church. The different applications that concern the soul are always the object of a 'third exposition' or a 'third category of exposition,' which depends on the mystery of the Church."

the *Expositio super Isaiam*, the application of a biblical theme to the faithful soul is framed by its application both to the Church on earth and to the Church in heaven. For example, according to Aquinas, the "feast of fat things" promised in Isaiah 25:6 can be understood either as the "domestic" feast of the Church Militant, the "private" feast of the soul, or finally the "solemn" feast of the heavenly court, each of these interpretations being generally illustrated by a verse of the Song.[4] Saint Thomas does not consider the present relations of the individual soul to God either outside of their ecclesial context here below or as cut off from their eschatological fulfillment in heaven.

With regard to the personal relationships of the soul with the Lover, the quotations of the Song are first of all used to evoke the nature and effects of love in general, and then the nature and effects of charity, which is the supernatural and perfect form of love. Charity is essentially ecclesial because it is nourished by the teaching of the true faith and by the sacraments, particularly the Eucharist, in which communion with Christ is consummated. Union with Christ in charity here on earth finds its fulfillment—at the end of our journey, about which the amorous play of the Song suggests some hidden depths—in the rest of contemplation. Nevertheless, this contemplation cannot fail to redound upon our preaching.

OF LOVE AND ITS EFFECTS

Sensitive Affectivity and Spiritual Affectivity

Authentic amorous passion is certainly not reducible to a feast of the senses. It engages us much more, and more intimately. Even so,

4. See *In Is.*, c. 25 (p. 122) [no. 2]. See also the interpretation of the vine in *In Is.*, c. 5 (p. 39) [no. 105]. The vine can have four meanings. The first, the vine of earthly concupiscence, is negative. The three others are positive and refer to (a) the faithful soul, (b) the Church militant and (c) the celestial Fatherland. See again *In Is.*, c. 23 [no. 112]: "first of his own conscience, calling to mind his sins.... Second, of the Church militant, imitating the example of the just.... Third, of the heavenly homeland, contemplating the reward of the saints: '*I will rise, [and will go about the city, in the streets and the broad ways I will seek him whom my soul loves]*' (Song 3:2)."

it is profoundly "sensual," and there is no reason for surprise at the preponderant place occupied by feelings and sensations in the Song: perfumes, colors, sounds, kisses, and so on. The mutual attraction and union of the lovers are expressed through the categories of sensual pleasures. Aquinas has no scruples about integrating this celebration of feeling into the order of spiritual love. The latter, in fact, is by no means a "platonic," disembodied love, but it assumes into its own order the sensual dimension of all human love. The solid Aristotelian empiricism of Saint Thomas could only encourage this assumption of the sensible into the spiritual.

For Saint Thomas, a passion—as, for example, love—consists of two aspects: a material or physiological aspect and a formal or psychological aspect.[5] In the strict sense, passion belongs only to sensitive affectivity. However, we find in the spiritual affectivity movements that correspond analogically to the formal element of sensible passion. There is thus a strictly spiritual love that bears on a rational good, just as sensible love bears on a sensible good.[6] The relations between the sensible affectivity and these movements of spiritual affectivity are complex. On one hand, without ever being able to determine it totally, the passions influence the will, for good as well as evil: a sensible love can turn the will from its rational authentic good, just as it can support and strengthen an upright spiritual love. On the other hand, the orientations taken at the level of spiritual

5. See *ST* I, q. 20, a. 1, ad 2: "In the passions of the sensitive appetite there may be distinguished a certain material element—namely, the bodily change—and a certain formal element, which is on the part of the appetite. Thus in anger, as the Philosopher says (*De Anima* iii. 15, 63, 64), the material element is the kindling of the blood about the heart; but the formal, the appetite for revenge." On the passions according to Saint Thomas, see Kevin White, "The Passions of the Soul: (Ia IIae, qq. 22–48)," in *The Ethics of Aquinas*, ed. Stephen J. Pope (Washington, D.C.: Georgetown University Press, 2002), 103–15; Robert Miner, *Thomas Aquinas on the Passions: A Study of "Summa Theologiae," 1a2ae 22–48* (Cambridge: Cambridge University Press, 2009); Nicholas Lombardo, OP, *The Logic of Desire: Aquinas on Emotions* (Washington, D.C.: The Catholic University of America Press, 2011); Serge-Thomas Bonino, OP, "Les passions dans la théologie de saint Thomas d'Aquin: L'enseignement de la *Lectura super Ioannem*," in *Le emozioni secondo san Tommaso*, ed. S.-T. Bonino and G. Mazzotta (Rome: Urbaniana University Press, 2019), 7–25.

6. See *ST* I-II, q. 22, a. 3.

affectivity, natural and supernatural, spill over into the domain of feelings and sometimes even determine them. So charity can arouse and maintain a real loving passion for Christ, without being reduced to it.

Some Effects of Love: "Summa theologiae" I-II, q. 28, a. 5

The strongest concentration of quotations of the Song in the *Summa theologiae* occurs in I-II, question 28, which is about the effects of the passion of love. This is also where Dionysius's influence is also particularly marked since most of the *sed contra* arguments of this question are borrowed from the Areopagite. Love causes the union (article 1) and mutual indwelling of the lovers (article 2). It brings ecstasy, in that it makes the lover go out of himself, in the direction of the beloved (article 3). It excites good zeal, that is, a healthy jealousy (article 4), and is the driving force of all the person's action (article 6). In article 5, Saint Thomas asks if love is a wound in the lover (*laesiva amantis*). He responds that love, of itself, when it bears on the authentic good, far from destroying the lover, perfects him. Love promotes him in being; that is, it carries him to a richer, more intense life.[7] Our Dominican nevertheless admits that accidentally and indirectly, because of their physiological repercussions, the effects of the passion of love can introduce negative consequences for the one that loves, similar to how a light too intense can damage the eyes.[8] It is the same with the four next ef-

7. See *ST* I-II, q. 28, a. 5: "Love denotes a certain adapting of the appetitive power to some good. Now nothing is hurt by being adapted to that which is suitable to it; rather, if possible, it is perfected and bettered. But if a thing be adapted to that which is not suitable to it, it is hurt and made worse thereby. Consequently love of a suitable good perfects and betters the lover; but love of a good which is unsuitable to the lover, wounds and worsens him. Wherefore man is perfected and bettered chiefly by the love of God: but is wounded and worsened by the love of sin, according to [Hosea] 9:10: *They became abominable, as those things which they loved*. And let this be understood as applying to love in respect of its formal element, i.e., in regard to the appetite."

8. See *ST* I-II, q. 28, a. 5: "But in respect of the material element in the passion of love, i.e., a certain bodily change, it happens that love is hurtful, by reason of this change

fects of love—languor, enjoyment, melting of the heart, and fervor. Of themselves, explains Saint Thomas in the response to the objections, these effects are good and necessary to love, but they can have negative physiological consequences.[9]

Now, the three "objections" that were intended to support the idea that a wound is inherent to love are all, systematically, based on verses of the Song. It seems that this connection between the effects of love and certain verses of the Song is an invention of Saint Thomas himself. He uses the Song as a mine of information on the passion of love.

Here is the first of these objections:

> For languor denotes a hurt in the one that languishes. But love causes languor: for it is written (Song 2:5): "*Stay me up with flowers, compass me about with apples; because I languish with love.*" Therefore love is a wounding passion.[10]

In the response to the objection, Saint Thomas defines languor as the sadness caused by the absence of the beloved.[11] Evoked in several verses of the Song, languor consists in being consumed, in the "drying" of love, because of the heat love produces.[12] Languor certainly represents a corporeal waning of strength, but it is a healthy waning, caused by the promptness or vigor of love.[13]

---

being excessive: just as it happens in the senses, and in every act of a power of the soul that is exercised through the change of some bodily organ."

9. *ST* I-II, q. 28, a. 5, ad 1: "these are the effects of love considered formally, according to the relation of the appetitive power to its object. But in the passion of love, other effects ensue, proportionate to the above, in respect of a change in the organ."

10. *ST* I-II, q. 28, a. 5, obj. 1 [no. 86].

11. *ST* I-II, q. 28, a. 5, ad 1: "If, then, the beloved is present and possessed, pleasure or enjoyment ensues. But if the beloved be absent, two passions arise; viz., sadness at its absence, which is denoted by *languor* . . . and an intense desire to possess the beloved, which is signified by *fervor*."

12. The effect of charity is to "consume" and "dry up" from love. See *In Is.*, c. 30 (p. 140) [no. 85]: "charity is called fire first because it gives light. . . . Second, because it blazes out: '*stay me up with flowers, encircle me with apples, for I am faint with love*' (Song 2:5)."

13. See *In Matth.*, c. 26, lect. 5 (n° 2237) [no. 198]: "A good weakness, according to which the body fails in readiness, as is said, *I adjure you, O daughters of Jerusalem, if you find my beloved, that you tell him that I languish with love* (Song 5:8)."

Another effect of love, which the second objection lifts up, is melting. The lover "melts with love":

Melting is a kind of dissolution. But love melts that in which it is: for it is written (Song 5:6): *"My soul melted when my beloved spoke."* Therefore love is a dissolvent: therefore it is a corruptive and a wounding passion.[14]

The response to the objection explains very well in what sense this melting is essential in love:

Of these the first is *melting*, which is opposed to freezing. For things that are frozen, are closely bound together, so as to be hard to pierce. But it belongs to love that the appetite is fitted to receive the good which is loved, inasmuch as the object loved is in the lover.... Consequently the freezing or hardening of the heart is a disposition incompatible with love: while melting denotes a softening of the heart, whereby the heart shows itself to be ready for the entrance of the beloved.[15]

If Thomas's tracking of love's other effects comes from Dionysius, the idea of melting as an effect of love seems connected, in Saint Thomas's work, to his reading of Song 5:6. Nevertheless he often presents melting not so much as what makes the lover ready to welcome in himself the beloved but more as what allows him to expand and spread himself to the beloved, as required by the ecstatic character of love:

Alternately, it is to be said that the melting is a result of love. Cant. 5: *"My soul melted."* A thing before it becomes liquid, is hard and compacted in itself; if it melts, it spills out and tends from itself towards another.[16]

14. *ST* I-II, q. 28, a. 5, obj. 2 [no. 195]. In *In* III *Sent.*, d. 27, q. 1, a. 1, obj. 4 [no. 194] (trans. Benjamin Martin), the melting virtue of love, emphasized by Song 5:6, and some other effects of love are rather seen as so many objections to the *vis unitiva* of love, that is, to its ability to conjoin lovers: "Furthermore, Dionysius, sets among the properties of love that it is acute and fervent, he also states that liquefaction is an effect of love; Cant. 5:6: *My soul is melted.* Dionysius also states that ecstasy is an effect of love, that is a going out of oneself. But all these things seem to pertain to division, inasmuch as it pertains to the acute to penetrate by division, to that which is fervent (boiling) to be resolved by evaporation; moreover, liquefaction is a sort of division opposed to freezing: for that which goes outside of itself is divided from itself. Therefore, love is more a divisive than a unitive force."

15. *ST* I-II, q. 28, a. 5, ad 1.

16. *In Ps.* 21, 11 [no. 196] (trans. Benjamin Martin). Saint Thomas comments on "My

As a remedy to hardness of heart, which is an obstacle to love, the idea of melting can be likened to that of sweetness,[17] to which Saint Thomas seems to be particularly sensitive, given that the vocabulary of sweetness (*dulcedo, mansuetudo, suavitas...*) is omnipresent in the context of his use of the Song. Sweetness evokes an objective harmony, subjectively perceived and tasted, between the subject that senses (touch, taste, hear) and the sensed object. This happy co-adaptation that is sweetness is thus particularly suited to signifying the mutual complaisance of lovers.[18]

A third effect of love, identified by Dionysius, also seems to be damaging to health: fervor.

> Further, fervor denotes a certain excess of heat; which excess has a corruptive effect. But love causes fervor: for Dionysius (*Coel. Hier.* vii) in reckoning the properties belonging to the Seraphim's love, includes "hot" and "piercing" and "most fervent." Moreover it is said of love (Song 8:6) that "*its lamps are fire and flames.*" Therefore love is a wounding and corruptive passion.[19]

Song 8:6—"the lamps thereof are fire and flames"—is one of the most quoted verses of the Song in Thomas's corpus (fourteen

---

heart is become like wax melting in the midst of my bowels," which he applies to Christ in his Passion. It is interesting to observe that, in the text, the melting is attributed to the action of the Holy Spirit, as it is the principle of the blazing charity of Christ as Head of the Church. Among other texts that mention the "centrifugal" aspect of the melting of love, see *In Matth.*, c. 13, lect. 1 (n° 1089) [no. 197]: "The second is hardness of heart; *his heart shall be as hard as a stone, and as firm as a smith's anvil* (Job 41:15). And this is opposed to charity, because it belongs to love to melt the heart; *my soul melted when he spoke* (Song 5:6). For that is hard which is constrained within itself, and bound to its own measurement. Love works to transfer the one loving into the one loved; hence the one loving is spread out"; also *In 1 ad Co.*, c. 13, lect. 2 (n° 773): "just as fire by melting metal makes it flow, so charity inclines a person not to keep the good things he has, but makes them flow to others."

17. The rapprochement between the Name compared to an oil that spreads (Song 1:3; Song 1:2 Vulgate) and mercy falls under the same logic that links love and melting. See *In Is.*, c. 56 [no. 4]; *In Ps.* 19, 1 [no. 6]; *In Ioan.*, c. 1, lect. 15 (n° 285) [no. 9].

18. The words of Christ are sweet for those who love him but hard for those who do not love him (see *In Ioan.*, c. 8, lect. 5 (n° 1238) [no. 100]); in passing from slavery to the devil to the yoke of Christ, man passes from hardness to sweetness (Thomas Aquinas, "*Veniet Desideratus,*" in *The Academic Sermons*, 31 [no. 213]).

19. *ST* I-II, q. 28, a. 5, obj. 3 [no. 276].

times), right after Song 2:2. It assists the comparison of love, in every shape and form, to a fire: "For fire is commonly used to symbolize the fervor of love, as we read in the Song of Songs, '*his lamps are fire and torches*' (Song 8:6)."[20] This comparison, commonplace as it is, allows Saint Thomas to bring up several aspects of love (natural and supernatural) that correspond to properties of fire, as conceived by ancient physics or common experience. The commentary on John 5:35, where the Lord Jesus describes Saint John the Baptist as "a burning and a shining light," outlines an ordering of these correspondences between fire and love:

Its burning signifies love for three reasons.

- First, because fire is the most active of all bodies; so too is the warmth of charity, so much so that nothing can withstand its force: "the love of Christ spurs us on" (2 Cor 5:14).
- Second, because just as fire, because it is very volatile, causes great unrest, so also this love of charity makes a person restless until he achieves his objective: "*its light is fire and flame*" (Song 8:6).
- Third, just as fire is inclined to move upward, so too is charity; so much so that it joins us to God: "he who abides in love abides in God, and God in him" (1 John 4:16).[21]

Although in the text of the *Lectura super Iohannem* Song 8:6 is used to describe the second of these effects of love (the heating of fervor), Saint Thomas uses it elsewhere to illustrate indifferently any one of these three effects of love.

Fire is then, first of all, an eminently active element that is always developing: fire communicates itself, and to anything to which it is communicated it transmits its own communicative dynamism. Likewise, love is a principle of action that is always developing.[22] It leads the subject whom it affects to communicate himself, among other reasons because it makes him "melt" and therefore spread himself.

20. Thomas Aquinas, *Expositio super Iob ad litteram* [*In Iob*], c. 18 (p. 109) [no. 281].

21. *In Ioan.*, c. 5, lect. 6 (n° 812) [no. 283].

22. See *ST* II-II, q. 24, a. 10, s.c. [no. 277] (regarding charity, which, as such, can never diminish).

Thus the love of God is the principle of all his action *ad extra*, that is, regarding creatures:

The cause of our salvation is God's love: "but God, who is rich in mercy, out of the great love with which he loved us, even when we were dead through our trespasses, made us alive together with Christ" (Eph 2:4). This charity is described, first, in its intensity; second, in its effect. The inward intensity of charity is designated by *benignity*, which is from *bonus*, which means 'good,' and *ignis*, which means 'fire.'[23] Now fire signifies love: "*love is strong as death, its flashes are flashes of fire*" (Song 8:6). Therefore, *benignity* is an internal love, which expresses itself outwardly in good works. Now this love was present in God from all eternity, because his love is the cause of all things.[24]

Thus, the fire of love stirs to action (*stimulare, urgere, sollicitare . . .*) those whom it enkindles.[25] It is, for example, the principle and the driving force of apostolic activity:

"The charity of Christ presses us" to this. He says, "presses," because it is the same as stimulates. As if to say: the love of God, as a goad, stimulates us to do what charity commands, namely, to procure the salvation of our neighbor. "*Those who are led*," i.e., stirred, "by the Spirit of God are sons of God" (Rom 8:14); "*its flashes are flashes of fire*" (Song 8:6).[26]

Fire, as heat that subsists, is the cause of all heat wherever it is found, according to the principle of the causality of the maximum.[27] In what it touches, it provokes a heating, which seeks to be expressed and puts its subject under tension.[28]

Finally, fire tends upward as toward its natural place. Likewise, love raises the beloved from her bed to seek her beloved (Song 3:1), and charity raises to God.[29]

23. This fanciful etymological explanation of the word "benignity" as "good fire" is frequent in Thomas's work. See *ST* I-II, q. 79, a. 3; *In Ps.* 51, 2 (p. 352); *In 1 ad Co.*, c. 13, lect. 2 (n° 773); *In ad Ga.*, c. 5, lect. 6 (n° 332); *In ad Col.*, 3, lect. 3 (n° 160).

24. *In ad Tit.*, c. 3, lect. 1 (n° 88) [no. 288].

25. See *In Ps.* 26, 3 (p. 237) [no. 279]; *In Ioan.*, c. 20, lect. 1 (n° 2473) [no. 285].

26. *In 2 ad Co.*, c. 5, lect. 3 (n° 181) [no. 287].

27. See *In ad He.*, c. 1, lect. 3 (n° 58) [no. 289].

28. Charity fixes in God the intention of the will. See *In Ioan.*, c. 14, lect. 6 (n° 1942) [no. 284].

29. See *In Is.*, c. 30 [no. 109].

All these effects, attributed to love by virtue of its comparison with fire, fall under the action of the Holy Spirit when they concern the supernatural order of charity. The Spirit is the Fire sent by the ascended Christ, so great that nothing escapes its heat (Ps 18:7).[30] The Spirit "fuels and nourishes the heat of love within us."[31]

> [The Spirit] is called fire because it lifts up our hearts by its ardor and heat: "ardent in Spirit" (Rom 12:11), and because it burns up sins: "*its light is fire and flame*" (Song 8:6).[32]

Ecstasy

To clarify certain effects of love, particularly its ecstatic character, Saint Thomas also has recourse to the theme of wine and of drunkenness, a theme very present in the Song. As Dionysius the Areopagite brings to light, love leads the lover to come out of himself, to transfer himself to the beloved by giving himself to her. The beloved then takes possession, in a way, of the lover and his actions: the lover no longer belongs to himself.[33] This effect of love is analogous to that of the drunkenness produced by wine. Both drunkennesses, that of wine and that of love, make the subject cease to be his own measure, according to the supposed etymology of the word "inebriation" that would have to do with "measure."[34] Regarding the "chalice that inebriates" the Lord's faithful (Ps 22:5), Saint Thomas explains:

> This chalice is the gift of divine love which inebriates; because the one who is inebriated is not said to be so either in himself, or according to himself, but according to the power of the wine; so he who is full of divine love is said to be inebriated according to God: for he has entered an ecstatic state. Cant. 5: "*Eat, my friends, and be drunk.*" Isa. 55: "As the rain and

30. See *In Ps.* 18, 4 [no. 278].

31. *In Ps.* 44, 5 [no. 280] (trans. Martin).

32. *In Ioan*, c. 4, lect. 2 (n° 577) [no. 282].

33. See *ST* I-II, q. 28, a. 3; Dionysius, *The Divine Names*, ch. IV, 13, in Pseudo-Dionysius, *The Complete Works*, trans. Colm Luibheid with Paul Rorem (New York: Paulist Press, 1987), 47–131, at 82.

34. See *In 2 ad Co.*, c. 5, lect. 3 (n° 179) [no. 180]; *In I Sent.*, Prol. [no. 159]. On the supposed etymology of "bria," see Thomas Aquinas, *Commentaire de la Deuxième Epitre aux Corinthiens*, 147n7.

the snow fall from heaven, and water the earth, and cause it to sprout; so shall the word be which shall come forth from my mouth." Jer. 23: "I have become like a drunken man, like a man sodden with wine from the face of the Lord."[35]

The invitation to get drunk, addressed to the "dearly beloved" (*charissimi*)—"Be inebriated, my dearly beloved" (Song 5:1)—is therefore an invitation to charity (*charitas*), to the love of God above all things. "And those who are drunk, are not so within themselves, but without themselves. Thus, those who are filled with the spiritual gifts have their entire intention fixed on God."[36] It is "that inebriation which is from the Holy Spirit and draws men to divine things and about which it is said: '*eat, O friends, and drink: drink deeply, O lovers!*' (Song 5:1)."[37]

CHARITY

Indeed, the most perfect form of love is charity, spread in hearts by the Holy Spirit. It gives the spiritual creature a supernatural participation in the love with which God infinitely loves himself, and all things in this love. The love described by the Song between Christ the Bridegroom and the Church/soul-Bride is then, ultimately, charity. Charity takes up in an eminent manner the already-mentioned effects of love in general. Nevertheless, Saint Thomas draws on many verses of the Song to illustrate certain aspects that are proper to charity as such. I will examine two.

Song 2:4—"He set in order charity in me"[38] (*Ordinavit in me caritatem*)—brings together the notions of charity and order. Saint Thomas invokes it, particularly in his systematic works, each time when he deals with the question of order among the persons that we

35. *In Ps.* 22, 2 [no. 173] (trans. Benjamin Martin). See *In Ioan.*, c. 2, lect. 1 (nº 347) [no. 167]; *In Is.*, c. 28 (p. 130) [no. 171].

36. *In Ps.* 35, 4 [no. 174] (trans. Benjamin Martin).

37. *In 2 ad Co.*, c. 5, lect. 3 (nº 179) [no. 180].

38. The Revised Standard Version translates: "his banner over me was love."

must love with charity: first God, because he is the very cause of this order, that is, he is the reason to love in charity all that is not God; next, ourselves, and then, our neighbor; the closest neighbor first, such as our parents, and then the more distant neighbor.[39] Thus, "we must love ordinately; that is, we must not love him [the neighbor] above God or as much as God, but next to him in the way you must love yourself: '*he ordered love in me*' (Song 2:4)."[40] The association of the order of charity with Song 2:4 dates back at least to Origen, and had become classic in medieval theology; one finds it not only in the *Glossa ordinaria* but also in the *Sententiae* of Peter Lombard.[41]

Song 8:6—"Love is strong as death" (eight occurrences)—and Song 8:7—"Many waters cannot quench charity" (nine occurrences)—both celebrate the force of charity, and Saint Thomas connects them to the hymn to charity in 1 Corinthians 13, and to the praise of the invincible love of God in Romans 8:31–38. He refers to these verses to highlight the solidity of the spiritual edifice, as much personal as ecclesial, when it is founded on the love of charity, a fruit of the Spirit:

> "Being rooted and founded in charity" which "bears all things, believes all things, hopes all things, endures all things. Charity never falls away" (1 Cor 13:7–8), "*for love is strong as death*" (Song 8:6). A tree without roots, or a house lacking a foundation are destroyed easily. In a similar manner, a spiritual edifice not rooted and founded in charity cannot last.[42]

39. See *ST* II-II, q. 26, a. 1, s.c. [no. 79]; q. 44, a. 8 [no. 80]; Thomas Aquinas, *Quaestiones disputatae de virtutibus* [*Q. de virt.*], q. 2 (*De caritate*), a. 9, s.c. [no. 78]; *In* III *Sent.*, d. 29, q. 1, a. 6 (p. 938) [no. 80'].

40. Thomas Aquinas, *De decem preceptis*, VIII [no. 82]. See Thomas Aquinas, *Lectura super epistolam ad Romanos* [*In ad Ro.*], c. 13, lect. 2 (n° 1057) [n° 81]; *In 1 ad Tim.*, c. 5, lect. 1 (n° 191) [no. 83].

41. See Origen, III, 7, in *The Song of Songs: Commentary and Homilies*, 187–93; Hélène Pétré, "*Ordinata caritas*: un enseignement d'Origène sur la charité," *Recherches de science religieuse* 42 (1954): 40–57; "II, 24 and 28," in *The Glossa ordinaria on the Song of Songs*, 39–40; Peter Lombard, *Sententiae*, III, d. 29, c. 1, 171.

42. *In ad Ep.*, c. 3, lect. 4 (n° 172) [no. 272]. See also, regarding the faithful, *In ad Ep.*, Prol. (n° 1) [no. 273] and, regarding the Church as such, *In Ps.* 47, 6 (p. 334) [no. 270].

Although we can never rule out the loss of charity through sin,[43] the more intense the charity, the less it is susceptible to destruction in us:

"Who then shall separate us from the love of Christ?".... God bestows great benefits on his holy ones, and when we consider them, such love of Christ burns in our hearts that nothing can quench it: "*many waters cannot quench love*" (Song 8:7).[44]

By the force it represents, charity is revealed to be the principal source of the patience that is so necessary to stay on track when faced with assaults of evil:

Therefore, in regard to enduring evil he says, "charity is patient" (1 Co 13:4), i.e., makes one endure evils patiently. For when a man loves someone on account of the beloved's love, he endures all difficulties with ease; similarly, a person who loves God patiently endures any adversity for love of him. Hence it is said: "*many waters cannot quench love, neither can floods drown it*" (Song 8:7).[45]

Charity, then, makes it possible to resist temptations,[46] to overcome trials,[47] and even to find joy in the love that unfurls in a trial.[48] Indeed, when trials overcome evil desires and false loves,[49] trials have as their indirect effect the growth of charity:

43. Song 8:6 appears (wrongly) as one of the objections to the doctrine according to which sin can destroy charity in its subject. See *Q. de virt.*, q. 2, a. 6, obj. 6 [no. 268] (trans. Benjamin Martin): "that which is strongest, cannot be driven out by that which is weakest. But charity is the strongest, '*for love is as strong as death*,' as it says in Cant. vii, 6: and sin is the weakest, because evil is weak and impotent, as Dionysius says. Therefore, mortal sin does not drive out charity; and thus, it is able to coexist with it"; *Q. de virt.*, q. 2, a. 12, obj. 11 [no. 269].

44. *In ad Ro.*, c. 8, lect. 7 (n° 722) [no. 294].

45. *In 1 ad Co.*, c. 13, lect. 2 (n° 772) [no. 295].

46. Thomas Aquinas, *Collaciones in orationem dominicam*, p. 6 (n° 1100) [no. 292]: "He guides man by the fervor of charity, lest man be led into temptation, for the very least degree of charity is able to resist any sin whatsoever: 'Many waters cannot quench charity.'"

47. *In 2 ad Co.*, c. 2, lect. 1 (n° 49) [no. 296].

48. Thomas Aquinas, *Lectura super I epistolam ad Thessalonicenses* [*In ad 1 Th.*], c. 1, lect. 1 (n° 16) [no. 303].

49. *In 1 ad Th.*, Prol. (n° 1) [no. 298].

It is clear that when we carry heavy burdens for the sake of the one we love, love itself is not destroyed, but rather grows. Hence, "*Many waters,*" that is, tribulations and adversities, "*could not extinguish charity*" (Song 8:7). And therefore holy men who put up with adversities for the sake of God are more firmly rooted in his love, just as a craftsman loves more the work he puts more effort into.[50]

Finally, charity leads one to subordinate everything to the love of God, as religious life attests in its radical way:

When the mind becomes attached to a thing with intense love and desire, the result is that it sets aside other things. So, from the fact that man's mind is fervently inclined by love and desire to divine matters, in which it is obvious that perfection is located, it follows that he casts aside everything that might hold him back from this inclination to God: not only concern for things, for wife, and the love of offspring, but even for himself. And the words of Scripture suggest this, for it is said in the Canticle of Canticles (8:7): "*if a man should give all the substance of his house for love, he will account it as nothing.*"[51]

THE DOCTRINE OF FAITH AND THE SACRAMENTS, FOODS OF LOVE

The intrinsically ecclesial dimension of the spiritual life of the believer, which can unfold only within the Church of Jesus Christ led by the Spirit, is clearly indicated by the fact that charity—to be born, grow, and reach its perfection—needs to receive the doctrine of faith and the sacraments from and in the Church. The soul-bride does not go to Christ and unite with him except in the Church-Bride. In Psalm 44, a mirror of the Song, the virgins are led to the bridegroom in the wake of the queen:

Virgins, interiorly, namely faithful souls, who have not been corrupted through sin; will be led to the king, that is Christ, who is the king of kings.

50. *De decem praeceptis*, IV [no. 293].

51. *SCG* III, c.130, (n° 3023) [no. 299]. Translation taken from *Summa Contra Gentiles: Book Three: Providence Part II*, trans. Vernon J. Bourke (Notre Dame, Ind.: University of Notre Dame Press, 1975). See also *De perfectione spiritualis vitae*, c. 16 (p. B 88) [no. 300]; *In Matth.*, c. 13, lect. 4 (n° 1192) [no. 301].

I say they will be led, because they shall not come of themselves. John 6: "No one comes to me," etc, and therefore it says in Cant. 1: "*Draw me after you.*" But they shall be drawn after her, namely the universal Church, for no one shall come or be led to Christ except he follow the doctrine of the Church.[52]

The union of the soul to God supposes adhesion by faith to the doctrine of the Church, which transmits and authentically interprets the Word of God. This is why the beloved asks to be taught by her spouse.[53] It is then vital to dismiss all the deformations of the doctrine of faith introduced by heresies, and Saint Thomas uses, twice, the traditional exegesis of Song 2:15, which connects the little foxes, destructive of the vines, to heretics and schismatics:

In the Song of Songs 2:15 we read: "*Catch us the little foxes.*" By which words the Gloss understands, "Pursue and overcome schismatics and heretics." "For (as another Gloss explains) it will not suffice for us to spend our lives in preaching and setting a good example, unless we correct those that are in error, and preserve the weak from their snares."[54]

To fight them, the Church has at its disposal, according to Saint Thomas, a coercive power, but she mainly turns to the arguments (*rationes*) and to the authorities (*auctoritates*) of the Fathers, who are compared to shields hung on the fortified tower of David (Song 4:4), that is, pendants that adorn the neck of the beloved.[55]

52. *In Ps.* 44, 10 (p. 325) [no. 14] (trans. Benjamin Martin). See the observation of de Lubac, *Medieval Exegesis*, 146, on Origen's commentary of Ps. 44: "There the queen adorned with garments of gold is the Church. It is to the Church that the Father addresses himself as to his daughter. It is the Church that is led to Christ, and it is in her that souls, united by faith and virtue, are made one."

53. See *In Is.*, c. 2 (p. 21) [no. 261]; *In Matth.*, c. 25, 1 (n° 2017) [no. 8]. The profession of the true Christological faith—Christ is God—is the "sign" that the beloved carries ceaselessly on her heart (Song 8:6). See *In Ioan.*, c. 3, lect. 6 (n° 539) [no. 266].

54. Thomas Aquinas, *Contra impugnantes*, c. 16, 1. 83 (p. A 147) [no. 104]. See also *In 2 ad Co.*, c. 11, lect. 3 (n° 405) [no. 103]. In *In Is.*, c. 4 (p. 36) [no. 102], the little foxes refer rather to "false virtues." Both interpretations, personal and ecclesial, have Origen for their source. See Origen, *The Song of Songs: Commentary and Homilies*, 254–63.

55. See *In Sent.*, Prol., div. Text. [no. 129]; *In Ier.*, c. 1, 5 [no. 130]. This interpretation of the fortified tower of David is already found in "IV, 47," in *The Glossa ordinaria on the Song of Songs*, 84: "Fortifications are those unbreakable statements in the holy scriptures by means of which those who defend themselves from incursions from a distance are

Founded on faith, union to the Bridegroom is realized through the action of the sacraments of the Church. They are streams, springing from the pierced side of Christ, that water the garden of the Church and make holiness sprout.[56] They are remedies and help for the believer.[57] The beloved bears the mark (*signaculum*, Song 8:6) or character of the Cross she received at baptism,[58] during which she was purified and renewed:

> "*Your teeth are like a shorn flock*" (Song 4:2). Hairs are sins: the shorn flock that ascends from the bath consists of those who have been cleansed from sin through Baptism, and these ascend.[59]

But it is in the sacrament of the Eucharist, to which all the other sacraments are ordered because it substantially contains Christ himself,[60] that the union of charity between Christ and the faithful is realized and consummated. Song 5:1—"Eat, O friends, and drink, and be inebriated, my dearly beloved" (thirteen occurrences)[61]—is copiously put to use here by Saint Thomas. The Eucharistic use of this verse is not found explicitly either in the *Glossa ordinaria* or in the *Postilla* of Hugh of Saint-Cher,[62] and so it is not impossible that we are dealing with one of the biblical verses that expresses and nurtures the intense personal Eucharistic devotion of

---

safe. The shield is that most stable reason by means of which they go forth against heretics with willing trust, and defend themselves when heretics assail them."

56. See *In I Sent.*, Prol. (p. 309) [no. 152].

57. See *In Ier.*, c. 1, 5 (p. 582) [no. 305].

58. See *In Ps.* 4, 5 (p. 159) [no. 265].

59. See "*Beatus Vir*," in *The Academic Sermons*, 320–21 [no. 128]. Song 4:2, with its baptismal interpretation, is one of the texts of the Song most quoted by Saint Augustine: see La Bonnardière, "Le Cantique des cantiques dans l'œuvre de saint Augustin," 232.

60. See *ST* III, q. 65, a. 3.

61. Song 5:1 is also quoted outside of an explicitly Eucharistic context to evoke the drunkenness of divine love that satisfies the heart, already here on earth but above all in the eschatological beatitude. See Thomas Aquinas, "*Puer Jesus*," in *The Academic Sermons*, 181 [no. 168].

62. See "V, 4," in *The Glossa ordinaria on the Song of Songs*, 103; Hugh of Saint-Cher, *Postilla in Cantica*, c. 5 (f. 128vb–129ra). Alan of Lille (*Elucidatio in Cantica canticorum*, V, PL 210, col. 84) says a lot concerning this verse about eating bread from heaven, but he interprets it in an anagogical, eschatological sense, since it is about eating *non in sacramento sed in re*.

Master Thomas.[63] Song 5:1 has the merit of uniting a whole sheaf of themes associated with the Eucharist. First, the invitation to a double refreshment (eating and drinking) evokes the twofold matter of the Eucharistic meal: bread and wine, that become the Body and Blood of Christ. Secondly, the invitation is doubly associated with the theme of love: on one hand, it is addressed to friends, to dear ones,[64] and on the other hand, the drink leads to drunkenness, which we have already pointed out signifies one of the major effects of love, namely its ecstatic character. It is not, then, surprising that this verse of the Song is closely associated with Saint Thomas's commentary on Saint Matthew's narrative of the institution of the Eucharist,[65] and that it would be brought up to highlight the effect of the grace of Eucharistic communion:

> Through this sacrament, as far as its power is concerned, not only is the habit of grace and of virtue bestowed, but it is furthermore aroused to act, according to 2 Cor. 5:14: "The charity of Christ presseth us." Hence it is that the soul is spiritually nourished through the power of this sacrament, by being spiritually gladdened, and as it were inebriated with the sweetness of the Divine goodness, according to Song 5:1: "*Eat, O friends, and drink, and be inebriated, my dearly beloved.*"[66]

63. Another element of the long verse 1 of ch. 5 ("I have eaten the honeycomb with my honey, I have drunk my wine with my milk") receives, as well, a Eucharistic sense, since Saint Thomas uses it in the Office of Corpus Christi. See *Officium de festo Corporis Christi* [no. 164]. On the Eucharistic devotion of Saint Thomas, see Torrell, *Initiation à saint Thomas*, 173–81 [*Saint Thomas Aquinas: The Person and His Work*, 152–60, 332]; Jean-Pierre Torrell, *Saint Thomas d'Aquin: Maître spirituel*, 3rd ed. (Paris: Cerf, 2017), 285–90 [*Saint Thomas Aquinas*, vol. 2, *Spiritual Master*, 2nd ed., trans. Robert Royal (Washington, D.C.: The Catholic University of America Press, 2003), 295–96, 375–76].

64. Those who have set themselves against the unity founded on ecclesial charity-friendship cannot participate in the Eucharistic meal, whose purpose is to express and reinforce this unity. See *In 1 ad Co.*, c. 11, lect. 4 (n° 630) [no. 179]: "*For this sacrament*, says Augustine in *On John*, *is the sacrament of unity and love*. Therefore, it is not suited to dissenters; *eat, O friends and drink; drink deeply, O lovers* (Song 5:2)."

65. See *In Matth.*, c. 26, lect. 3 (n° 2180) [no. 175]; ibid., lect. 4 (n° 2199) [no. 176].

66. *ST* III, q. 79, a. 1, ad 2 [no. 169].

THE JOURNEY OF THE SOUL TO GOD

Like flames that always rises higher, charity in us is a dynamic reality in perpetual growth.[67] This growth, however, has thresholds and therefore stages. There are "ages" or hierarchical spiritual states that correspond to different levels of charity.[68] The Song endeavors to describe, through the figure of the beloved, the final stage, the state of the "perfect," of those who reach the highest form of union with God possible *in via*.

Love and Moral Rectitude

Charity, carried to incandescence, is the formal and determining element of the spiritual life of the "perfect" Christian. However, this perfect life must nevertheless integrate all the other virtues, informed by charity. For example, we mentioned above, with regard to the great waters of trial that cannot extinguish love (Song 8:7), the importance of the virtue of patience nourished by charity. For that matter, charity can neither subsist nor develop in the absence of a fundamental moral rectitude, which charity at once supposes and establishes by fixing on God the deepest intention of the will.[69] So love purifies and rectifies, as indicated by Aquinas's observations on Song 1:3, "The righteous love thee":

> It is impossible for an impure heart to be prompt in regard to charity: because a thing loves that which is in conformity with it. But an impure heart loves that which conforms to it among the passions. Therefore, it needs to be freed of the passions: "*the righteous love you*" (Song 1:3).[70]

67. See *ST* II-II, q. 24, a. 10, s.c. [no. 277].

68. See for example, *ST* II-II, q. 24, a. 9; Torrell, *Saint Thomas d'Aquin: Maître spirituel*, "Les degrés de la charité," 456–60 [Torrell, *Saint Thomas Aquinas: Spiritual Master*, "The Degrees of Charity," 359–62].

69. See *In Is.*, c. 44 (p. 188) [no. 36]: "righteous by love."

70. *In 1 ad Tim.*, c. 1, lect. 2 (nº 15) [no. 37]. See also *In Ps.* 50, 6 (p. 348) [no. 35] (trans. Benjamin Martin): "Therefore, just as the spirit is rendered unclean by turning to some changeable good, so by turning away from its end is it disordered; and the rectitude by which man is directed to God is opposed to a disordering of this kind. Cant. 1:

Contemplative union with Christ demands, therefore, a moral purification as its precondition.[71] The Song is reached only after the reader has passed through Proverbs and Ecclesiastes! In the sermon for Advent *Lauda et laetare,* Saint Thomas warns that to become "daughters of Zion," that is, true contemplatives, souls must start by purifying themselves:

Such are the daughters of Zion, and therefore the sight of his coming through contemplation is announced and promised to them. Zechariah 9:9 says: "Exult greatly, daughter of Zion." And Song 3:11 reads: "*Go out, daughters of Zion, and see (King Solomon; look upon the crown with which his mother has crowned him).*" "*Go out,*" from the rags of vices [cf. Eph 4:21–31], and be "*daughters of Zion,*" through contemplation of the things that are above, and thus you will be able to see "*King Solomon,*" meaning the Lord of the angels [cf. Heb 1:5], in "*the crown with which his mother has crowned him,*" that is, according to a gloss, in the humanity[72] [cf. Ps 8:6] assumed from Judah's posterity [Heb 7:14, 8:8].[73]

In this perspective, some verses of the Song can receive a moral or tropological interpretation. They contain a teaching on how the faithful must live virtuously in Christ. Indeed, for Saint Thomas, the moral sense of Scripture is of a "mystical" nature, that is to say, it is intrinsically linked to the mystery of Christ: these are the moral and spiritual attitudes of Christ, which the believer is called to reproduce in himself, insofar as he is a member of this body whose head is

The upright love you, and therefore it says, *renew a right spirit,* that is grant anew what I have lost through sin: Eph. 4: *You are renewed by the spirit of your mind.*"

71. See *ST* II-II, q. 182, aa. 3–4, on the role of the active life in relation to the contemplative life.

72. In other texts, Saint Thomas rather sees in the royal diadem of Song 3:11 the divinity of Christ. See *In Ps.* 20, 3 [no. 122]; *In Is.*, c. 33 (p. 147) [no. 121].

73. Thomas Aquinas, "*Lauda et Laetare,*" in *The Academic Sermons,* 36 [no. 125]. See "III, 92," in *The Glossa ordinaria on the Song of Songs,* 76. In *In Ioan.*, c. 10, lect. 2 (n° 1392) [no. 124], where Saint Thomas comments on the gospel of the Good Shepherd, he interprets the "going out" to which the daughters of Zion are invited as the movement of the Church Militant, where the sheep find the pastures of doctrine and of grace, to the contemplation of the Church Triumphant in glory. This general interpretation comes from Augustine and from Gregory the Great but without the reference to Song 3:11. See Augustine, XLV, 15, in *Homilies on the Gospel of John,* 255; Gregory the Great, *Homélies sur Ezéchiel,* II, homily 1, 16 (SC 360), 84–85.

Christ.[74] Thus, regarding the myrrh that permeates the clothing of the royal spouse (Ps 44:9), Saint Thomas moves naturally from the Christological signification, which he finds in Song 5:5, to a moral meaning applied to "saints" or members of Christ:

Myrrh has bitterness; and thus, if it is referred to the body of Christ, it symbolizes the bitterness of his passion. Cant. 5: "*his fingers*" fixed to the wood, "*are full of purest myrrh.*" But if they are referred to the saints, it symbolizes repentance: Eccl. 24: "*As choice myrrh I have given forth the sweetness of my fragrance.*"[75]

Nevertheless, the Christological grounding of the moral meaning sometimes remains implicit, and Saint Thomas is content to establish links—which can be judged a little artificial—between a description contained in the Song and the moral virtues that the Christian must cultivate. For example, in Sermon XXI, preached in honor of Saint Martin of Tours, our Dominican applies Song 3:6 to the moral progress that must (should?) accompany all promotions in the ecclesiastical hierarchy.[76] He attributes a moral meaning to each component of the column of smoke that rises in the desert:

So it is necessary that someone who ascends according to the state also ascends in merit. About this ascent it is said in Song 3:6: "*Who is she who ascends through the desert, like a little twig of smoke from the scents of myrrh and frankincense and every powder of the merchant?*" "*Who goes up like a twig of smoke,*" not of terrifying smoke, but of fragrant smoke. But whence does that smoke come? Certainly "*from the scents of myrrh,*" that is, the morti-

74. See, for example, *ST* I, q. 1, a. 10: "so far as the things done in Christ, or so far as the things which signify Christ, are types of what we ought to do, there is the moral sense."

75. *In Ps.* 44, 6 [no. 193] (trans. Benjamin Martin). See, in a similar sense, *In Matth.*, c. 2, lect. 3 (n° 201) [no. 191]. The gifts taken to Bethlehem by the Magi can in a mystical sense signify first the content of the Christological or Trinitarian faith, then what concerns our action: "For wisdom can be indicated through gold.... Through frankincense, devoted prayer.... Through myrrh, the mortification of the body: 'mortify therefore your members which are upon the earth' (Col 3:5); '*my hands dropped with myrrh*' (Song 5:5)."

76. Other examples of interpretation of the verses of the Song according to the moral meaning: *In Ps.* 44, 6 [no. 210] (Song 5:14; ivory, symbol of chastity); *In Ioan.*, c. 13, lect. 2 (n° 1762) [no. 188] (Song 5:3; washing the feet signifies purifying the inferior affections).

fication of the flesh [cf. Mt 2:11, Jn 19:39], *"and of frankincense,"* that is, devotion [cf. Ps 141:2, etc.], *"and of every powder of the merchant,"* namely, all virtues.[77]

Seeking the One Whom the Heart Loves

Let us focus instead—given the specificity of the Song—on charity itself. Love, affective union, can take a double form. It is desire as long as the effective union with the beloved person is not realized; it becomes joy and fruition as soon as it is realized in some manner.[78] This is why the spiritual life here below alternates between the search for Christ, the Beloved—desired above all things—and rest in union with the Christ who is already possessed in some manner. The various stages of the games of love, played by the beloved and the lover in the Song, offer, according to Saint Thomas, an eloquent image of this alternation.

First of all, desire. It is desire that stimulates the spiritual life of the Christian. Henceforth the spiritual life presents itself as a permanent quest, stimulated and borne by love. "In my bed by night I sought him whom my soul loveth: I sought him, and I found him not" (Song 3:1). This first verse of chapter 3 happily unites the theme of love and that of the persevering search. It indicates with what in-

77. Thomas Aquinas, *"Beatus Vir,"* in *The Academic Sermons*, 323–24 [no. 119]. See "III, 52," in *The Glossa ordinaria on the Song of Songs*, 69: "Note that, bringing to mind perfumes, first he puts myrrh, then incense, and afterwards all the powder of the perfume-maker, because first it is necessary to mortify the concupiscence of the flesh, then to offer to God the pleasing vows of the heart, and afterwards as a consequence to grow in humility in every kind of virtue"; Hugh of Saint-Cher, *Postilla in Cantica*, c. 3 (f. 121ra): "The powder of perfume mortifies evil movements and preserves the movements of penitents from the corruption of sin. Incense is the devotion of prayer. All the powder is perfect and integrates humility or the totality of virtues"; *Postilla in Cantica*, c. 3 (f. 121rb): "Myrrh and incense, which are perfumes, that is, the mortification of the flesh and the devotion of prayer."

78. On fruition or pleasure, see Thomas Aquinas, *Lectura super epistolam ad Philemonem* [*In ad Philem.*], lect. 2 (nº 28) [no. 77]: "For to enjoy is to make use of the fruit, and thus as to use is to the useful, so is to enjoy to the fruit. It implies the sweetness of the fruit: *and his fruit was sweet to my palate* (Song 2:3), as well as the end, because the ultimate produce of the tree is its fruit. Therefore, to enjoy, properly speaking, is to have something that is pleasant and final."

tensity and purity of intention our prayers and requests should be made, born of a spiritual desire that wants to be fulfilled: "Just as he who seeks something places there his whole concentration. Hence to this pertains what the spouse says, '*I sought him whom my soul loves*' (Song 3:1)."[79]

This amorous quest for the Lover is punctuated by "revivals." At times Christ manifests his presence to the soul but, by withdrawing almost immediately, he arouses the desire of the latter who, from then on, looks for him with more intensity. It is in this sense that Saint Thomas interprets the loving game of chapter 5 between the lover and the beloved: he approaches her; she is late in joining him; he leaves; she searches for him. In this way Christ touches the soul with his grace—"My beloved put his hand through the keyhole, and my bowels were moved at his touch" (Song 5:4)[80]—but he withdraws to be better desired. Thus, with regard to the absence of Christ when the disciples struggle on the lake in the heart of the storm (Jn 6:17):

> Jesus left his disciples alone for this length of time so that they might experience his absence; and they did indeed experience it during the storm at sea: "know and realize, that it is evil and bitter for you to have left the Lord" (Jer 2:19). He left them, in the second place, so that they might look for him more earnestly: "*where has your beloved gone, most beautiful of women? We will search for him with you*" (Song 5:17).[81]

In a similar way, on the evening of Holy Thursday, Simon Peter expresses the desire to follow Christ (Jn 13:36–37) but Jesus delays the fulfillment of this desire on the grounds that Simon Peter is still

79. *In Matth.*, c. 7, 1 (nº 642) [no. 111]. See *In Is.*, c. 26 (p. 124) [no. 108]; *In Ps.* 39, 7 (p. 304) [no. 110].

80. See *In Ier.*, c. 1, 5 (p. 581) [no. 190] (trans. Benjamin Martin): "God touches some by reproving them.... By cleansing them from sin.... By infusing grace. '*My beloved put forth his hand through the hole, and my belly trembled at his touch*' (Song 5:4). By strengthening with grace.... By stirring up fervor."

81. *In Ioan.*, c. 6, lect. 2 (nº 877) [no. 214]. See John Chrysostom, *Homilies on the Gospel of John*, XLIII, 1, trans. G. T. Stupart, in *Chrysostom: Homilies on the Gospel of Saint John and the Epistle to the Hebrews*, ed. Philip Schaff, NPNF (1st ser.) 14 (Peabody, Mass.: Hendrickson, 1995), 1–334, at 155, 372–73, but without a reference to the Song.

imperfect. Saint Thomas connects the desire expressed by Simon Peter to that of the young girls in Song 5:17: "Whither is thy beloved gone, O thou most beautiful among women? Whither is thy beloved turned aside, and we will seek him with thee."[82] In the exegetical tradition, the young girls (*adolescentulae*) that escort the beloved represent the beginner or progressing souls, those who are still imperfect.[83] It is possible that Saint Thomas was led to quote Song 5:17 in this passage of *Lectura super Ioannem* because of this theme of imperfection, common to Simon Peter and to the young girls.

Seizing Christ: Here Below, and in Heaven

The spiritual quest of the faithful, driven by the desire aroused by Christ, is entirely completed by union to the same Christ and, through Christ, to God himself. But the texts of the Song that celebrate the union of the lover and the beloved have, in the interpretation of Saint Thomas, a double meaning: they first refer to the union with God already accessible here below in contemplation, and then to its full eschatological fulfillment in the beatific vision. Union with Christ here below is a participation in, a foretaste of, the definitive vision that characterizes Heaven, and union with Christ is intrinsically ordained to this definitive vision. All the images and themes in the Song that evoke union with Christ are to be understood in this double sense. We could not better indicate the resolutely eschatological orientation of Saint Thomas's spirituality, entirely directed toward the Vision.[84]

82. See *In Ioan*, c. 13, lect. 8 (n° 1841–1842) [no. 215].

83. According to "Prefaces, II," in *The Glossa ordinaria on the Song of Songs*, 1–2, the young girls represent "the throng of potential brides, to some degree having obtained salvation." In "I, 34," in *The Glossa ordinaria on the Song of Songs*, they are identified with those who are "unripe in faith." The idea clearly comes from Origen. See for example Origen, I, 4, in *The Song of Songs Commentary and Homilies*, 77. In *In Matth.*, c. 14, 2 (n° 1255) [no. 7], the young girls represent the crowds attracted by Jesus.

84. For Saint Thomas, the union to Christ and to God is above all a union by sight, that is to say by intelligence, that then spills over in fruition in the affective powers. It is significant that the theme of the "kiss" conveyed by the first verse of the Song, which has often held the attention of the interpretive tradition, is absent from Saint Thomas. He mentions it only one time in passing, in relation to the liturgical practice of the kiss

The idea of "holding" or "seizing" receives this double meaning. Song 3:4—"I held him: and I will not let him go"—is generally associated by Saint Thomas with the vision of the divine essence by the blessed:

But when we see him by direct vision we shall hold him present within ourselves. Thus in the Song of Solomon 3:4, the spouse seeks him whom her soul loves; and when at last she finds him she says: "*I held him, and I will not let him go.*"[85]

Nevertheless, a "holding" of Christ is already possible here below, although it is still threatened, unlike the definitive holding of the Vision.[86] Twice in the *Lectura super Ioannem*, Saint Thomas, taking up an idea of Origen, contrasts the perverse will of the wicked who want to apprehend Christ—in the sense of getting their hands on him—with the attitude of the faithful who want to seize Christ "with piety," according to Song 7:8: "I will go up into the palm tree, and will take hold of the fruit thereof":

of peace. See *In ad Ro.*, c. 16, lect. 1 (n° 1211) [no. 1]. Likewise, the embrace evoked in Song 2:6 and 8:3 ("His left hand under my head, and his right hand shall embrace me") is interpreted as evoking the double perfection of both the contemplative life and the active life. See *In Matth.*, c. 20, 2 (n° 1656) [no. 87]. Aquinas is a man of sight, the most "spiritual" of senses, more than of touch.

85. See *Comp. theol.* II, c. 9 [no. 116]. It is in the sense of this final embrace at the end of a journey, evoked by Song 3:4, and not in the sense of an exhaustion of the infinite intelligibility of the divine essence by the created intellect, that the "comprehension" by which the beatific vision is defined must be understood. See *ST* I, q. 12, a. 7, ad 1 [no. 115]: "*comprehension* is taken more largely as opposed to *non-attainment*; for he who attains to anyone is said to comprehend him when he attains to him. And in this sense God is comprehended by the blessed, according to the words, "*I held him, and I will not let him go*" (Cant. 3:4)"; *In ad Ph.*, c. 3, lect. 2 (n° 127) [no. 118].

86. In John 6:37, Jesus Christ affirms that he will not cast out the one who comes to him. It follows paradoxically that the possibility of being cast out from within (*intrinsecum*) exists. See *In Ioan.*, c. 6, lect. 4 (n° 921) [no. 30]: "What is interior is twofold. The first is the most profound, and is the joy of eternal life. From this interior no one is cast out. The other interior is that of an upright conscience; and this is a spiritual joy. We read of this: "when I enter into my house I will enjoy repose" (Wis 8:16); and "*the king has brought me into his storerooms*" (Song 1:3). It is from this interior, that some are cast out." See also *In Matth.*, c. 24, 3 (n° 1992) [no. 53]. The seizing possible here below is sometimes attributed to prayer. See *In Is.*, c. 64 (p. 249) [no. 117].

They became angry, feigning that they did know him. And so they formed the evil plan of seizing him, so that they could crucify and kill him: "go after him, and seize him" (Ps 70:11). Yet there are some who have Christ within themselves, and still seek to seize him in a reverent manner: "*I will go up into the palm tree and seize its fruit*" (Song 7:8). And so the Apostle says: "I will go after it to seize it, wherein I am also apprehended by Christ Jesus" (Phil 3:12).[87]

This union with God, begun here below in order to be completed in heaven, is evoked by Saint Thomas through several images and themes drawn from the Song. We can note four of these: A first theme is the entrance of the beloved into the intimacy of the cellars of the king (Song 1:3). For Saint Thomas, Song 1:3 often illustrates the idea of a centripetal movement, wholly directed toward spiritual and interior goods, rather than the union itself.

And why does he say, "enter into the joy" (Mt 25, 21), not "accept"? One should say that there are two joys: joy over exterior goods and joy over interior goods. The one who rejoices over exterior goods does not enter into joy, but rather joy enters into him; but the one who rejoices over spiritual things enters into joy. "*The king has brought me into his storerooms*" (Song 1:3).[88]

A second bundle of images evokes the contemplative union with Christ as "rest" (*quies*).[89] The union is the goal of a movement that finds therein its end, in a double sense: as term and as fulfillment. This contemplative rest is associated with a certain "sleep," so much

87. *In Ioan.*, c. 7, lect. 3 (nº 1067) [no. 247]. See also *In Ioan.*, c. 7, lect. 5 (nº 1104) [no. 248]. This theme comes from Origen, in whom is already found the link between Song 7:8 and Song 3:4. See Origen, *Commentaria in Evangelium secundum Matthaeum*, t. 17, PG 13, col. 1515 (Paris: Migne, 1862); Thomas Aquinas, *Catena in Matthaeum*, 21, 7 [no. 248'].

88. *In Matth.*, c. 25, 2 (nº 2054) [no. 29]. See also: *In Ps.* 36, 19 (p. 287) [no. 27]; *In ad He.*, c. 4, lect. 1 (nº 201) [no. 31]; *In Matth.*, c. 7, 2 (nº 665) [no. 28]; *In Ioan.*, c. 6, lect. 4 (nº 921) [no. 30].

89. To the theme of the meal can be joined the theme of peace that brings union in love: see *In ad Ga.*, c. 5, lect. 6 (nº 330) [no. 306]: "For it is then that the lover has peace, when he adequately possesses the object loved: *I am become in his presence as one finding peace* (Song 8:10)." Properly, this peace already attainable here below is ordered to the perfect peace of beatitude, when "there will be nothing further to be desired": see *In ad He.*, c. 12, lect. 4 (nº 706) [no. 308].

so that, according to Aquinas, "the state of contemplation is signified by the bed. It says about this: *our bed is flourishing* (Song 1:15)."[90] The paradoxical verse "I sleep, and my heart watcheth" (Song 5:2) indicates that this rest of contemplation consists in a certain suspension of exterior activity to the benefit of an intense though peaceful interior attention fixed upon God.[91] Here again, the contemplative rest is presented in relation with the eternal rest of the Vision, which it anticipates:

> We should note that the word "sleep" can be understood in several ways. Sometimes it refers to a natural sleep.... Again, it can mean the repose of contemplation: "*I slept, but my heart was awake*" (Song 5:2). It can also signify the rest of future glory: "in peace I will both lie down and sleep" (Ps 4:8).[92]

Or again, regarding the exhortation of Saint Paul to rise from sleep (Rom 13:11):

> Nor is it a reference to the sleep of grace, sometimes called the repose of eternal glory, as in a psalm: "in peace I will lie down and sleep" (Ps 4:9) and sometimes the rest of contemplation even in this life: "*I slept, but my heart was awake*" (Song 5:3).[93]

The two first themes—the entrance into the cellar and rest—place us on the side of the soul. The third invites consideration of contemplative union from the side of Christ. Indeed, Christ never ceases to come before his people in order to unite himself with them, now through the invisible missions, then at the hour of death,

90. *In Matth.*, c. 24, 3 (nº 1992) [no. 53]. See Hugh of Saint-Cher, *Postilla super Cantica*, c. 3 (f. 119v), regarding Song 3:1: "In the moral sense, this is understood as the bed of contemplation."

91. Saint Augustine applied Song 5:2 to the contemplative life. See, for example, Augustine, LVII, 3, in *Homilies on the Gospel of John*, 304: "'I sleep, and my heart waketh': I rest from troublesome business, and my mind turns its attention to divine concerns (*or* communications)."

92. *In Ioan.*, c. 11, lect. 3 (nº 1495) [no. 184].

93. *In ad Ro.*, c. 13, lect. 3 (nº 1062) [no. 185]. See also *In Matth.*, c. 24, lect. 4 (nº 1994) [no. 182]; *In Matth.*, c. 26, lect. 5 (nº 2244) [no. 183]. Saint Thomas also reads into Song 5:2 the sleep of death, which does not suppress the activity of the immortal soul: see *In 1 ad Th.*, c. 4, lect. 2 (nº 93) [no. 186].

and finally at the end of time through his glorious return. Each time, he delights in his people. Saint Thomas interprets several verses of the Song in this sense: the lover comes into his garden to taste its fruits (Song 5:1), graze there, and gather the lilies (Song 6:1).[94] Contemplation is the joy of Christ himself.

Fourth and finally, contemplative union is associated with the theme of a shared meal, the biblical symbol par excellence of the communion of people and the communion between God and believers. Here again, our Dominican underlines the continuity between the feast of contemplation of grace here below and its full accomplishment in glory:

> Christ prepared for us a refreshment that pertains to our affection. Thus we read in Song 5:1: "*Eat, my friends!*" that is, here and now, through grace, "*and get drunk, my dear!*" that is, in the future, through glory. Christ makes this refreshment for us insofar as he has the fullness of divinity, as Ps 84:12 reads: "The Lord will give grace and glory."[95]

Regarding the "feast of fat things, a feast of wine" prophesied by Isaiah 25:6, the commentary of Saint Thomas, in a *nota* (already mentioned above to underscore the link between the ecclesial and personal dimension of the figure of the beloved), describes three feasts:

> The banquet is threefold.
>
> a. The first is the domestic [banquet] of the Church. [...]
>
> b. The second is the private banquet of the soul. Three things are proposed:
>
> 1. the wine of love: "*your breasts are better than wine*" (Song 1:1);
> 2. the honey of contemplation: "how sweet are your words to my palate, more than honey to my mouth" (Ps 118:103).
> 3. the milk of purification (which is ordered to the increase in perfection): "desire the rational milk without guile, [that by it you might increase into salvation]" (I Pet 2:2).

94. See *In Ioan.*, c. 14, lect. 1 (n° 1861) [no. 218]; *In Is.*, c. 35 (p. 154) [no. 217]; *In I Sent.*, Prol. (p. 309) [no. 159].

95. Thomas Aquinas, "*Homo Quidam Fecit Cenam Magnam*," in *The Academic Sermons*, 181 [no. 168].

c. The third is the solemn banquet of the heavenly court. Three things are proposed:

1. wine for inebriation: "*eat friends, and drink, and be inebriated, [my dearly beloved]*" (Song 5:1)
2. honey for fullness, "I will be satisfied when thy glory shall appear" (Ps 16:15);
3. milk for the perfection of body and soul: "*your eyes are as doves [upon brooks of waters, which are washed with milk]*" (Song 5:12).[96]

CONTEMPLATA ALIIS TRADERE

Contemplation is an end in itself. It cannot be subordinated to anything else. However, for Thomas Aquinas, friar of the Order of Preachers, contemplation overflows (super)naturally in preaching for the salvation of souls. *Contemplata aliis tradere* (hand down to others the fruits of contemplation). Such is the necessary effect of charity, that lamp of fire, which burns in the heart of the contemplative:

"The charity of Christ presses us" (2 Co 5, 15) to this. He says, "presses," because it is the same as stimulates. As if to say: the love of God, as a goad, stimulates us to do what charity commands, namely, to procure the salvation of our neighbor. "Those who are led," i.e., stirred, "by the Spirit of God are sons of God" (Rom 8:14); "*its flashes are flashes of fire*" (Song 8:6).[97]

By his action, the preacher imitates the "condescension" of Christ, the Beloved who descends into his garden:

Some are devoted only to themselves, that they may live in peace and advance in wisdom, but do not want to reach out to others. Such people can advance in grace with God, but not with people. But Jesus advanced in grace and wisdom "with God and the people" [Lk 2:52]. This is signified in his coming down [to be] with them: Jesus remained in Jerusalem during his time, but he came down when he wanted. Hence it says in Song 6:2: "*My beloved* (dilectus) *has come down into his garden*," that is, the garden of delights. And on the ladder that Jacob saw, he saw the "angels of God going

96. *In Is.*, c. 25 (p. 122) [no. 2].
97. *In 2 ad Co.*, c. 5, lect. 3 (n° 181) [no. 287].

up and down"; Gn 28:12. Thus we also should go up by a spiritual progress and go down by devotion to our neighbor.[98]

Central to Dominican spirituality, the theme of the necessary overflow of contemplation into preaching is admirably displayed in the collation at Vespers of Sermon IX, *Exit qui seminat*. This sermon, preached in February 1270, is meant to be—like the *Contra retrahentes*—a rejoinder to the attacks of Gerard of Abbeville against the Dominicans. In the sermon, the texts of the Song serve to illustrate both the contemplative ideal itself and the necessity that it overflow into preaching.[99] Saint Thomas first of all describes the intimacy of contemplative union by relying on Song 7:10 and 6:3:

A preacher ought to go out from hidden contemplation and go to the public [field] of preaching, for a preacher first ought to draw in contemplation what he will pour out later on in preaching. Hence it says in Is 12:3–4: "With joy you shall draw water," that is, with the joy of contemplation, "from the fountains of the Savior,"—that is, from divine wisdom [cf. Wis 1:5 (Vg)]—"and then you will say on that day," after you have drawn: "Give thanks to the Lord" [e.g., Ps 33:2, 106:1], et cetera. This going out is very similar to the Savior's going out from the secret dwelling place of the Father to the public area of what is visible. Therefore, it says in Song 7:10: "*I am (here) for my beloved* (dilectus), *and he is turned towards me*," namely, in the hidden realm of contemplation. There are two things that can turn the soul toward God: devout prayer and contemplation; and through internal speech God is turned to the soul. Hence the soul says: "*My beloved* (dilectus) *is mine, and I am his*" [Song 6:3].[100]

Immediately after this description of the secret (*occultum, secretum*) of contemplation, supported by a text from the Song (Song 7:10–12), the Dominican continues:

98. Thomas Aquinas, "*Puer Jesus*," in *The Academic Sermons*, 105–6 [no. 216].

99. In Homily 57 on the Gospel of John, Saint Augustine had, as well, called upon the Song to urge contemplatives to preach for the salvation of souls. But he relied above all on the exegesis of Song 5:3: "I have washed my feet, how shall I defile them?" See Augustine, LVII in *Homélies sur l'évangile de Jean*, ed. Marie-François Berrouard, Bibliothèque Augustinienne 74A (Turnhout: Brepols, 1993), 86–101, with the complementary note 6, 407–11: "Le dialogue de l'Eglise et du Christ d'après Cant. 5, 2–3 et le problème du ministère de la prédication."

100. Thomas Aquinas, "*Exiit Qui Seminat*," in *The Academic Sermons*, 120 [no. 107].

But will we not always be here? No. Therefore, he says : "*Come, my beloved* (dilectus), *let us go out into the field*" [Song 2:10], meaning: the public field of the preaching; "*let us remain*," when we preach, "*in the country houses*" [Song 7:11], that is, with the people who are open to the preaching [cf. Lk 10:5–9]. Note that when he says "let *us* remain," a particular familiarity of God with the preacher is indicated; "Let *us* go out": I by inspiring you, and you by preaching.[101] When shall we go out? Let us go out early in the morning to the vineyards; in the same way Christ went out early in the morning, as we read in the Gospel: "He went out most early in the morning to hire workers for his vineyard" [Mt 20:1].[102]

A similar theme, associated with the same verse of the Song, is found in the commentary on John 21. After the Resurrection of Christ, the apostles, in Galilee, "go out" to go fishing. This "going out" signifies, according to Saint Thomas, that preachers must leave all life of sin and all attachment to carnal things, but also "the quiet of contemplation: '*let us go forth into the fields, and lodge in the villages; let us go out early to the vineyards*' (Song 7:11)."[103] This office of preaching requires a mandate from the Church.[104]

The *Glossa ordinaria* had already connected this going out toward the country and toward the vines described in Song 7:11–12 with the preaching that follows upon contemplation.[105] It is especially interesting to observe how much Hugh of Saint-Cher in his *Postilla* on the Song had already made this theme into an argument for the defense and illustration of the Order of Preachers. He attacks the

101. This beautiful formula comes from the *Glossa ordinaria*. See "VII, 90," in *The Glossa ordinaria on the Song of Songs*, 154: "Because the night of faithlessness has passed and the light of faith appears, proceeding from the early-morning resurrection of Christ, let us labor from that same early morning of resurrection, you inspiring, me preaching."

102. Thomas Aquinas, "*Exiit Qui Seminat*," in *The Academic Sermons*, 120–21 [no. 107].

103. *In Ioan.*, c. 21, lect. 1 (nº 2582) [no. 253]. See also *In Matth.*, c. 24, lect. 3 (nº 1992) [no. 53]: "The prelates are signified by the field into which the men go out to work; *come, my beloved, let us go forth into the field* (Song 7:11)."

104. See *In ad Ro.*, c. 10, lect. 2 (nº 840) [no. 239].

105. See "VII, 87–89," in *The Glossa ordinaria on the Song of Songs*, 153: "'*let us go out*,' I shall go out from the secrecy of the heart, in which I have been contemplating, to those who from the beginning until now [wait] to be ploughed and cultivated. '*Let us linger*,' by earnest preaching. '*In the villages*,' in those already instructed in how to live lawfully."

"pure" contemplatives, who in his view are the philosophers of the Faculty of Arts rather than religious of contemplative orders,[106] to exalt the objective perfection of the vocation of the Order of Preachers. Solomon, says the Song, made himself a litter (Song 3:9). A litter, comments Hugh, is not a simple bed (*lectulum*), a fixed piece of furniture, but a vehicle that carries the King (Christ) everywhere it goes: "It is evident by this that the state of preaching is higher, greater, and more dignified than the state of contemplation."[107] Preaching demonstrates the fecundity of contemplation, as Hugh emphasizes concerning Song 7:11:

Come, therefore, my beloved, let us go out into the field, as though you are with me in the bed, where by mutual intercourse I have already been made pregnant by you; but now, I wish to go forth that I may give birth.... By the field is meant the Church generally, to which the one imbued with the divine Wisdom should go forth to instruct.[108]

Hence the insistent invitation of the French Dominican, who makes of the exegete a sergeant recruiter:

The Bridegroom is to be sought on the field of battle and of labor, not on the bed of contemplation; for behold we have heard of him in Ephratha, we found him in the field of the forest (Ps 131:6). They manifestly err, who consider the bed of their own slothfulness to be the habitation of philosophy, and their own inactivity the strenuous labor of philosophizing, or, as Apuleius says, showing or philosophizing merely with their ears and eyes. Therefore, there is so great a multitude of Parisians seeking the bridegroom, night and day, inspecting the skins of goats,[109] yet they find nothing. Why? Because they never go out into the field to labor. Therefore,

106. See the concise interpretation that Hugh of Saint-Cher gives to Luke 17:34 in *Postilla super Canticum*, c. 3 (f. 120v). On the day of Judgment two people will be in same bed (symbol of contemplation) and one will be taken, the other left: "Indeed, there are two kinds of contemplatives, the philosophers and the religious. The first will be left behind and the second taken."

107. Hugh of Saint-Cher, *Postilla super Cantica*, c. 3 (f. 122 r) (trans. Benjamin Martin).

108. Hugh of Saint-Cher, *Postilla super Cantica*, c. 3, c. 8 (f. 135 v) (trans. Benjamin Martin).

109. The skins of goats refer to the skins that Michal, wife of David, placed with a mannequin in the bed in place of David, threatened by Saul, to save his life; see 1 Sam 19:13.

most advisedly the Bride subjoins: "*I will arise*," from the bed of the body, from the bed of leisurely investigations. And "*I shall go round about the city*," that is, the Church, preaching everywhere by word and example.[110]

No doubt Friar Thomas Aquinas, like Friar Hugh of Saint-Cher and the first Dominicans, had received the call of the Song to "go out" as the very expression of their ideal of religious life, devoted to the salvation of souls through preaching.

110. Hugh of Saint-Cher, *Postilla super Cantica*, c. 3 (f. 120r) (trans. Benjamin Martin).

Conclusion

At the end of this investigation of the citations of the Song in Saint Thomas Aquinas, it is appropriate, following the example of the bride of the Song, to gather the "fruits: the new and the old" (Song 7:13): they concern Thomistic studies, the spiritual doctrine of Saint Thomas, and finally his own spiritual life.

As far as Thomistic studies are concerned, we have tried through this work to open a third methodological way to "biblical Thomism," which is today the subject of strong attention. The expression "biblical Thomism" does not reflect a distinct part of the teaching of Saint Thomas, alongside, for example, dogmatic Thomism or moral Thomism. Rather it means to point out an essential property of the Angelic Doctor's ensemble of writings: the determining role of the Scriptures and their interpretation in the work of understanding the faith.[1] This dimension of Thomas's theology, although essential, has long been neglected, first because of the continental drift splitting exegesis and theology that began at the end of the Middle Ages and has worsened continually ever since. Next, because of philosophic tropism that marked the neo-Thomist project of the nineteenth century. Neo-Thomism required of Saint Thomas a philosophy capable of offering an alternative to the philosophy of modernity, while adopting for apologetic reasons the modern model

1. On the notion of biblical Thomism, see Piotr Roszak and Jörgen Vijgen, "Towards a 'Biblical Thomism': Introduction," in *Reading Sacred Scripture with Thomas Aquinas*, vii–xvi.

of a separate philosophy. In this perspective, the biblical impregnation of Thomas's thought mattered little, and could even constitute an obstacle. For several decades now, but each day more decidedly, the biblical dimension of Thomas's thought has held the attention of the disciples of Saint Thomas. This evolution results from a more frank consideration of the essentially theological nature of the work of Saint Thomas and from the concern to propose Thomism as a credible theology in a theological context in which the place given to Scripture has become, quite rightly, a determining criterion.

In this perspective, recent Thomistic studies are interested not only in the Thomistic theory of biblical inspiration—already profitably put to use at the time of the modernist crisis—or in the general doctrine of the senses of Scripture, but also in the concrete exegetical method of Saint Thomas and above all in the fruitful interaction between his practice of biblical exegesis and the work of understanding the faith more systematically. In his recent dissertation, Stéphane Loiseau has demonstrated that for Saint Thomas, biblical commentary is the cardinal place of mediation between the divine science (which is communicated in the sacred texts) and theological science (which is subordinate to the divine science). Through the reading of the Bible, the theologian makes sure of the truths of the faith that form the principles of his science.[2]

To a degree, the relations between biblical exegesis and systematic theology have a parallel in the noetic of Saint Thomas. It is through sensory experience and the images that express it that the human person elaborates, by abstraction, under the light of the agent intellect, the universal concepts that, then, through a movement of return to the images (*conversio ad phantasmata*), allow him to think more deeply about the real. In an analogous way, Christian theology comes into contact with its object in the Scriptures, which constitute for theology a permanent foundation. Theology then develops the content, the *res*, according to the exigencies proper to all

2. See Loiseau, *De l'écoute a la parole.*

science, which leads it to "lift away" from the inspired text. But this movement has for its purpose a better return to the biblical text. Indeed, by a sort of *conversio ad Scripturas*, the theologian returns to the Bible, on one hand to verify the conformity of his theology to the permanent standard that is the Word of God, and on the other hand to deepen the understanding of the Scriptures by means of perspectives opened up by theological contemplation. Convinced of the fundamental unity of truth, Thomas Aquinas never hesitates to illuminate the meaning of the Word of God from the later developments of Tradition or even from metaphysical or anthropological truths established by natural reason.[3] Thus, in interacting with Scripture, Saint Thomas "aims to discover the *res* to which the letter of the text refers and . . . the letter is interpreted by the understanding of the *res*."[4] Thomas's exegesis is an integral exegesis.[5]

Biblical Thomism has so far taken two principal approaches. The first is the systematic study of the biblical commentaries of Saint Thomas: hermeneutical method, the place of patristic sources, the specific doctrinal contents, and so on. The long-awaited critical editions of the commentaries on the New Testament and the work in progress on the *Catena aurea* should allow the exponential development of this type of study. The second approach consists in studying

3. See Matthew Levering, *Scripture and Metaphysics: Aquinas and the Renewal of Trinitarian Theology* (Oxford: Wiley-Blackwell, 2004). Levering contests "the alleged opposition between metaphysical analysis and exegesis of Scripture by exploring how Saint Thomas's use of metaphysics illumines the meaning of scriptural revelation" (8).

4. Marc Aillet, *Lire la Bible avec S. Thomas. Le passage de la* littera *à la* res *dans la "Somme théologique"* (Fribourg: Editions universitaires, 1993), 200.

5. See Michael Dauphinais and Matthew Levering, eds., *Reading John with St. Thomas Aquinas: Theological Exegesis and Speculative Theology* (Washington, D.C.: The Catholic University of America Press, 2005); Matthew Levering and Michael Dauphinais, eds., *Reading Romans with St. Thomas Aquinas* (Washington, D.C.: The Catholic University of America Press, 2012); Matthew Levering, Piotr Roszak, and Jörgen Vijgen, *Reading Job with St. Thomas Aquinas* (Washington, D.C.: The Catholic University of America Press, 2020); Thomas F. Ryan, *Thomas Aquinas as Reader of the Psalms* (Notre Dame, Ind.: University of Notre Dame Press, 2000); Thomas Prügl, "Thomas Aquinas as Interpreter of Scripture," in *The Theology of Thomas Aquinas*, ed. Rik Van Nieuwenhove and Joseph Wawrykow (Notre Dame, Ind.: University of Notre Dame Press, 2005), 386–415.

the place and the role of citations and biblical themes in the works of theological synthesis, by the model mapped out by Valkenberg.[6] Yet, it seemed to me possible, even fruitful, to take, in addition to these two principal approaches, a "little way" as it were: the study of Thomas's citations of the biblical books on which he did not comment. The aim is twofold: to extract what this use of citations suggests about Thomas's interpretation of the book in question, and to benefit from the harmonies that arise in the rapprochement between these citations and the theological themes with which Saint Thomas associates them. A similar work to that which we have here undertaken could be conducted on the citations of other biblical books, in particular the wisdom literature.[7]

Our study of the citations of the Song also opens up some beautiful perspectives on the spirituality of Saint Thomas, in both of the senses (subjective and objective) that were spoken about by Father Jean-Pierre Torrell:[8] "the quality of a life [here, that of friar Thomas Aquinas] conducted by the movement of the Spirit"[9] and "a spiritual doctrine" that, in Saint Thomas, proves to be "an implicit and necessary dimension of his theology."[10] Indeed, the study of the citations of the Song highlights several remarkable aspects of the spiritual doctrine of Saint Thomas. First, the perspective of the Song confers upon this doctrine a dynamic tonality, since the poem describes a "history" of love, a process, a path toward union with God. We have underscored its Christocentric and profoundly ecclesial character: it is by participating in the mystery of the wedding of Christ and the Church that each believer tends toward the perfection of the Christian life, which consists in charity. Three other aspects

6. See Valkenberg, *Words of the Living God.*

7. It would also be interesting to examine the manner in which Saint Thomas uses in his other works the biblical books upon which he commented, for example the epistles of Saint Paul. Does the interpretation of a verse in his commentary on the book correspond to his use of the verse in other works?

8. See Torrell, *Saint Thomas d'Aquin: Maître spirituel,* 17–40 [*Spiritual Master,* 1–21].

9. Torrell, *Saint Thomas d'Aquin: Maître spirituel,* 37 [*Spiritual Master,* 18].

10. Torrell, *Saint Thomas d'Aquin: Maître spirituel,* 38 and 40 [*Spiritual Master,* 21].

of Aquinas's spiritual doctrine stand out in his use of citations of the Song and should be underlined here. The first is the omnipresence of eschatological tension: the "holding" of Christ accessible here below in contemplation or Eucharistic communion is intrinsically ordered to the plenary union of the beatific vision. "Thomas places the whole spiritual life under the sign of hope in the eschatological fulfillment."[11] The second aspect to emphasize is the attention to the affective or amorous dimension of the spiritual life, more marked than we might think in a theologian sometimes judged too "intellectual." Not only has the Song nourished the general reflection of Saint Thomas on amorous passion, but also it illustrates to his eyes how, without ever having to take leave of understanding, love is the driving force of the journey of the soul toward Christ. Finally, the third aspect of Saint Thomas's spiritual doctrine worthy of note here—the intimate connection that unites contemplation and preaching—leads us to his personal spiritual experience as a friar of the Order of Preachers.

Indeed, everything indicates that the Song nourished the spirituality of Saint Thomas, in the sense that "spirituality" designates the mystery of the believer's personal life in the Spirit. Like so many readers of the Song through the ages, Friar Thomas made his own, in meditation and prayer, the words of the beloved. They informed his spiritual experience, which was expressed and molded in them. His reading of the Song, doubtless, is a "reading which takes up the 'I' and the 'you' into a subjective dialogue in which the reader is involved."[12] In his questions on prayer in the *Summa theologiae,* Saint Thomas asks himself if it is appropriate to ask of God something definite, or whether, as Socrates suggested, it is better to leave it to God to give us what he knows to be best for us. Saint Thomas responds that, in what concerns temporal goods, such as riches, health,

11. Torrell, *Saint Thomas d'Aquin: Maître spirituel,* 285. [*Spiritual Master,* 332: "That all this is gathered here under the sign of hope shows to what extent Thomas sees in it the virtue of *homo viator,* of man on the way to beatitude."]

12. Pelletier, *Lectures du Cantique,* 416.

or success, which are not directly linked to beatitude and which we can put to good or evil use, it is legitimate to ask for them—seeing as it is up to us to cooperate as responsible persons with the divine government—but always with reserve, leaving God to decide ultimately what is best. Nevertheless, for the goods of salvation "which are the object of beatitude or whereby we merit it" and which we can never misuse, there is no hesitation. They can and must be asked for without any restriction. The "saints" in Scripture "absolutely" ask for them in their prayer, and Saint Thomas gives two examples of this drawn from the Psalms: "Show us Thy face, and we shall be saved" (Ps 89:4); "Lead me into the path of thy commandments" (Ps 118:35).[13] We can be sure that the words of the "beloved" of the Song, which express these goods as unconditionally desirable and as to be consumed without moderation, often rose to the heart and lips of the holy Doctor.

13. See *ST* II-II, q. 83, a. 5.

Appendix 1

List of Citations of the Song of Songs in Thomas's Corpus

The list is broken down by chapters in the Song of Songs; only those verses to which Saint Thomas refers are included. In the first column, the references are numbered, for convenience; an asterisk indicates a text from Thomas's corpus in which the quotation of the Song appears inside another quotation (for example, in the *Catena aurea*) or a text that makes only an allusion to the Song. The second column indicates the place in which the quotation or allusion appears. The third column gives the text of the quotation and its immediate context. The fourth column indicates the scriptural text that is the object of the commentary, or the title of the textual unit in which the quotation appears. The fourth column indicates also, when possible, the exact references to the authors or works to which the text of Saint Thomas refers.

APPENDIX TABLE 1

1		**osculetur me osculo oris sui**	
1	*In ad Ro.*, c. 16, lect. 1 (n° 1211)	Deinde ostendit modum quo se generaliter salutent, dicens 'Salutate invicem in osculo sancto', quod dicitur ad differentiam osculi libidinosi, de quo dicitur Prov. VII, 13 'Apprehensum deosculatur iuvenem'. Et etiam dolosi, de quo dicitur Prov. XXVII, 6: 'Meliora sunt vulnera diligentis, quam fraudulenta oscula inimici'. Osculum autem sanctum est quod in signum sanctae Trinitatis datur. Cant. I, 1: '***Osculetur me osculo oris sui***'. Exinde autem mos in Ecclesia inolevit ut fideles inter Missarum solemnia invicem dent oscula pacis.	Rom 16:16
		quia meliora sunt ubera tua vino	
2	*In Is.*, c. 25, lines 111–36 [125] (p. 122)	Nota super illo verbo, 'convivium pinguium', quod est triplex convivium. Primum familiare militantis Ecclesie. [...] Secundum est convivium privatum anime: in quo proponit tria: primo vinum amoris. Cant. i '***Meliora sunt ubera tua vino***'. Secundo mel contemplationis. Ps. 'Quam dulcia faucibus meis eloquia tua! Super mel ori meo'; tertio lac depurationis adhuc ad crescendum in perfectum II Petri i 'Rationabiles sine dolo, lac concupiscite'. Tertium est convivium solempne celestis curie, in quo proponit tria: primo vinum ad ebrietatem. Cant. iv '***Comedite amici, et bibite et inebriamini***'; secundo mel ad satietatem. Ps. 'Satiabor cum apparuerit gloria tua'; tertio lac ad perfectionem corporis et anime, Cant. iv '***Oculi tui sicut columbe***'.	Is 25:6
3	*In Is.*, c. 66, lines 83–96 [93] (p. 254)	Secundo promittit congregatis immensam consolationem. Et primo invitat alios ad congratulationem 'Letamini cum Jerusalem', in ea, sicut in obiecto gaudii, ponens conditionem congratulantium quantum ad affectum, 'qui diligitis'. Cant. v '***Comedite amici, et bibite, et inebriamini carissimi***'; quantum ad affectus signum, 'qui lugetis'. Matth. v 'Beati qui lugent, quoniam ipsi consolabuntur'; et congratulationis fructum quantum ad participationes laetitie vel pacis, 'ut sugatis [et repleamini ab ubere consolationis ejus]', Cant. i: '***Meliora sunt ubera tua vino***'; quantum ad participationem glorie, ut mulgeatis, 'quasi mulgentes' lac, Iob xxii: 'Tunc super Omnipotentem deliciis afflues'.	Is 66:10
2		**oleum effusum nomen tuum; ideo adulescentulae dilexerunt te**	
4	*In Is.*, c. 56, lines 105–14 [113–14] (p. 224)	Item nota quod nomen Dei est diligendum [...] quarto quia copiosum ad miserendum, Cant. i '***Oleum effusum nomen tuum***'.	Is 56:6

5	*In Ps.* 7, 3 (p. 169)	'Exsurge' ergo 'in hoc praecepto', idest appare humilis altus existens; quasi dicat: ita humilitatem accipias ut altitudinem non deseras: vel 'exsurge' a mortuis, et sic 'synagoga populorum circumdabit te', congregatio scilicet beatorum qui remunerabuntur, et malorum qui punientur. Cant. 1 '***Oleum effusum nomen tuum'*** et cetera.	Ps 7:7–8
6	*In Ps.* 19, 1 (p. 212)	Iste ergo, 'protegat te': Prov. 18 'Turris fortissima nomen domini': Psalm. 30 'Proteges eos in tabernaculo tuo' et cetera. Hoc nomen est omnipotens: Exod. 15 'Qui potest salvare' et cetera. Item est nomen misericordiae: Luc. 1, 'sanctum', idest misericors, 'nomen ejus': Can. 1 '***Oleum effusum nomen tuum***'. Sic ergo ex potentia et misericordia Dei protegimur.	Ps 19:2
7	*In Matth.*, c. 14, 2 (n° 1255)	'Unde statim impulit eos intrare naviculam'. Unde statim facto miraculo voluit separari a turbis [...]. Item ostendit affectum turbarum, scilicet cum quo ardore sequebantur eum; Cant. I, 2 '***Oleum effusum nomen tuum, ideo adolescentulae dilexerunt te***'.	Mt 14:22–23
8	*In Matth.*, c. 25, 1 (n° 2017)	Secundum aenem per oleum sancta doctrina signatur; Cant. I, 2 '***Oleum effusum nomen tuum***'. Oleum iustitiae rectam doctrinam signat; Ps. CXVIII, 11 'In corde meo abscondi eloquia tua'. Unde virgines dicuntur qui continentiam servant, qui faciunt misericordiam, qui gaudium interius quaerunt, qui rectam doctrinam assumunt.	Mt 25:3 Origen, *Commentaria in Evangelium secundum Matthaeum*, c. 25 (PG 13; col. 1699–1702)
9	*In Ioan.*, c. 1, lect. 15 (n° 285)	Secundo vero quod cum Ioannes dignitatem Christi commendans dixit 'ante me factus est', et quoniam 'non sum dignus solvere corrigiam calceamenti eius', nullus conversus est; sed quando humilia de Christo, et incarnationis mysterio locutus est, tunc secuti sunt eum discipuli: quia humilia, et quae pro nobis passus est Christus, magis movent nos; et ideo dicitur Cant. I, 2 '***Oleum effusum nomen tuum***', idest misericordia, qua salutem omnium procurasti; et ideo statim sequitur '***Adolescentulae dilexerunt te nimis***'.	Jn 1:37 John Chrysostom, *Homelia XVIII in Ioannem*, 1 (PG 59, col. 115)
10	*In ad Ro.*, prol. (n° 3)	Hoc autem vas, de quo nunc agitur, plenum fuit pretioso liquore, scilicet nomine Christi, de quo dicitur Cant. I, 2 '***Oleum effusum nomen tuum***'. Unde dicitur 'ut portet nomen meum'. Totus enim videtur fuisse [Paulus] hoc nomine plenus.	Acts 9:15 (theme of the Prologue)
11	*In de div. nom.*, c. 4, lect. 11 (n° 443)	Quaerit ergo primo quid voluerint significare editores sacrae Scripturae, quos theologos vocat, quod Deum, 'aliquando quidem' nominaverunt 'dilectionem et amorem', sicut patet I Ioan. I 'Deus charitas est'; 'aliquando' vero nominant 'ipsum amabilem et diligibilem': Cant. I '***Adolescentulae dilexerunt te nimis***'.	Dionysius, *De divinis nominibus* IV, 14 (PTS 33, p. 712)

3		**trahe me post te, curremus in odorem unguentorum tuorum.**	
12	*In Symbolum Apostolorum*, 6 (n° 946)	Et licet sancti in caelum ascendant, non tamen sicut Christus: quia Christus sua virtute, sancti vero attracti a Christo. Cant. I, 3 '***Trahe me post te***'.	
13	*De decem preceptis*, X (p. 81)	Aliquando enim peccamus nec Deum querimus: et Deus trahit nos ad se vel infirmitate vel aliquo huiusmodi. Prov. [?] 'Sepiam viam tuam spinis'. Sic quidem Paulus tractus fuit. Ps. 'Erravi sicut ovis que periit', etc; Cant., '***Trahe me***' etc.	
14	*In Ps.* 44, 10 (p. 325)	Virgines interius, scilicet fideles animae non corruptae per peccatum; 'adducentur regi', scilicet Christo qui est rex regum. Adducentur, dico, quia non per se venient. Joan. 6 'Nemo venit ad me' etc.: et ideo dicit Cant. 1 '***Trahe me post te***'. Sed adducentur post eam, scilicet universalem Ecclesiam, quia nullus veniet nec adducetur ad Christum nisi sequatur doctrinam Ecclesiae.	Ps 44:15
15	*In Is.*, c. 40, lines 289–301 [293] (p. 172) (Collatio 9)	Sancti comparantur aquilis: [...] propter odoris subtilitatem, Luce xvi 'Ubicumque fuerit corpus' etc., in quo fervor dilectionis, Cant. primo '***Trae me post te***' etc.; [...] propter membrorum pulcritudinem, Ez. Xvij 'Aquila grandis' etc., in quo decor virtutum, Cant. iiij '***Tota pulcra es***' etc.	Is 16:1
16	*In Ioan.*, c. 6, lect. 5 (n° 935)	Si enim, ut dicit Augustinus, 'trahit sua quemque voluptas', quanto fortius debet homo trahi ad Christum, si delectatur veritate, beatitudine, iustitia, sempiterna vita, quod totum est Christus? Ab isto ergo si trahendi sumus, trahamur per dilectionem veritatis; secundum illud Ps. XXXVI, 4 'Delectare in domino, et dabit tibi petitiones cordis tui'. Hinc sponsa dicebat, Cant. I, 3 '***Trahe me post te; curremus in odorem unguentorum tuorum***'.	Jn 6:44 Augustine, *In Iohannis evangelium tractatus CXXIV*, XXVI, 4–5 (p. 261)
17	*In Ioan.* c. 12, lect. 5 (n° 1673)	Sic ergo exaltatus 'Omnia traham', per caritatem, ad meipsum: Ier. XXXI, 3 'In caritate perpetua dilexi te, ideo attraxi te, miserans'. In hoc etiam maxime apparet caritas Dei ad hominem, inquantum pro ipsis mori dignatus est; Rom. V, 8 'Commendat Deus suam caritatem in nobis, quoniam cum adhuc peccatores essemus secundum tempus, Christus pro nobis mortuus est.' In hoc complevit quod sponsa petit Cant. I, 3 '***Trahe me post te, et curremus in odorem unguentorum tuorum***'.	Jn 12:32

18	*In Ioan.*, c. 14, lect. 1 (n°1859)	Praeparavit autem dominus per recessum suum nobis locum quinque modis. [...]. Quarto sursum attrahendo; Cant. I, 3 '***Trahe me post te***'; Coloss. III, 1 'Si consurrexistis cum Christo, quae sursum sunt quaerite'.	Jn 14:3
19	*In Ioan.*, c. 15, lect 5 (n° 2055)	Nullus enim potest ad Christum venire per fidem nisi tractus; supra VI, 44: 'Nemo potest venire ad me, nisi pater, qui misit me, traxerit eum'. Et ideo Cant. I, 3, dicit sponsa '***Trahe me post te: curremus in odorem unguentorum tuorum***'.	Jn 15:24
* 19'	*Catena in Ioan.* 6, 6	Augustinus. Trahit sua quemque voluptas, quanto fortius nos dicere debemus trahi hominem ad Christum, qui delectatur veritate, beatitudine, iustitia, sempiterna vita, quod totum Christus est? [...] Sed quare voluit dicere quem traxerit pater? Si trahendi sumus, ab illo trahamur cui dicit quaedam quae diligit '***Trahe me post te***'.	Augustine, *In Iohannis evangelium tractatus CXXIV*, XXVI, 4–5 (p. 261)
20	*In ad Ep.*, c. 5, lect. 1 (n° 20°	Et hoc 'in odorem suavitatis'. Alludit autem hic, quod dicitur Lev. III, 5 s. Sed certe ille odor non erat tunc Deo acceptus secundum se, sed secundum suam significationem, inquantum significabat oblationem odoriferam corporis Christi filii Dei. Gen. II 'Ecce odor filii mei, sicut odor agri pleni'. Cant. I, 3 '***Trahe me post te, curremus in odorem unguentorum tuorum***'.	Eph 5:2
21	*In ad Ph.*, c. 2, lect. 2 (n° 52)	'Hoc sentite', id est experimento tenete quod fuit 'in Christo Iesu'. Notandum quod quinque modis debemus hoc sentire, scilicet quinque sensibus. [...] Tertio odorare gratias suae mansuetudinis, ut ad eum curramus. Cant. I, 3 '***Trahe me post te, curremus in odorem unguentorum tuorum***'.	Phil 2:5
22	*In Is.*, c. 3, lines 412–19 [418–19] (p. 30)	'Et olfactoriola'. Hic ponuntur ea quae pertinent ad organa sensus: et primo quantum ad olfactum. 'Olfactoriola', quaedam pixides in quibus ponebant muscum et hujusmodi, vel etiam quaedam vasa, sicut poma de argento facta, perforata ad modum thuribuli, in quibus ponitur ignis et aliquid odoriferum, Cant. I '***Curremus in odorem unguentorum tuorum***'.	Is 3:20
23	*In Is.*, c. 16, lines 78–90 [88–89] (p. 97)	Nota super illo verbo, 'de petra deserti', quod beata Virgo dicitur petra, primo propter gratiae firmitatem, Eccl. xxxvi 'Fundamenta aeterna'; secundo propter continentie frigiditatem, infra xxxii 'Sicut umbra petrae prominentis in terra deserta'; tertio propter fructus ubertatem, Iob xxxix 'Petra fundebat rivos olei'. Et nota, quod ista petra fuit singularis deserti, quia precipua quantum ad primum, Cant. iv '***Tota pulcra es, amica mea***'; secundo, quia prima quantum ad secundum, Cant. ii '***Curremus in odorem unguentorum tuorum***'; virgo quantum ad tertium, supra vii 'Ecce virgo concipiet et pariet filium'.	Is 16:1

24	*In Matth.*, c. 25, 1 (n° 2011)	Secundum Hieronymum, duplicantur secundum quod ad diversos sensus referuntur: sunt enim quidam sensus exteriores, et quidam interiores. De visu interiori dicitur Io. IV, 1 2 'Deum nemo vidit umquam'. De gustu dicitur Ps. XXXIII, 9 'Gustate et videte quoniam suavis est dominus'. De olfactu dicitur Cant. I, 3 '***In odorem unguentorum tuorum currimus***'. Et sic sunt omnes decem, qui ad iudicium veniunt.	Mt 25:1 Jerome, *Commentariorum in Matheum libri IV*, 25, 2 (CCSL 77, p. 236)
* 24'	*Catena in Matthaeum*, 25, 1	Hieronymus. Sunt enim quinque sensus, qui festinant ad caelestia, et superna desiderant. De visu autem et auditu et tactu specialiter dictum est: 'Quod vidimus, quod audivimus quod oculis nostris perspeximus et manus nostrae palpaverunt'. De gustu: 'Gustate, et videte quoniam suavis est dominus'. De odoratu: '***In odorem unguentorum tuorum currimus***'.	Mt 25:1 Jerome, *Commentariorum in Matheum libri IV*, 25, 2 (CCSL 77, p. 236)
* 24''	*Catena in Lucam*, 12, 2	Origenes. [...] Mystice autem quinque passeres spirituales sensus iuste significant, qui excelsa et supra homines sentiunt, Deum intuentes, vocem audientes divinam, gustantes panem vitae, olfacientes ***odorem unguentorum*** Christi, palpantes vivum verbum.	Lk 12:6 Origen: not identified
25	*In Ioan.*, c. 12, lect. 1 (n° 1596)	Effectus autem obsequii tangitur consequenter, cum dicit 'et domus impleta est ex odore unguenti': per quod insinuatur unguenti bonitas, cuius odor totam domum implevit; Cant. I, 3 '***Curremus in odorem unguentorum tuorum***'.	Jn 12:3
26	*In 1 ad Co.*, c. 12, lect. 3 (n° 741)	Et, iterum: 'si' totum corpus esset 'auditus', id est instrumentum audiendi, 'ubi' esset 'odoratus' ? et cetera. Per quem possunt in Ecclesia intelligi illi qui, et si non sint capaces verborum sapientiae, percipiunt tamen quaedam eius indicia a remotis, quasi odorem. Unde et Cant. I, 3 dicitur '***In odorem unguentorum tuorum currimus***'.	1 Cor 12:17
		introduxit me rex in cellaria sua	
27	*In Ps.* 36, 19 (p. 287)	Sed est sensus, 'inhabita', quasi intus habita. Sensibilia dicuntur exteriora bona, quia exteriori sensu capiuntur. Interiora bona sunt spiritualia et intelligibilia. Cum ergo dicit, 'inhabita', dicit intra possessionem spiritualium bonorum habitabis: Cant. 1 '***Introduxit me rex in cellaria sua***'.	Ps 36:27
28	*In Matth.*, c. 7, 2 (n° 665)	Sed notandum, quod per hoc quod dicit 'regnum' tangitur remuneratio aeterna; unde dicit 'intrabit'. Illud enim regnum in bonis spiritualibus est, non in bonis exterioribus; ideo dicit 'intrabit'. Ideo Cant. I, 4 '***Introduxit me rex in cellaria sua***'.	Mt 7:21
29	*In Matth.*, c. 25, 2 (n° 2054)	Et quare dicit 'intra in gaudium', non accipe? Dicendum quod duplex est gaudium: de bonis exterioribus et de bonis interioribus; qui gaudet de bonis exterioribus, non intrat in gaudium, sed intrat gaudium in ipsum; qui autem gaudet de spiritualibus intrat in gaudium. Cant. I, 5 '***Introduxit me rex in cellaria sua***'.	Mt 25:21

30	*In Ioan.*, c. 6, lect 4 (n° 921)	Ergo duplex est intrinsecum. Unum est profundissimum, scilicet gaudium vitae aeternae [...]. Et ab hoc intrinseco nullus eiicietur [...]. Aliud intrinsecum est rectitudo conscientiae, quae est spirituale gaudium; et de hoc dicitur Sap. VIII, 16 'Intrans in domum meam, conquiescam'. Et Cant. I, 3 '***Introduxit me rex in cellaria sua***'. Et de isto aliqui eiiciuntur.	Jn 6:37
31	*In ad He.*, c. 4, lect. 1 (n° 201)	Est autem duplex requies. Una in bonis exterioribus, et ad istam egreditur homo a requie mentis; alia est in bonis spiritualibus, quae est intima, et ad istam ingreditur. Matth. XXV, 21 'Intra in gaudium domini tui'. Cant. I, 3 '***Introduxit me rex in cellaria sua***'.	Heb 4:3
		exultabimus et letabimur in te, memores uberum tuorum super vinum	
32	*In Is.*, c. 41, lines 83–88 [88] (p. 174)	Ponens etiam exaltationis beneficium [...] quantum ad eorum exultationem, 'et tu exultabis' etc., Cant. primo '***Letabimur et exultabimus***' etc.	Is 41:16
33	*In Ps.* 20, 1 (p. 214)	Similiter si dicatur de David 'O domine Deus, rex', scilicet David et alii sancti, 'laetabuntur in virtute tua': Can. 1 '***Laetabimur et exultabimus in te: memores uberum tuorum***'.	Ps 20:2
		recti diligunt te	
34	*In Ps.* 30, 21 (p. 256)	'Diligite dominum sancti eius'. Primo inducit eos ad diligendum Deum [...]. Et qui sunt qui diligere debent, ostendit: quia, 'sancti': Cant. 1 '***Recti diligunt te***'.	Ps 30:24
35	*In Ps.* 50, 6 (p. 348)	Sicut ergo per conversionem ad aliquod commutabile bonum animus efficitur immundus, ita per aversionem a fine deordinatur; et hujusmodi deordinationi opponitur rectitudo qua homo dirigitur in Deum : Cantic. 1 '***Recti diligunt te***': et ideo dicit, 'et spiritum rectum innova'	Ps 50:12
36	*In Is.*, c. 44, lines 160–63 [163] (p. 188) (Collatio 20)	Sancti sunt electi per praedestinationem [...], formati per gratiae infusionem [...], recti per dilectionem, Cant. primo: '***Recti diligunt***' etc..	
37	*In 1 ad Tim.*, c. 1, lect. 2 (n° 15)	Impossibile est quod cor impurum sit promptum ad charitatem, quia unicuique est diligibile quod sibi est conforme. Cor impurum diligit illud, quod competit ei secundum passionem; ergo necesse est quod sit expeditum a passionibus. Cant. I, 3 '***Recti diligunt te***'.	1 Tm 1:5
38	Sermo XVII, lines 400–17 [415] (p. 271)	Isti recti scitis quid faciunt? [...]. Secundo, recti corde Deo adherent per dilectionem. Unde in Cantico '***Recti diligunt te***'; Psalmista : 'Innocentes et recti adheserunt michi', scilicet per fervorem et habitum caritatis.	

4		**nigra sum sed formosa, filiae Jerusalem**	
39	*In Ier.*, c. 38, 1 (p. 662)	Primo describit petentem, 'Abdemelech' [...]. 'Aethiops', propter carnis mortificationem. Psalm. 67 'Aethiopia praeveniet manus ejus Deo'. Cant. 1 '***Nigra sum, sed formosa***'.	Jer 38:7
5		**filii matris meae pugnaverunt contra me**	
40	*In Ier.*, c. 12, 1 (p. 609)	Secundo quantum ad sanguine junctos, commemorans pristinam injuriam: 'nam et fratres', scilicet Idumaei, 'et domus', scilicet Moabitae et Amonitae. Cant. 1 '***Filii matris meae pugnaverunt contra me***'.	Jer 12:6
41	*In ad Ga.*, c. 1, lect. 4 (n° 41)	'Ex utero matris meae', scilicet synagogae, cuius uterus est collegium Pharisaeorum, qui nutriebant alios in Iudaismo. Matth. XXIII, 15: 'Circuitis mare et aridam, ut faciatis', et cetera. Sic ergo mater sua fuit synagoga. Cant. I, 5: '***Filii matris meae pugnaverunt contra me***', et cetera.	Gal 1:15
6		**indica mihi, quem diligit anima mea, ubi pascas, ubi cubes in meridie**	
42	*In Ioan.*, c. 1, lect. 15 (n° 290)	Moraliter autem interrogant 'Ubi habitas?' Quasi vellent scire, quales debent esse homines qui digni sunt quod Christus habitet in eis; de quo habitaculo dicitur Eph. II, 22 'Aedificamini in habitaculum Dei', et Cant. I, 6 '***Indica mihi, quem diligit anima mea, ubi pascas, ubi cubes in meridie***'.	Jn 1:38
7		**si ignoras te, o pulcherrima inter mulieres**	
43	*In Ioan.*, c. 13, lect. 1 (n° 1743)	Et ideo Christus sciebat ea quae sibi data erant a Deo. Hoc autem ideo dicit ut humilitas magis sit commendabilis. Quandoque enim contingit quod aliquis magnae dignitatis est, et tamen, propter simplicitatem suam, dignitatem suam non recognoscit. Talis ergo si faceret aliquid humile, non reputaretur sibi ad magnam laudem, secundum illud Cant. I, 7 '***Si ignorans te, pulcherrima inter mulieres***'.	Jn 13:3
10		**murenulas aureas faciemus tibi, vermiculatas argento**	
44	*In Is.*, c. 3, lines 403–8 [407–8] (p. 30)	Secundo ponit ornamenta colli immediata, cum dicit, 'murenulas', scilicet quedam catene virgulis aureis et argenteis vermiculate in modum murene, quae ponuntur circa collum. Cant. i '***Murenulas aureas faciemus tibi, vermiculatas argento***'.	Is 3:20
11		**dum esset rex in accubitu suo, nardus mea dedit odorem suum.**	
45	*In Ioan.*, c. 12, lect. 1 (n° 1596)	Circa primum tria tangit. Primo quantitatem unguenti, quia multum fuit, unde dicit 'libram unguenti'; Tob. IV, 9 'Si multum tibi fuerit, abundanter tribue'. Secundo materiam, quia fuit ex nardo confectum; unde dicit 'nardi'; Cant. I, 11 '***Dum esset rex in accubitu suo, nardus mea dedit odorem suum***'. Est autem nardus herba brevis et spicosa et nigra, ex qua fit unguentum, quod vim confortandi habet ex sua aromaticitate.	Jn 12:3

* 45’	*Catena in Marcum* 14, 2	Hieronymus. Mystice […] mulier autem cum alabastro ecclesiasticam fidem, quae dicit : ‘***Nardus mea dedit odorem suum***’. Pistica nardus dicitur, idest fidelis et pretiosa..	Mk 14:3 Jerome, *Tractatus in Marci Evangelium*, XIIII (CCSL 78, p. 498)
13		**botrus cypri dilectus meus mihi in vineis Engaddi**	
46	*In Is.*, c. 63, lines 93–104 [102–3] (p. 245)	Primo assignat ruboris rationem […]. Circa primum tria. Primo narrat singularem victoriam: ‘Torcular’, scilicet crucem in qua pondere passionis pressus, hostes, ‘calcavi solus’, patiens, et vincens; ‘et de gentibus non est vir mecum’, in auxilium, quia eo relicto omnes fugerunt. Et dicit signanter, ‘vir’, propter beatam Virginem, in qua fides nunquam defecit. Cant 1 ‘***Botrus Cipri dilectus meus michi in vineis Engaddi***’. Thren. 1 ‘Torcular calcavit’.	Is 63:2–3
14		**ecce tu pulchra es, amica mea.**	
47	*In Is.*, c. 11, lines 72–76 [74–75] (p. 78–79)	Nota super illo verbo, ‘et flos de radice’, quod Christus dicitur flos: primo propter Marie puritatem. Cant. i ‘***Ecce tu pulcra es, amica mea***’, Cant. ii ‘***Ecce tu pulcer es, dilecte mi***’ etc, et infra ‘***Ego flos campi, et lilium convallium***’.	Is 11:1
15		**ecce tu pulcher es, dilecte mi, et decorus**	
48	*In Ps.* 44, 2 (p. 320)	‘Speciosus forma prae filiis hominum’ […]. Quarta est pulchritudo corporis: et haec etiam Christo infuit. Cant. 1 ‘***Ecce tu pulcher es dilecte mi***’.	Ps 44:3
49	*In Is.*, c. 11, line 75 (p. 79)	See [no. 47]	
50	In de div. nom., c. 4, lect. 5 (n° 334)	Dicit ergo, primo, quod hoc supersubstantiale bonum quod est Deus ‘laudatur a sanctis theologis’ in sacra Scriptura ‘sicut pulchrum’; Cant. I ‘***Ecce tu pulcher es, dilecte mi***’; ‘et sicut pulchritudo’; Psalm. 95 ‘Confessio et pulchritudo in conspectu eius’; ‘et sicut dilectio’: I Ioan. 4 ‘Deus caritas est’, ‘et sicut diligibile’, ut in auctoritate Canticorum inducta; ‘et quaecumque aliae sunt convenientes’ Dei ‘nominationes’, ad pulchritudinem pertinentes.	Dionysius, *De divinis nominibus* IV, 7 (PTS 33, pp. 150–51)
		lectulus noster floridus	
51	Sermo VIII, lines 544–52 [546–47] (p. 111)	Unde et Christus ‘descendit in Nazareth’ quod interpretatur ‘flos’, per quod significatur puritas, unde in Cantico: ‘***Lectulus noster floridus***’ est. Beatus qui in consciencia sua nichil habet fetidum vel infamia dignum, sed solum odorem bone fame, unde in Cantico [=*Si* 24, 23]: ‘Flores mei fructus honoris et honestatis’. Fructus sint in merito, unde Apostolus: ‘Habetis fructum in sanctificationem’; flores sunt un futura patria.	

52	*In Ps.* 27, 7 (p. 245)	In primo homine floruit caro ejus per innocentiae puritatem, sed peccando inquinata est. Sed in Christo refloruit in resurrectione: fuit enim de Spiritu sancto sine peccato concepta. Isa. 11 'Flos de radice ejus ascendet'. Item in primo statu natura humana floruit, quia erat incorruptibilis: sed per peccatum est subjecta corruptioni: Rom. 8 'Corpus per peccatum mortuum est'. Sed Christus refloruit in resurrectione: Cant. '***Et lectulus noster floridus est***'.	Ps 27:7
53	In Matth., c. 24, 3 (n° 1992)	Sunt tria genera hominum, quidam contemplativi, quidam praelati, quidam activi. Nullus status securus est, quin aliqui damnentur in statu aliquo. Status contemplationis per lectum significatur. De hoc in Cant. I, 15: '***Lectus noster floridus***'; et tamen aliqui in hoc statu damnantur. [...] Per agrum in quem homines exeunt ad laborandum, signantur praelati; Cant. VII, 11 '***Veni, dilecte mi, egrediamur in agrum***'. Et in talibus quidam assumuntur, et quidam relinquuntur.	Mt 24:40–41

APPENDIX TABLE 2

1		**ego flos campi et lilium convallium**	
54	*In Is.*, c. 11, lines 25–28 [26–27] (p. 78)	Quantum ad processum filii ex matre virgine, 'et flos', Christus. Cant ii '***Ego flos campi, et lilium convallium***', 'ascendet', quia qui de caelo venit, 'super omnes est'. Joan. 3.	Is 11:11
55	*In Is.*, c. 11, lines 74–75 (p. 78–79)	See [no. 47]	
56	*In Is.*, c. 35, lines 74–78 [78] (p. 154) (Collatio 3)	Hec lilia Christus vestit quantum ad virtutum dona. Mt vj 'Considerate lilia agri etc.; colligit ad eterna premia. Cant vj '***Dilectus meus descendit in ortum***' etc.; in eis requiescit per complacentiam, Cant. ij '***Dilectus meus mihi***' etc.; et ideo ipse lilium. Cant. ij: '***Ego flos campi***' etc	
57	*In Matth.*, c. 2, 4 (n° 240)	Vel potest dici, quod per Nazarenum interpretatur floridus; et hoc habetur Is. XI, 1: 'Egredietur virga de radice Iesse, et flos de radice eius ascendet' etc.; et convenit cum eo, quod dicitur Cant. II, 1 '***Ego flos campi et lilium convallium***'.	Mt 2:23

* 57’	*Catena in Matthaeum*, 21, 2	Hieronymus. Aliis autem vel ambigentibus vel interrogantibus, nisi plebecula confitetur: unde sequitur ‘Populi autem dicebant : hic est Iesus propheta a Nazareth Galilaeae’. [...] A Nazareth autem Galilaeae, quia ibi educatus fuerat, ut ***flos campi*** nutriretur in flore virtutum.	Mt 21:11 Jerome, *Commentariorum in Matheum libri IV*, III, 21, 11 (CCSL 77, p. 186)
58	*In Ioan.*, c. 19, lect. 4 (n° 2420)	Hoc vero quod dicit ‘Nazarenus’, quod interpretatur floridus, pertinet ad patientis innocentiam; Cant. II, 1 ‘***Ego flos campi, et lilium convallium***’ Is. XI, 1: ‘et flos de radice eius ascendet’.	Jn 19:19
2		**sicut lilium inter spinas, sic amica mea inter filias.**	
59	*ST* IIa-IIae, q. 108, a. 1, obj. 2	Praeterea, ille de quo vindicta sumitur, non toleratur. Sed mali sunt tolerandi, quia super illud Cant. II ‘***Sicut lilium inter spinas***’, dicit Glossa, ‘non fuit bonus qui malos tolerare non potuit’. Ergo vindicta non est sumenda de malis.	“Utrum vindicatio sit licita?” *Glossa ordinaria in Canticum*, II, 7 (CCCM 170, p. 141)
60	*Contra impugnantes*, c. 20, lines 129–38 [136–37] (p. A 154–A 155)	Non ergo propter hoc infamandum est religiosorum collegium si aliqui ex eorum numero gravia etiam peccata committunt: alias simili modo etiam apostolorum collegium vituperabile fuit propter hoc quod dicitur Ioan. VI, 71 ‘Nonne duodecim vos elegi, et unus ex vobis diabolus est?’ Unde etiam Cant. II, 2, dicitur ‘***Sicut lilium inter spinas, sic amica mea inter filias***’. Glossa Gregorii ‘Nec mali sine bonis, nec boni sine malis esse possunt’.	*Glossa ordinaria in Canticum*, II, 7 (CCCM 170, p. 141)
61	*In Is.*, c. 35, lines 69–73 [70] (p. 154) (Collatio 2)	Sancti comparantur liliis propter stipitis altitudinem, ex quo constantia in adversis, Cant ij ‘***Sicut lilium inter spinas***’ etc.; [...]; propter connexionem, ex quo sanctorum caritas. Cant. vij ‘***Venter tuus quasi***’, etc.	
62	*In Matth.*, c. 9, 2 (n° 762)	E contrario similiter aliqui commorantur cum peccatoribus ad sui probationem: unde tentatio est sui probatio, ut habetur Eccli. XXVII, 6 et II Petri II, 8 ‘Aspectu enim et auditu iustus erat habitans apud eos’. Et Cant. II, 2 ‘***Sicut lilium inter spinas, sic amica mea inter filias***’. Et ibi dicit Glossa: ‘Non fuit bonus, qui malos tolerare non potuit’.	Mt 9:11; “Utrum sunt vitanda peccatorum consortia?” *Glossa ordinaria in Canticum*, II, 7 (CCCM 170, p. 141)
63	*In Matth.*, c. 10, 1 (n° 812)	Item est alia ratio, ad notandum quod vix contingit quin in multa congregatione sit aliquis malus; et ideo ita ponitur, ut ostendatur quod boni aliquando non sunt sine malis; Cant. II, 2 : ‘***Sicut lilium inter spinas, sic amica mea inter filias***’.	Mt 10:5

64	*In Matth.*, c. 13, 2 (n° 1156)	Quamdiu durat tempus istud, mali cum bonis sunt, zizania cum tritico, '***lilium inter spinas***', ut habetur Cant. II, 2.	Mt 13:30
65	*In Matth.*, c. 13, 4 (n° 1199)	Modo mali sunt inter bonos, zizania in medio tritici, '***lilium inter spinas***', sed separabuntur ex communione bonorum	Mt 13:49
66	*In Matth.*, c. 25, 3 (n° 2088)	Notate quod quamdiu mundus durat, mali sunt bonis permixti. Vix autem est aliqua societas, quin aliqui sint mali; Cant. II, 2 '***Sicut lilium inter spinas, sic amica mea inter filias***'. Sed in illo iudicio mali erunt ad unam partem, boni ad aliam.	Mt 25:32
67	*In Ioan.*, c. 12, lect 1 (n° 1605)	Sed quaeritur quare dominus Iudae, quem furem sciebat, custodiam loculorum commisit? Ad quod respondendum est tripliciter. Primo quidem, secundum Augustinum, hoc fecit Christus, ut eius Ecclesia cum fures patitur toleraret: non enim est bonus qui malos tolerare non potuit, unde dicitur Cant. II, 2 '***Sicut lilium inter spinas, sic amica mea inter filias***'.	Jn 12:6 Augustine, *In Iohannis evangelium tractatus CXXIV*, L, 11 (pp. 437–38)
68	*In Ioan.*, c. 13, lect. 3 (n° 1791)	Ideo autem dominus Iudam, quem futurum noverat esse malum, elegit, ut daret intelligere quod nulla societas hominum sine alicuius mali admixtione futura erat: Cant. II, 2 '***Sicut lilium inter spinas, sic amica mea inter filias***'.	Jn 13:18
69	*In 1 ad Co.*, c. 5, lect. 2 (n° 241)	Et ideo Corinthiis non erat gloriandum de peccato unius, sed magis cavendum, ne peccato unius omnes inquinarentur ex eius consortio, secundum illud Cant. II, 2 '***Sicut lilium inter spinas, sic amica mea inter filias***', ubi dicit Glossa: 'Non fuit bonus, qui malos tolerare non potuit'.	1 Cor 5:6 *Glossa ordinaria in Canticum*, II, 7 (CCCM 170, p. 141)
70	*In 1 ad Co.*, c. 11, lect. 4 (n° 625)	Alii vero non erant contentiosi, ex quorum persona ibi subditur 'Ego autem Christi'. Unde et Cant. c. II, 2 dicitur '***Sicut lilium inter spinas, sic amica mea inter filias***', id est, boni inter malos.	1 Cor 11:18
71	*In 2 ad Co.*, c. 6, lect. 3 (n° 243)	Sed Donatistae dicunt quod debemus corporaliter deserere malam societatem, quod non est verum. Unde quod Apostolus dicit, intelligendum est de separatione spirituali. Et ideo sic exponit: 'Exite', spiritualiter, non sequendo vitam eorum. Cant. II, 2 '***Sicut lilium inter spinas***', et cetera. Et hoc ideo, ut vitemus ipsas peccatorum occasiones ab eis datas.	2 Cor 6:17
72	*In ad Ga.*, c. 4, lect. 9 (n° 275)	In mundo enim isto boni sunt malis permixti, et mali bonis. Cant. II, 2 '***Sicut lilium inter spinas***', et cetera. Sed in aeterna patria non erunt nisi boni.	Gal 4:30

* 72'	*Catena in Matthaeum*, 6, 19	Remigius. [...] Per lilia sancti viri intelliguntur, qui absque labore legalium caeremoniarum, sola fide Deo placuerunt; de quibus dicitur: '***Dilectus meus mihi, qui pascitur inter lilia***'. Sancta etiam Ecclesia per lilium intelligitur, propter candorem fidei et odorem bonae conversationis; de qua dicitur: '***Sicut lilium inter spinas***'. Per foenum designantur infideles; de quibus dicitur: 'Aruit foenum et flos eius cecidit'.	Mt 6:28–30 Remigius of Auxerre: not identified
3		**sub umbra illius quam desideraveram sedi,**	
73	*In Thren.*, c. 4, 20 (p. 683)	Quarto excludit protectionem regum: 'Spiritus oris nostri', quo respirabamus inter angustias, 'Christus dominus', Josias, 'captus est', interfectus est ab Aegyptiis, 4 Reg. 24, 'pro peccatis nostris', quia ipse justus erat. Vel potest exponi de Sedecia, secundum consequentiam historiae. Vel melius de Christo. Isa. 53: 'Ipse vulneratus est propter iniquitates nostra'. 'In umbra', protectione. Cantic. 2 '***Sub umbra illius, quem desideraveram, sedi***'.	Lam 4:20
3		**et fructus eius dulcis gutturi meo.**	
74	*In Is.*, c. 3, lines 301–7 [302] (p. 28–29)	[Fructus iusti] quem quaerit: in fruitione Dei, Cant. ii '***Fructus eius dulcis gutturi meo***'; in societate caelestis chori, Ez. Xxxvi 'Montes Israel ramos vestros germinetis, et fructum vestrum afferatis populo meo Israel'; in perceptione divini doni, Cant. iv '***Emissiones tue paradisus malorum punicorum cum pomorum fructibus***'.	Is 3:10
75	*In Ioan.*, c. 15, lect. 1 (n°1979)	Sed vitis est ipse; unde dicit per quamdam similitudinem, 'Ego sum vitis', quia sicut vitis, licet despecta videatur, omnia tamen ligna excedit in dulcedine fructus, ita Christus etsi mundo despectus videretur, quia pauper erat et ignobilis videbatur et ignominiam sustinens, tamen dulcissimos fructus protulit; secundum illud Cant. II, 3 '***Fructus eius dulcis gutturi meo***'.	Jn 15:1
76	*In ad Ga.*, c. 5, lect. 6 (n° 328)	Opera autem spiritus dicuntur fructus non ut adepti sive acquisiti, sed ut producti; fructus autem qui est adeptus, habet rationem ultimi finis, non autem fructus productus. Nihilominus tamen fructus sic acceptus duo importat, scilicet quod sit ultimum producentis, sicut ultimum quod producitur ab arbore est fructus eius, et quod sit suave sive delectabile. Cant. II, 3 '***Fructus eius dulcis gutturi meo***'.	Gal 5:22
77	*In ad Philem.*, lect. 2 (n° 28)	Nam frui est uti fructu, et sicut est uti ad utile, sic frui ad fructum. Importat autem fructus dulcedinem. Cant. II, 3 '***Et fructus eius dulcis gutturi meo***'. Item finem, quia ultimum de arbore est fructus. Et ideo proprie est habere aliquid ut delectabile et finale.	Philem 20

4		**introduxit me in cellam vinariam; ordinavit in me caritatem.**	
78	*Q. de virt.*, q. 2, a. 9, s.c.	Sed contra, est quod dicitur Cantic. II, 4 '***Introduxit me rex in cellam vinariam, ordinavit in me caritatem***'.	"Utrum ordo aliquis sit in caritate?"
79	*ST* IIa-IIae, q. 26, a. 1, s.c.	Sed contra est quod dicitur Cant. II '***Introduxit me rex in cellam vinariam; ordinavit in me caritatem***'.	"Utrum sit aliquis ordo in caritate?"
80	*ST* IIa-IIae, q. 44, a. 8	Sed Deus causat in nobis ordinem caritatis, secundum illud Cant. II, '***Ordinavit in me caritatem***'.	"Utrum ordo caritatis cadat sub praecepto?"
* 80'	*In* III *Sent.*, d. 29, q. 1, a. 6 (p. 938)	Et ideo Ambrosius (super illud Cantic. cap. 2: '***Ordinavit in me caritatem***') hunc ordinem dilectionis ponit, ut primo diligantur consanguinei, ad quos habetur prima amicitia: secundo domestici...	"Utrum ex caritate magis debeat diligere extraneos quam propinquos?" Ambrose (?), according to *Glossa ordinaria in Canticum*, II, 24 (CCCM 170, p. 149); Peter Lombard, *Sententiae*, III, d. 29, c. 1 (p. 171)
81	*In ad Ro.*, c. 13, lect. 2 (n°1057)	Quod autem dicit 'sicut teipsum', non est referendum ad aequalitatem dilectionis, ut scilicet aliquis teneatur diligere proximum aequaliter sibi: hoc enim esset contra ordinem charitatis, quo quilibet plus tenetur suam, quam aliorum salutem curare. Cant. II, 4: '***Ordinavit in me charitatem***'.	Rom 13:9
82	*De decem preceptis*, VIII (p. 77)	Secundum est quod debemus eum [=proximum] diligere ordinate, ut scilicet non diligamus eum supra Deum nec quantum Deum set iuxta, sicut et teipsum debes diligere, Cant. '***Ordinavit in me caritatem***'.	
83	*In 1 ad Tim.*, c. 5, lect. 1 (n° 191)	Circa hoc instruatur vidua, quia hoc est de necessitate. Et ideo dicit 'suorum', quorum scilicet cura ei incumbit, et 'maxime domesticorum'. Cant. II, 4: '***Ordinavit in me charitatem***'.	1 Tm 5:8
* 83'	*Catena in Matthaeum*, 10, 14	Hieronymus. Quia ante praemiserat: 'Non veni pacem mittere, sed gladium', et dividere hominem adversus patrem et matrem et socrum, ne quis pietatem religioni auferret, subiecit, dicens 'Qui amat patrem aut matrem plusquam me, non est me dignus'. Et in Cantico legimus canticorum: '***Ordinavit in me caritatem***'. Hic enim ordo in omni affectu necessarius est.	Mt 10:34–37 Jerome, *Commentariorum in Matheum libri IV*, I, 10, 37 (CCSL 77, p. 74)

5		**fulcite me floribus, stipate me malis, quia amore langueo.**	
84	*In Ps.* 44, 1 (p. 318)	Hieronymus habet sic, 'Victoria pro liliis filiorum Core, canticum pro dilectissimo'. Et quod dicit 'pro liliis', ostendit quod agit hic Psalmus pro deliciis sponsi et sponsae. Et hoc signatur per flores, rosas et lilia: Cant. 2 '***Fulcite me floribus***' et cetera. Et competit virginibus quae sunt quasi lilia.	Ps 44:1
85	*In Is.*, c. 30, lines 324–29 [328–29] (p. 140)	Item super illo verbo, 'lingua ejus quasi ignis', quod caritas dicitur ignis : primo quia illuminat. Eccl. ii: 'Qui timetis Deum diligite eum, et illuminabuntur corda vestra'; secundo quia exestuat. Cant. ii: '***Fulcite me floribus, stipate me malis, quia amore langueo***'.	Is 30:27
86	*ST* Ia-IIae, q. 28, a. 5, obj. 1	Languor enim significat laesionem quandam languentis. Sed amor causat languorem, dicitur enim Cant. II, '***Fulcite me floribus, stipate me malis, quia amore langueo***'. Ergo amor est passio laesiva.	"Utrum amor sit passio laesiva?"
6	(cf. 8, 3)	**leva eius sub capite meo et dextera illius amplexabitur me.**	
* 86'	*Contra impugnantes*, c. 11, lines 119–29 [128–29] (p. A 133)	Item, quod non solum studio litterarum sacrarum sed etiam studio litterarum saecularium laudabiliter vacare possint, expresse habetur per Ieronymum in epistola ad Pammachium monachum 'Si adamaveris captivam mulierem, id est sapientiam saecularem, et eius pulcritudine captus fueris, decalva eam et illecebras crinium atque ornamenta verborum cum remotis unguibus seca, lava eam prophetali nitro, et tunc requiescens cum illa dicito: '***Sinistra eius sub capite meo et dextera illius amplexabitur me***'.	Jerome, *Epistola 66 ad Pammachium*, 8 (CSEL 54, p. 648)
* 86"	*In Boet. de Trin.*, q. 2, a. 3, s.c. 3 (p. 98)	Preterea Ieronimus in epistola ad Pammachium de dormitione Pauline: 'Si adamaveris captivam [. . .] et requiescens cum illa dicito '***Sinistra eius sub capite meo et dextera illius amplexabitur me***', et multos tibi captiva fetus dabit. . .'	Jerome, *Epistola 66 ad Pammachium*, 8 (CSEL 54, p. 648)
87	*In Matth.*, c. 20, 2 (n° 1656)	Unde per dexteram spiritualia significantur, terrena per sinistram. Vel possumus intelligere per dexteram et sinistram activam vitam et contemplativam; ideo petit istos perfici in utraque vita; Cant. c. II, 6: '***Laeva eius sub capite meo, et dextera illius amplexabitur me***'.	Mt 20:23
8		**ecce iste venit, saliens in montibus, transiliens colles.**	
88	Sermo II, lines 149–56 [154–55] (p. 23)	In hoc enim modo loquendi [. . .] demonstrat eius novitatem ut attendamus et admiremur. Et sic loquitur sponsa Cantici II '***Ecce*** ille ***venit saliens in montibus***'. Et in Ysaia 'Ecce nova facio omnia et nunc orietur'.	Zec 2:10

89	*In Ioan.*, c. 1, lect. 14 (n° 261)	Quasi dicat: licet post me venerit ad praedicandum, tamen 'ante me' idest praelatus mihi factus est dignitate. Cant. II, 8 '***Ecce iste venit saliens in montibus, transiliens colles***'. Collis unus fuit Ioannes Baptista, quem Christus transilivit: quia, ut dicitur infra III, 30 'Me oportet minui, illum autem crescere'.	Jn 1:30
9		**en ipse stat post parietem nostrum**	
90	*In ad Ep.*, c. 2, lect. 5 (n° 112)	In isto autem agro est paries, quia quidam sunt ex una parte, quidam ex alia; hic autem paries potest dici lex vetus secundum carnales observantias, in qua Iudaei conclusi custodiebantur, ut dicitur Gal. c. III, 23 'Sub lege custodiebamur conclusi in eam fidem, quae revelanda erat'. Cant. II, 9 '***Ipse stat post parietem nostrum***'; quia videlicet Christus per veterem legem figurabatur.	Eph 2:14
11		**jam enim hiems transiit, imber abiit, et recessit**	
91	*In Ioan.*, c. 10, lect. 5 (n° 1435)	Et ideo ut hoc designet, describit tempus in speciali, dicens 'et hiems erat': quod etiam causam mysticam habet. Ut Gregorius dicit, II Moral., idcirco Evangelista hiemis curavit tempus exprimere, ut inesse auditorum cordibus, scilicet Iudaeorum malitiae, frigus indicaret; Ier. VI, 7 'Sicut frigidam facit cisterna aquam suam, ita frigidam fecit malitiam suam'. De hac hieme dicitur, Cant. II, 11 '***Iam enim hiems transiit, imber abiit et recessit***'.	Cf. Gregory the Great, *Moralia in Iob, Libri I-X*, II, II, 2 (CCSL 143, pp. 59–60)
13		**ficus protulit grossos suos**	
* 91'	*Catena in Lucam*, 6, 11	Ambrosius. In spinis istius mundi ficus illa reperiri non potest; quae quia fecundis fructibus melior est, bene species ei resurrectionis aptatur: vel quia, ut legisti: '***Ficus dederunt grossos suos***'; quod immaturus et caducus et inutilis in synagoga fructus ante praecessit.	Lk 6:44 Ambrose, *Expositio evangelii secundum Lucam*, V, 81 (CCSL 14, pp. 161–62)
92	*In Matth.*, c. 24, 3 (n° 1977)	Vel potest exponi in bono. Per ramum virtus et fortitudo sanctorum. Quando Ecclesia incipiet finiri, virtus Christi et sanctorum apparebit qui sustinebunt eam; Cant. II, 13 '***Ficus protulit grossos suos***'.	Mt 24:32
13–14		**surge amica mea speciosa mea et veni columba mea in foraminibus petrae**	
93	*In Is.*, c. 2, lines 257–65 [264–65] (p. 23)	Bernardus exponit de Christo. 'Petra enim erat Christus' I ad Co. X; in ipso est intrandum per devotionis affectum. Dicit ergo 'Ego fidenter quod michi deest usurpo de visceribus Ihesu Christi. Viscera enim misericordie affluxerunt, nec desunt foramina per que effluant: 'Foderunt enim manus ejus, et pedes ejus perforaverunt' [21, 17]. Cant. ii '***Surge, propera amica mea,et veni in foraminibus petre***'.	Bernard, *Sermones super Cantica canticorum*, Sermo 61, 4 (in *Opera omnia*, vol. 2, pp. 150–51).

		ostende mihi faciem tuam, sonet vox tua in auribus meis; vox enim tua dulcis et facies tua decora.	
94	*In Ps.* 44, 2 (p. 320)	Nota quod duo sensus vigent in homine principaliter, scilicet visus et auditus: unde per haec duo aliquis gratiosus apparet; per pulchritudinem visui, per gratiosum verbum auditui. Unde haec duo praecipue fuerunt in Christo: unde Cant. 2 '***Ostende mihi faciem tuam, sonet vox tua in auribus meis: vox enim tua dulcis et facies tua decora***'. Ipse enim pulcher fuit et eloquens in his quae decuit suam eloquentiam.	Ps 44:2
95	*In Is.*, c. 53, lines 42–48 [48] (p. 214)	Habebat siquidem speciem, quia 'speciosus forma prae filiis hominum', sed latebat propter infirmitatem assumptam; habebat decorem, quia 'fortitudo et decor indumentum ejus', Prov. ult., sed latebat propter paupertatem servatam : unde Cant. ii '***Sonet vox tua in auribus meis***'.	Is 53:2
96	*In Is.*, c. 55, lines 95–113 [112–13] (p. 222)	[Divina doctrina primo dicitur aqua… secundo dicitur vinum…] Tertio dicitur lac: et hoc primo propter pulcritudinem, Gen. ult. 'Neptalim cervus emissus dans eloquia pulcritudinis; secundo propter dulcedinem, Cant. ii '***Sonet vox tua in auribus meis, vox enim tua dulcis***'.	Is 55:1
97	*In ad He.*, c. 3, lect. 2 (n° 174)	Nam sequitur 'Si vocem eius audieritis', quia audimus vocem eius, quod non erat in veteri testamento, in quo audiebantur tantum verba prophetarum. Supra I, 1 s. 'Olim Deus loquens patribus in prophetis, novissime vero diebus istis locutus est nobis in filio'. Is. LII, 6 'Propter hoc sciet populus meus nomen meum in die illa, quia ego ipse qui loquebar ecce adsum'. Cant. II, 14 '***Sonet vox tua in auribus meis***'.	Heb 3:7
98	*In Ps.* 45, 5 (p. 328)	'Dedit vocem suam'. Supra dixit, 'in fortitudine': in veteri autem testamento dicit, 'dedit vocem', sed per prophetas sed postea per seipsum. Psalm. 17 'Intonuit de caelo' et cetera. Cant. 2: '***Sonet vox tua in auribus meis***'.	Ps 45:7
99	*In Ioan.*, c. 7, lect. 5 (n° 1108)	'Numquam sic locutus est homo'. Et hoc rationabiliter: quia non solum homo erat, sed etiam Dei verbum; et ideo verba sua erant virtuosa ad commovendum; Ier. c. XXIII, 29 'Numquid non verba mea quasi ignis sunt, dicit dominus, et quasi malleus conterens petram?' Et ideo dicitur Mt. VII, 29, quod 'erat docens sicut potestatem habens'. Erant etiam sapida ad dulcorandum; Cant. II, 14 '***Sonet vox tua in auribus meis, vox enim tua dulcis***'; Ps. CXVIII, 103 'Quam dulcia faucibus meis eloquia tua'.	Jn 7:46

100	*In Ioan.*, c. 8, lect. 5 (n° 1238)	Quod autem non diligunt, manifestant per effectum: nam effectus dilectionis alicuius est quod diligens libenter audit verba dilecti. Unde Cant. II, 14 '***Sonet vox tua in auribus meis; vox enim tua dulcis***'. Et Cant. ult., 13 '***Fac me audire vocem tuam: amici auscultant te***'. Quia ergo isti Christum non diligebant, durum videbatur eis etiam vocem eius audire; supra VI, 61 'Durus est hic sermo: quis potest eum audire?' Sap. II, 15 'Gravis est nobis etiam ad videndum'.	Jn 8:43
101	*In Ioan.*, c. 10, lect. 1 (n° 1376)	Et hoc ideo, 'quia [oves] vocem eius', idest cognoscunt et delectantur in ea; Cant. II, 14 '***Sonet vox tua in auribus meis: vox enim tua dulcis***'.	Jn 10:4
15		**capite nobis vulpes parvulas quae demoliuntur vineas**	
102	*In Is.*, c. 4, lines 231–43 [242–43] (p. 36)	Tertio donorum perfectio per Christum [...] quantum ad amotionem erroris: 'Aufer opprobrium nostrum' quod patimur a falsis virtutibus que nostrum nomen subripiunt, Ro. xiii 'Nox precessit, dies autem appropinquavit; abiciamus ergo opera tenebrarum et induamur arma lucis', Cant. ii '***Capite nobis vulpes parvulas que demoliuntur vineas***'.	Is 4:1
103	*In 2 ad Co.*, c. 11, lect. 3 (n° 405)	'Subdoli', id est, callidi et vulpini, sub specie religionis decipientes. Ez. XIII, 4 'Quasi vulpes in desertis', et cetera. Cant. II, 15 '***Capite nobis vulpes parvulas, quae demoliuntur vineas***', et cetera. Matth. VII, 15 'Veniunt ad vos in vestimentis ovium', et cetera.	2 Cor 11:13
104	*Contra impugnantes*, c. 16, lines 59–89 [83] (p. A 147)	Sed quod sancti viri poenas aliquibus inferant vel inferri procurent, probatur [...]. Item. Cant. II[15] '***Capite nobis vulpes parvulas***'. Glossa: 'Debellate et comprehendite schismaticos et haereticos': quia, ut in alia Glossa ibidem dicitur, non sufficit nobis vitam nostram aliis in exemplum proponere, et bonam praedicationem facere, nisi et errantes corrigamus, et infirmos ab insidiis aliorum defendamus.	*Glossa ordinaria in Canticum*, II, 159–60 (CCCM 170, p. 187) [Bede] and 154 (pp. 185 and 187) [Bede]

		nam vinea nostra floruit.	
105	*In Is.*, c. 5, lines 123–56 [133] (p. 39)	Nota super illo verbo 'Vinea facta est dilecto' quod vinea est multiplex. Primo carnalis concupiscentiae [...]. Secundo est vinea fidelis anime, Cant. ii '***Vinea nostra floruit***'. [...] Tertio est vinea militantis Ecclesie, Cant. ult. '***Vinea fuit pacifico in ea quae habet populos***': et huius vinee est vinum primo sacre ablutionis, Num. xv 'Et vinum ad liba fundenda eiusdem mensure'; secundo fructuose praedicationis, Ps. 'A fructu frumenti, vini et olei multiplicati sunt'; tertio devote confessionis, Cant. vii '***Guttur tuum sicut unicum optimum***'. Quarto est vinea celestis patrie, iii Regum xxi 'Vinea erat Naboth Iezrahelite': et huius vinee est vinum primo divine fruitionis, Cant. viii '***Comedi favum cum melle meo, bibi vinum cum lacte meo***'; secundo interioris repletionis, Hester i 'Vinum quoque ut magnificentia regia dignum erat, habundans e precipuum ponebatur'; tertio sanctorum congratulationis, Cant. ult.: '***Dabo tibi poculum ex vino condito.***'	Is 5:1
16		**dilectus meus mihi et ego illi, qui pascitur inter lilia**	
* 105'	*Catena in Matthaeum*, 6, 19	See [no. 72']	
106	*In Is.*, c. 35, line 77 (p. 154) (Collatio 3)	See [no. 56]	
107	Sermo IX, lines 341–69 [357] (pp. 124–25)	Debet predicator exire ab occulto contemplacionis ad publicum predicacionis. Debet enim predicator in contemplacione prius haurire quod postea in predicacione effundat, unde Ysaie XII: 'Haurietis aquas in gaudio, scilicet contemplacionis, de fontibus salvatoris, id est de divina sapiencia, et tunc dicetis in illa die, scilicet quando hauseritis, confitemini domino et cetera. Iste exitus simillimus est exitui Salvatoris a secreto Patris ad publicum visibilitatis, unde in Cantico '***Ego dilecto meo, ad me conversio eius***' [7, 10], scilicet in occulto contemplacionis. Per duo convertitur anima ad Deum, per devotam oracionem et per contemplacionem; et Deus convertitur ad animam per internam locucionem, unde dicit '***Dilectus meus mihi et ego illi***'. Sed numquid semper erimus hic? Non. Unde dicit '***Veni dilecte mi, egrediamur in agrum***', id est predicacionis publicum, '***commoremur***, scilicet per instanciam predicacionis, ***in villis***', id est in hominibus dispositis ad predicandum. Notate: cum dicit '***commoremur***', significat quandam familiaritatem Dei cum predicatore; '***egrediamur***', ego inspirando et tu predicando. Quando exibimus? '***Mane*** egrediamur ***ad vineas***' [7, 11] et quo modo Christus exivit mane, unde in Evangelio 'Exiit summo mane conducere operarios in vineam suam' (*Mt* 20, 1).	cf. *Glossa ordinaria in Canticum*, VII, 90 (CCCM 170, p. 375)

APPENDIX TABLE 3

1		**in lectulo meo per noctes quesivi quem diligit anima mea; quesivi illum et non inveni.**	
108	*In Is.*, c. 26, lines 68–79 [77–78] (p. 124)	Secundo afflictorum expectationem, proponens tria [...]; expectantium desiderium [...]; desiderii assiduitatem : quia die et 'nocte', idest omni tempore, vel in prosperis et adversis, 'anima mea', Cant. iii '***In lectulo meo quesivi quem diligit anima mea'***, Ps. 'Deus Deus meus, ad te de luce vigilo'.	Is 26:9
109	*In Is.*, c. 30, lines 325–36 [334–36] (p. 140)	Caritas dicitur ignis: [...] quinto quia sursum trahit. Cant. iii '***In lectulo meo quesivi quem diligit anima mea, quesivi illum et non inveni.***'	Is 30:27
110	*In Ps.* 39, 7 (p. 304)	Pro bonis petit quod gaudeant de auxilio suo et de liberatione, et laudent Deum: et quantum ad primum dicit, 'Exultent et laetentur omnes quaerentes te'. Quantum ad secundum, 'Et dicant semper, magnificetur dominus qui diligunt salutare tuum'. Ubi quatuor ponit, quae conveniunt bonis. Primo, ut diligant salutare Dei, quod est Christus. Luc. 2 'Viderunt oculi mei salutare tuum'. Secundo, ut quaerant dilectionis actus. Can. 3 '***In lectulo meo quaesivi***' et cetera. Isa. 55 'Quaerite dominum dum inveniri potest'.	Ps 39:17
111	*In Matth.*, c. 7, 1 (n° 642)	Requiritur enim ad petendum sollicita attentio; item fervens devotio: et haec duo innuit, cum dicit 'quaerite', idest orate. Vel 'petite', sicut qui aliquid quaerunt, totam intentionem ibi ponunt. Unde ad illum pertinet quod sponsa dicit in Cant. III, 1: '***Quaesivi quem dilexit anima mea***'. 'Et invenietis'; Ps xxvi, 4 'Unam petii ad Domino, hanc requiram'. Item 'quaerite' ad modum pulsantis: quia qui clamat ad ostium, si non exaudiatur, fortiter pulsat; Cant. VII, 11: '***Veni, dilecte mi, egrediamur in agrum, commoremur in villis***'.	Mt 7:7
2		**surgam, et circuibo civitatem**	
112	*In Is.*, c. 23, lines 137–45 [145] (p. 117)	Item nota super illo verbo 'Circui civitatem' quod debet homo circuire civitatem: primo proprie conscientie, recogitando peccata. [...]; secundo militantis Ecclesie, imitando iustorum exempla [...]; tertio celestis patrie, cogitando sanctorum praemia, Cant. iii '***Surgam, et circuibo civitatem'***.	Is 23:16
113	*In Ps.* 47, 6 (p. 334)	Dicit ergo, 'Circumdate', scilicet Ecclesiam militantem vel triumphantem oculo contemplationis: Cant. 3 '***Surgam et circuibo***' et cetera. Aliqui circumdant iniquo oculo ad impugnandum; sed nos circumducamus eam ad amandum	Ps 47:13

3		**invenerunt me vigiles qui custodiunt civitatem**	
114	*In Thren.*, c. 2, 19 (p. 677)	‘In principio vigiliarum’. Vigiliae noctis distinguebantur secundum custodias illorum qui civitatem custodiebant, sicut dicitur Cant. 3 ‘***Invenerunt me vigiles qui custodiebant civitatem***’.	Lam 2:19
4		**tenui eum, nec dimittam**	
115	*ST* Ia, q. 12, a. 7, ad 1	Alio modo comprehensio largius sumitur, secundum quod comprehensio insecutioni opponitur. Qui enim attingit aliquem, quando iam tenet ipsum, comprehendere eum dicitur. Et sic Deus comprehenditur a beatis, secundum illud Cant. III, ‘***Tenui eum, nec dimittam***’.	“Utrum videntes Deum per essentiam ipsum comprehendant?”
116	*Comp. theol.* II, c. 9 (p. 204)	Sed quando eum per essentiam videbimus, presentialiter eum in nobismet ipsis tenebimus, unde Cant. III, 4, sponsa querens quem diligit anima sua, tandem eum inveniens dicit ‘***Tenui eum nec dimittam***’.	“Secunda petitio, ut participes gloriae nos faciat”
117	*In Is.*, c. 64, lines 69–72 [71–72] (p. 249)	Secundo ostendit necessitatem quantum ad defectum auxilii. Et primo humani ‘Non est qui invocet, et teneat te’, precibus. Cant. iii ‘***Teneo eum, nec dimittam***’.	Is 64:7
118	*In ad Ph.*, c. 3, lect. 2 (n° 127)	Dicendum est, quod comprehendere uno modo est includere, sicut domus comprehendit nos. Alio modo idem est quod attingere et tenere [...]. Et ideo dicit ‘Sequor si quo modo comprehendam’, hoc intelligendo secundo modo, scilicet attingendo. Cant. ult. (?) ‘***Tenui eum, nec dimittam***’, et cetera.	Phil 3:12
* 118’	*Catena in Matthaeum*, 21, 7	Origenes in Matth. Deinde sciendum est, quoniam volentium Iesum tenere, differentia est. Aliter enim principes et Pharisaei quaerebant eum tenere; aliter sponsa quae dicit: ‘***Tenui eum, nec dimittam***’, adhuc tentura melius, sicut dicit: ‘***Ascendam in palmam, et tenebo altitudinem eius***’.	Origen, *Commentaria in Evangelium secundum Matthaeum*, vol. 17 (PG 13, col. 1515)
6		**quae est ista quae ascendit per desertum sicut virgula fumi ex aromatibus myrrhae, et thuris, et universi pulveris pigmentarii?**	
119	Sermo XXI, lines 310–20 [313–15] (p. 335)	Unde requiritur ut qui ascendit secundum statum, quod ascendat eciam in merito. De isto ascensu dicitur in Cantico ‘***Que est ista que ascendit per desertum sicut virgula fumi ex aromatibus mirre et thuris et universi pulveris pigmentarii?***’ ‘Que ascendit sicut virgula fumi’, non fumi horrendi sed fumi odoriferi. Set unde procedit iste fumus? Certe ‘***ex aromatibus mirre***’ id est mortificationis carnis, ‘***et thuris***’, id est devotionis, ‘***et universi pulveris pigmentarii***’, id est omnium virtutum.	

8		**uniuscuiusque ensis super femur suum**	
120	*In Ps.* 44, 3 (p. 321)	Primo ergo ponit fortem praeparationem armorum, cum dicit, 'accingere gladio tuo': secundum aliam litteram dicit, 'super femur tuum potentissime'. Ubi designatur virtus armorum: Cant. 3 '***Uniuscujusque ensis super femur suum***'.	Ps 44:4
9		**ferculum fecit sibi rex Salomon de lignis Libani**	
* 120'	Sermo XVIII, line 489	Lignum crucis [...] est sicut ***ferculum Salomonis***	
11		**egredimini et videte, filiae Sion, regem Salomonem in diademate quo coronavit eum mater sua in die desponsionis illius, et in die laetitiae cordis eius**	
121	*In Is.*, c. 33, lines 115–23 [122–23] (p. 147)	Tertio ostendit huius habitationis utilitatem quantum ad quatuor. [...] Tertio quantum ad Dei visionem: 'Regem', idest Deum. Cant. iii '***Egredimini filie Syon et videte regem***	Is 33:17
122	*In Ps.* 20, 3 (p. 215)	'Posuisti in capite ejus coronam de lapide' etc. idest fecisti eum regem. Corona autem est signum regiae dignitatis: quia, ut dicitur Isa. 33 'Regem in decore suo videbunt': Cant. 3 '***Egredimini filiae Sion, et videte regem in diademate, quo coronavit eum mater sua***' : idest divinitas. Propter hoc dicit, 'de lapide pretioso', idest de divinitate.	Ps 20:4
123	*In Matth.*, c. 12, 4 (n° 1070)	'Dixit autem ei quidam: ecce mater tua et fratres tui foris stant quaerentes te'. Quare hoc dixerit, et qua necessitate, exponitur in Luca VIII, 19 quia tanta erat multitudo, quod non poterant intrare. Mystice per matrem significatur synagoga; unde Cant. III, 11 '***Egredimini, et videte regem Salomonem in diademate quo coronavit illum mater sua***'. 'Et fratres', idest Iudaei, qui foris stant derelinquentes Christum; Iob VI, v. 15: 'Fratres mei dereliquerunt me'.	Mt 12:47
124	*In Ioan.*, c. 10, lect. 2 (n° 1392)	Tertia expositio est etiam eiusdem [=Augustinus], et beati Gregorii super Ezech., ut sit sensus: 'Ingredietur', in Ecclesiam, credendo; Ps. XLI, 5 'Transibo in locum tabernaculi admirabilis', quod est ingredi in Ecclesiam militantem; 'et egredietur', scilicet de militante ad Ecclesiam triumphantem; Cant. III, 11 '***Egredimini, filiae Sion, et videte regem Salomonem in diademate, quo coronavit illum mater sua in die desponsationis illius***'; 'et pascua inveniet', in Ecclesia militante, scilicet doctrinae et gratiae; Ps. XXII, 2 'In loco pascuae ibi me collocavit': et in Ecclesia triumphante, scilicet gloriae; Ez. c. XXXIV, 14 'In pascuis uberrimis pascam eas'.	Jn 10:9 Augustine, *In Iohannis evangelium tractatus CXXIV*, XLV, 15 (pp. 396–97); Gregory the Great, *Homiliae in Hiezechielem prophetam*, II, Homelia I, 16 (CCSL 142, pp. 220–22)

125	Sermo II, lines 60–70 (p. 22)	Tales sunt filie Syon [=contemplatives], et ideo dicitur eis et promittitur sui adventus aspectus per contemplacionem. Zacharie IX: 'Exulta satis, filia Syon'. Cantici III: '***Egredimini, filie Syon, et videte*** etc'. '***Egrediemini***' a sordibus viciorum, et estote '***filie Syon***' per contemplacionem supernorum, et sic videre poteris '***regem Salomonem***', id est angelorum Dominum, '***in dyademate quo coronavit eum mater sua***' id est in humanitate de iudaica progenie sumpta, secundum Glosam	*Glossa ordinaria in Canticum*, III, n° 92 (CCCM 170, p. 221)

APPENDIX TABLE 4

1		**oculi tui columbarum**	
126	*In Is.*, c. 60, lines 221–40 [240] (p. 238)	Nota super illo verbo, 'qui sunt isti qui ut nubes et quasi columbae', quod apostoli dicuntur [...] columbe [...] quarto propter conscientie puritatem, Cant. v '***Oculi tui sicut columbe***'; Cant. '***Oculi tui columbarum***'.	Is 60:8
		capilli tui sicut greges caprarum	
127	*In 1 ad Co.*, c. 11, lect. 3 (n° 619)	Secundo ponit id quod est ex parte mulieris, dicens 'Mulier et si comam nutriat, gloria est illi', quia videtur ad ornatum eius pertinere. Unde dicitur Cant. VII, 5 '***Comae capitis eius sicut purpura regis***'. Et assignat consequenter rationem, cum dicit 'quoniam capilli dati sunt ei', scilicet mulieri, 'pro velamine'; et ideo eadem ratio est de capillis nutriendis, et de velamine artificiali apponendo. Cant. IV, 1 '***Capilli tui sicut grex caprarum***', et cetera.	1 Cor 11:15
2		**dentes tui sicut greges tonsarum quae ascenderunt de lavacro**	
128	Sermo XXI, lines 218–29 [225–27] (p. 334)	Beatus Martinus paravit sibi ascensionem per regeneracionis sacramentum [...]. De isto ascensu dicitur in Cantico '***Dentes tui sicut greges tonsarum***'. Pili sunt peccata; greges tonsi ascendentes '***de lavacro***' sunt qui per baptismum a peccato sunt mundati; et isti ascendunt, quod significatur per hoc quod Christus 'baptizatus acsendit de aqua'.	
4		**sicut turris David, collum tuum, quae aedificata est cum propugnaculis: mille clypei pendent ex ea; omnis armatura fortium**	
129	*In Sent.*, Prol., div. text. (p. 335)	'Davidice turris': hic sumitur Cant. iv '***Sicut turris David***' etc.—per David significatur Christus: turris ejus est fides vel Ecclesia, clypei sunt rationes et auctoritates sanctorum.	

130	*In Ier.*, c. 1, 5 (p. 582)	Item notandum, quod munitur Ecclesia, vel anima, divino auxilio [...]. Sanctorum Patrum exemplo, Cant. 4 '***Turris David collum tuum, quae aedificata est cum propugnaculis***' [...]. Sacramentorum remedio. Cant. 8: '***Ego murus, et ubera mea sicut turris, ex quo facta sum coram eo quasi pacem reperiens***'.	Jer 1
131	*In Is.*, c. 5, lines 75–80 [80] (p. 39)	Quantum ad sumptum edificii, quod pertinet ad defensionem, dicit 'Edificavit in medio ejus turrim'; in quo ostenditur regia dignitas, Ez. xvi 'Decora facta es vehementer nimis, et profecisti in regnum', Cant. iv '***Turris David edificata est cum propugnaculis***'.	Is 5:2
132	*In Is.*, c. 22, lines 89–95 [94–95] (p. 112)	Quarto quantum ad armamentarii destructionem : 'videbis armamentarium', idest 'domus saltus', in quo arma recondebantur, eversum; de cujus edificio iii Regum vii 'civitatis' David fortissime, vel ipsa Ierusalem cum forti muro in pluribus locis, Cant. iv '***Turris David edificata est cum propugnaculis***'.	Is 22:8
133	*Collaciones in salutationem angelicam* (n° 1118)	Magnum enim est in quolibet sancto, quando habet tantum de gratia quod sufficit ad salutem multorum; sed quando haberet tantum quod sufficeret ad salutem omnium hominum de mundo, hoc esset maximum: et hoc est in Christo, et in Beata Virgine. Nam in omni periculo potes salutem obtinere ab ipsa Virgine gloriosa. Unde Cant. IV, 4 '***Mille clypei*** (idest remedia contra pericula) ***pendent ex ea***'.	
7		**tota pulchra es, amica mea, et macula non est in te.**	
134	*In* III *Sent.*, d. 3, q. 1, a. 2, qla 2, s.c. 2 (p. 103)	Praeterea, Sap. i, 4, dicitur 'In malevolam animam non introibit sapientia, nec habitabit in corpore subdito peccatis'. Sed Dei sapientia non solum animam Virginis intravit, sicut et de ceteris dicitur Sap. vii, 27 'In animas sanctas se transfert'; sed et corpus ejus inhabitavit, carnem de ipsa assumens. Ergo in ea nullum peccatum fuit. Quod etam colligi potest ex eo quod dicitur Cant. iv, 7 '***Tota pulchra es, amica mea, et macula non est in te***'.	"Utrum beatissima Virgo per sanctificationem in utero fuerit totaliter ab originali mundata?"
135	*ST* IIIa, q. 27, a. 2, arg. 2	Praeterea, conveniens fuit, sicut Anselmus dicit, in libro De conceptu virginali, 'ut illa virgo ea puritate niteret qua maior sub Deo nequit intelligi', unde et in Cant. IV dicitur '***Tota pulchra es, amica mea, et macula non est in te***'. Sed maior puritas fuisset beatae Virginis si nunquam fuisset inquinata contagio originalis peccati. Ergo hoc ei praestitum fuit quod, antequam animaretur caro eius, sanctificaretur.	"Utrum beata Virgo sanctificata fuerit ante animationem?" Anselm, *De conceptu virginali et de originali peccato*, 18 (in *Opera omnia*, vol. 2, p. 159)

136	*ST* IIIa, q. 27, a. 3, s.c.	Sed contra est quod dicitur Cant. IV '***Tota pulchra es, amica mea, et macula non est in te***'. Fomes autem ad maculam pertinet, saltem carnis. Ergo in beata virgine fomes non fuit.	"Utrum beata Virgo fuerit emundata ab infectione fomitis?"
137	*ST* IIIa, q. 27, a. 4	Tum etiam quia singulari modo Dei filius, qui est Dei sapientia, in ipsa habitavit, non solum in anima, sed in utero. Dicitur autem Sap. I 'In malevolam animam non intrabit sapientia, nec habitabit in corpore subdito peccatis'. Et ideo simpliciter fatendum est quod Beata Virgo nullum actuale peccatum commisit, nec mortale nec veniale, ut sic impleatur quod dicitur Cant. IV '***Tota pulchra es, amica mea, et macula non est in te***', et cetera	"Utrum per sanctificationem in utero fuerit beata Virgo praeservata ab omni peccato actuali?"
138	*Comp. theol.*, I, c. 224, lines 12–13 (p. 175)	Et ideo credendum est eam ab omni labe actualis peccati fuisse immunem, non tantum mortalis sed etiam venialis, quod nulli sanctorum convenire potest post Christum, cum apostolus Iohannes dicat I Io. I 'Si dixerimus quia peccatum non habemus, nos ipsos seducimus, et veritas in nobis non est'. Sed de beata Virgine matre Dei intelligi potest quod in Cant. IV dicitur '***Tota pulcra es, amica mea, et macula non est in te***'. Nec solum a peccato actuali immunis fuit, sed etiam a peccato originali, speciali privilegio mundata.	"De sanctificatione matris Christi"
139	*In Is.*, c. 16, lines 85–86 (p. 97)	See [no. 23]	
140	*In Is.*, c. 40, line 301 (p. 172) (Collatio 9)	See [no. 15]	
141	*In Ps.* 17, 18 (p. 203)	'Deus meus impolluta via ejus' [...]. Vel via Dei est ipse Christus, quia peccatum non fecit: Isa. 35 'Via sancta vocabitur, et non transibit per eam pollutus: et erit via recta, ita ut stultus non erret per eam'. Vel via Christi est Virgo beata: Psal. 76 'In mari via tua' haec est impolluta: Cant. 4 '***Tota pulchra es, amica mea***' et cetera.	Ps 17:31
142	*In Ps.* 18, 3 (p. 208)	Quod ergo dicit, 'In sole posuit' etc. idest corpus suum posuit in sole, idest in beata Virgine, quae nullam habuit obscuritatem peccati: Cant. 4 '***Tota pulchra es amica mea, et macula non est in te***'.	Ps 18:6

143	*In Ps.* 45, 4 (p. 328)	'Adjuvabit eam Deus vultu suo', idest in contemplatione suae altitudinis. Et possunt haec referri ad b. Virginem, quia ipsa est civitas, in ipsa habitavit, ipsam fluminis impetus, scilicet spiritus sanctus, laetificavit, ipsam sanctificavit in utero matris suae, postquam formatum fuit corpus et creata anima [...]. Et est alia sanctificatio b. Virginis et aliorum sanctorum: quia alii sic sanctificati fuerunt quod nunquam mortaliter peccaverunt, tamen venialiter sic: 1 Joan. 1 'Si dixerimus quia peccatum non habemus 'et cetera. Beata autem Virgo nec mortaliter nec venialiter umquam peccavit: Cant. 4 '***Tota pulchra es amica mea***' et cetera. Et ideo dicit, 'non commovebitur', nec veniali peccato.	Ps 45:6
144	*In Matth.*, c. 12, 4 (n° 1073)	Haec positio partim sana est: nam quantum ad fratres sana est, quia sic habetur Io. VII, 5 'Neque enim fratres eius credebant in eum'. Sed de matre domini non sana est, quia creditur quod numquam peccavit, nec mortaliter, nec venialiter: de ea namque dicitur Cant. IV, 7 '***Tota pulchra es, amica mea, et macula non est in te***'. Et Augustinus: cum de peccato agitur, nullam prorsus volo de ea fieri mentionem.	Mt 12:47 Augustine, *De natura et gratia*, XXVI, 42 (CSEL 60), pp. 263–64.
145	*Collaciones in salutationem angelicam* (n° 1115)	Dicitur autem beata Virgo plena gratia quantum ad tria. Primo quantum ad animam, in qua habuit omnem plenitudinem gratiae. Nam gratia Dei datur ad duo: scilicet ad bonum operandum, et ad vitandum malum; et quantum ad ista duo perfectissimam gratiam habuit beata Virgo. Nam ipsa omne peccatum vitavit magis quam aliquis sanctus post Christum. Peccatum enim aut est originale, et de isto fuit mundata in utero; aut mortale aut veniale, et de istis libera fuit. Unde Cant. IV, 7 '***Tota pulchra es, amica mea, et macula non est in te***'. Augustinus in libro de natura et gratia: 'Excepta sancta virgine Maria, si omnes sancti et sanctae cum hic viverent, interrogati fuissent utrum sine peccato essent, omnes una voce clamassent: si dixerimus quia peccatum non habemus, ipsi nos seducimus, et veritas in nobis non est. Excepta, inquam, hac sancta virgine, de qua propter honorem domini, cum de peccato agitur, nullam prorsus volo quaestionem habere'.	
146	Sermo XXIV, lines 221–26 [224–25] (p. 286)	Set in beata Virgine nichil fuit inordinatum nec actu nec affectu, nec primos motus peccati habuit, unde in Cantico '***Tota pulcra est amica mea et macula non est in te***'. Et propter hoc dictum est ei: 'Concupiscet rex speciem tuam'.	
9		**vulnerasti cor meum, soror mea, sponsa**	
147	*In ad Ep.*, c. 1, lect. 8 (n° 69)	Quantum autem ad naturae conformitatem, Christus non est caput angelorum, quia non angelos apprehendit, sed semen Abrahae, ut dicitur Hebr. II, 16 sed est caput hominum tantum. Cant. IV, 9 '***Vulnerasti cor meum, soror mea***', scilicet per naturam, et '***sponsa***' per gratiam.	Eph 1:22

11		**favus distillans labia tua, sponsa**	
148	*In ad Ep.*, c. 3, lect. 1 (n° 138)	Et quantum ad hoc dicit 'Sicut scripsi in brevi', id est in paucis verbis, ita aperte, quod eo modo hoc 'potestis legentes intelligere'. Cant. IV, 11 '***Favus distillans labia tua***', et cetera. Labium quidem breve quid est. Et sic labia doctoris sunt favus distillans, quando brevibus et paucis verbis multa et magna insinuat.	Eph 3:3–4
		mel et lac sub lingua tua	
149	*In Is.*, c. 7, lines 333–40 [340] (p. 58)	Vel 'ut' est causale: 'ut sciat', idest ut ostendat se scire, quia per cibos perductus est ad perfectam etatis quantitatem, in qua ostendit se scire, Augustinus: per butyrum, humanitatem, quod de terre nutrimento venit; per mel, divinitatem, quod de rore celi colligitur, super illud Cant. iv '***Mel et lac***'.	Is 7:15 Cf. Alan of Lille, *Elucidatio in Cantica canticorum* (PL 210, col 81–82), rather than Augustine
150	*In Is.*, c. 28, lines 110–21 [120–21] (p. 130)	Item nota super illo verbo, 'ablactatos lacte', quod est quoddam lac quod debet deseri; et istud multiplex [...]. Et est lac quod debet amplecti: primo pure conscientie, Tren. iv: 'Candidiores nive, nitidiores lacte', propter nitorem; secundo sane doctrine propter dulcorem, Cant iv '***Mel et lac sub lingua ejus***'.	Is 28:9
		et odor vestimentorum tuorum sicut odor thuris.	
151	*In Is.*, c. 52, lines 91–106 [106] (p. 212)	Nota super illo verbo, 'induere vestimentis', quod sancti habent vestimenta virtutum de quibus gloriantur [...]. Haec vestimenta [...] debent esse [...] tertio odorifera per fame divulgationem, Cant. iv '***Odor vestimentorum tuorum sicut odor thuris***'.	Is 52:1
12		**hortus conclusus, soror mea, sponsa, hortus conclusus, fons signatus.**	
152	*In* I *Sent.*, Prol. (p. 309)	'Rigabo hortum plantationum'. Ortus enim iste Ecclesia est, de qua Cant. iv '**Ortus conclusus**' etc in qua sunt plantationes diverse, secundum diversos sanctorum ordines, quos omnes manus omnipotentis plantavit. Iste ortus irrigatur a Christo sacramentorum rivis, que ex ejus latere profluxerunt.	
* 152'	*In Ioan.*, c. 19, lect. 1 (n° 2468)	Ubi notandum, quod Christus in horto captus, et in horto passus, et in horto sepultus fuit: ad designandum quod per suae passionis virtutem liberamur a peccato quod Adam in horto deliciarum commisit, et quod per eum Ecclesia consecratur, quae est sicut **hortus conclusus**.	Jn 19:41
* 152"	Sermo XVII, lines 214–29 [227–29] (p. 268–69)	Quinto est lux mater generativa colorum; sic beata Virgo mater est virtutum. [...] Unde Bernardus: 'Si quid, inquit est nobis virtutis, si quid salutis et gracie, totum ab illa noverimus redundare que deliciis affluebat. Hic est enim ille ***ortus conclusus*** quem ***divinus Auster perflavit, et fluant aromata illius***, id est carismata graciarum'.	Bernard, "Sermo De nativitate beatae Mariae," *Sermones II* (in *Opera omnia*, vol. 5, pp. 278–79)

* 152'''	*Catena in Matthaeum*, 16, 1	Rabanus. Est autem Mageddan regio contra Gerasam, et interpretatur poma, vel nuntia; et significat hortum, de quo dicitur: ***hortus conclusus, fons signatus,*** in quo crescunt poma virtutum, et ubi nuntiatur nomen domini.	Mt 16:1 Rabanus Maurus, *Commentaria in Matthaeum*, V (PL 107, col. 986)
13		**emissiones tuae paradisus malorum punicorum, cum pomorum fructibus**	
153	*In Is.*, c. 3 (p. 29, lines 306–7)	See [no. 74]	Is 3:10
154	Sermo XVIII, lines 498–556 [553–55] (pp. 290–91)	De isto ligno [la Croix] dicitur quod est 'pomiferum' [Gn 1, 11]. Et que sunt eius poma? Dicitur in Cantico '***Omnia poma nova et vetera servavi tibi***'. Poma vetera sunt figure que referuntur ad lignum [...]. Poma nova que sunt? In Deuteronomio, in benedictione Ioseph, fit mentio de tribus pomis, scilicet 'de pomis celi, de pomis solis et lune et de pomis collium eternorum' [Dt 33, 13–15]. Quae sunt poma celi? Membra Christi. Crux membris Christi fuit ornata, sicut arbor ornatur pomis; non solum membris corporis Christi corporalis, set corporis mystici, quibus decet dicere: 'Confixus sum Christo cruci'. De pomis istis dicitur in Cantico '***Veniat dilectus meus in ortum suum et comedat fructum pomorum suorum***' (5, 1). Item poma solis et lune sunt exempla virtutis quae Christus in cruce demonstravit [...]. Ista sunt poma convallium de quibus in Cantico '***Descendi in hortum meum, ut viderem poma convallium***' (6, 10). Poma collium aeternorum que sunt? Dico quod sunt documenta doctorum qui sapientia sunt imbuti [...]. Ista sunt poma collium eternorum, de quibus in Cantico '***Emissiones tue paradisus malorum punicorum cum pomorum fructibus***' (4, 13) Est igitur lignum pomiferum.	
15		**fons hortorum, puteus aquarum viventium, quae fluunt impetu de Libano.**	
155	*In Ps.* 45, 3 (p. 327)	'Impetus fluminis'. Et hoc refertur ad duo. Primo, quia spiritus sanctus gratia perfundit subito cor. Act. 2 'Factus est repente de caelo sonus' et cetera. Alio modo, quia spiritus impetu sanctus amoris movet cor. Isa. 56 'Cum venerit quasi fluvius violentus'. Rom. 8 'Qui spiritu Dei aguntur, hi filii Dei sunt'. Cant. 4 '***Fons hortorum etc. quae fluunt impetu de Libano***'.	Ps 45:5

16		surge, aquilo; et veni auster; perfla hortum meum et fluant aromata illius.	
156	*In Ier.*, c. 1 (p. 582)	Item notandum, quod diabolus dicitur aquilo propter tentationis impetum. Eccl. 43 'Vox tonitrui ejus verberavit terram, tempestas Aquilonis, et congregatio spiritus'. Quia impedit boni operis fructum. Cant. 4 '***Surge aquilo et veni auster, perfla hortum meum, et fluent aromata illius***'.	Jer 1:14
157	*In Ier.*, c. 13, 2 (p. 612)	Item notandum, quod Spiritus Sanctus dicitur auster propter calorem. Job 37 'Nonne vestimenta tua calida sunt, cum perflata fuerit terra austro?' [...] Propter arborum fructificationem. Cant. 4 '***Veni auster, perfla in hortum meum, et fluent aromata illius.***'	Jer 13:19
158	*In Matth.*, c. 12, lect. 3 (n° 1058)	Per istam [=Regina austri] signatur Ecclesia ex fidelibus [...]. 'Regina' dicitur, quia regere se debet; Prov. XX, 8 'Rex qui sedet in solio iudicii, dissipat omne malum intuitu suo' et cetera. Et dicitur 'Austri' ratione Spiritus sancti; Cant. IV, 16 '***Surge, Aquilo, et veni, Auster, perfla hortum meum***' et cetera.	Mt 12:42
* 158'	Sermo XVII, lines 228–29 (p. 268–69)	See [no. 152'']	

APPENDIX TABLE 5

1		veniat dilectus meus in hortum suum, et comedat fructum pomorum suorum	
159	*In* I *Sent.*, Prol. (p. 309)	Inductio autem in gloriam notatur in hoc quod sequitur 'Et inebriabo partus mei fructus'. Partus ipsius Christi fideles Ecclesiae, quos suo labore quasi mater parturivit, de quo partu Ysa. ult. 'Numquid ego, qui alios parere facio' etc. Fructus autem istius partus sunt sancti qui sunt in gloria, de quo fructu Cant. 5 '***Veniet dilectus meus in ortum***' etc. Istos inebriat abundantissima sui fruitione; de qua fruitione et ebrietate Psalm. 35, 9 'Inebriabuntur ab ubertate domus tuae'. Et dicitur ebrietas, quia omnem mensuram rationis et desiderii excedit: unde Isa. 64, 4 'Oculus non vidit, Deus, absque te quae praeparasti expectantibus te'.	
160	*In Ier.*, c. 17, 4 (p. 621)	Nota, quod sancti fructificant per sapientiae contemplationem. Eccl. 6 'Quasi is qui arat, et qui seminat, accede ad eam, et sustine bonos fructus illius'. Per caritatis fervorem. Cant. 5 '***Veniat dilectus meus in hortum suum, ut comedat fructum pomorum suorum***'.	Jer 17:8

161	*In ad 2 Tim.*, c. 4, lect. 2 (n° 153)	Nam haec est corona gloriae, et haec duplex, scilicet animae; et haec redditur sanctis 'in illa die', scilicet in morte. [...] Alia est corporis, et haec reddetur 'in illa die', scilicet iudicii. I Cor. XV, 43 'Seminatur in ignobilitate', et cetera. Participes huius sunt omnes sancti, unde dicit 'non solum autem mihi', scilicet reponitur. Apoc. ult., 20 'Veni, domine Iesu'. Cant. V, 1 '***Veniat dilectus meus in hortum suum, ut comedat fructum pomorum suorum***'.	2 Tm 4:8
162	Sermo II, lines 192–200 [198] (p. 24)	'Venio', quasi dicat: non mitto angelum, non spiritum, non vicarium, sed venio per memet ipsum, in quo ostenditur maxima caritas. 'Venio', inquam, invitatus ab sanctis patribus; ipsum enim invitaverant omnes sancti ab origine mundi, quorum personam gerens sponsa dicebat Cantici II '***Veniat dilectus meus in ortum suum***'; et Apocalipsis ultimo 'Veni Domine Iesu'. Sic Ysaias, Ieremias et ceteri prophetarum.	Zec 2:10
163	Sermo XVIII, lines 513–14 (p. 291)	See [no. 154]	
		comedi favum cum melle; bibi vinum meum cum lacte meo.	
164	*Officium de festo Corporis Christi* (p. 279)	V/. ***Comedi favum cum melle meo***, alleluia. R/. ***Bibi vinum meum cum lacte meo***, alleluia.	
165	*In Is.*, c. 5, lines 151–52 (p. 39)	See [no. 105]	
166	*In Is.*, c. 55, lines 11–20 [19–20] (p. 221)	Secundo proponit promissionem, promittens futuram copiam in necessariis 'Omnes sitientes', idest vos ex Iudeis qui prius pre inopia sitientes eratis, 'emite', sine pretio, 'comedite' panem, et alia necessaria [...]; et in deliciis 'venite, emite', quasi: ac si emeretis accipite, vel 'absque argento', idest minus quam iusto pretio, Cant. v '***Bibi vinum meum cum lacte meo***'.	Is 55:1
167	*In Ioan.*, c. 2, lect. 1 (n° 347)	Ubi sciendum est, quod ante incarnationem Christi, triplex vinum deficiebat, scilicet iustitiae, sapientiae et caritatis, seu gratiae [...]. Vinum similiter inebriat, Cant. V, 1 '***Bibite, amici, et inebriamini, carissimi***', et secundum hoc caritas dicitur vinum, Cant. c. V, 1 '***Bibi vinum meum cum lacte meo***'. Et dicitur caritas etiam vinum ratione fervoris; Zach. IX, 17: 'Vinum germinans virgines'.	Jn 2:3
		comedite, amici, bibite; et inebriamini carissimi.	
168	Sermo XIII, lines 264–70 [265–67] (p. 201)	Tercio preparauit nobis Christus refeccionem pertinentem ad affectum, unde in Cantico '***Comedite amici mei***', scilicet hic per graciam, '***et inebriamini karissimi***', scilicet in futuro per gloriam. Istam refeccionem facit nobis Christus in quantum habet plenitudinem diuinitatis. Psalmista 'Graciam et gloriam dabit dominus'.	

169	*ST* IIIa, q. 79, a. 1, ad 2	Et ideo per hoc sacramentum, quantum est ex sui virtute, non solum habitus gratiae et virtutis confertur, sed etiam excitatur in actum, secundum illud II Cor. V 'Caritas Christi urget nos'. Et inde est quod ex virtute huius sacramenti anima spiritualiter reficitur, per hoc quod anima delectatur, et quodammodo inebriatur dulcedine bonitatis divinae, secundum illud Cant. V, '***Comedite, amici, et bibite; et inebriamini, carissimi***'.	"Utrum per hoc sacramentum [=eucharistia] conferatur gratia?"
170	*In Is.*, c. 25 lines 132–33 (p. 122)	See [no. 2]	
171	*In Is.*, c. 28, lines 76–88 [88] (p. 130)	Nota super illo 'ebriis', quod mali inebriantur vino [...]. Item inebriantur sancti [...] tertio, incentivo amoris, Cant. iv '***Comedite amici et inebriamini***'.	Is 28:1
172	*In Is.*, c. 66, lines 88–89 (p. 254)	See [no. 3]	
173	*In Ps.* 22, 2 (p. 226)	'Et calix tuus', vel meus, idest mihi datus, vel tuus, idest a te datus. Hic calix est donum divini amoris qui inebriat: quia ebrius non est in se, nec secundum se loquitur, sed secundum impetum vini; sic ille qui est plenus divino amore, loquitur secundum Deum: est enim in extasim factus. Cant. 5 '***Comedite amici, et inebriamini***'. Isa. 55: 'Quomodo descendit imber et nix de caelo, et inebriat terram, et germinare eam facit; sic erit verbum quod egredietur de ore meo'. Hier. 23 'Factus sum quasi vir ebrius, et quasi homo madidus vino a facie domini'.	Ps 22:5
174	*In Ps.* 35, 4 (p. 278)	Quantum ad primum dicit, 'inebriabuntur ab ubertate domus tuae'. Domus est Ecclesia [...]. Et haec domus, quae modo est in terris, quandoque transferetur in caelos: Ps. 121 'In domum domini laetantes ibimus'. In utraque est ubertas donorum Dei; sed in hac Ecclesia est imperfecta, sed in alia est perfectissima abundantia omnium bonorum, et hac satiantur spirituales viri: Psalm. 64 'Replebimur in bonis domus tuae'. Et quod plus est, inebriantur, inquantum supra omnem mensuram meriti desideria implentur: ebrietas enim excessus quidam est: Isa. 64 'Quod oculus non vidit' et cetera. Cant. 5 '***Inebriamini carissimi***'. Et qui sunt ebrii, non in se sunt, sed extra se. Sic qui repleti sunt spiritualibus charismatibus, tota eorum intentio fertur in Deum	Ps 35:9
175	*In Matth.*, c. 26, lect. 3 (n° 2180)	Item inducit ad comestionem, 'Comedite', non solum spiritualiter, sed etiam sacramentaliter; Cant. V, 1 '***Comedite, amici, et bibite***'.	Mt 26:26

176	*In Matth.*, c. 26, lect. 4 (n° 2199)	Tunc iniungit usum. Et primo ponit usum; secundo verba consecrationis sanguinis; tertio resurrectionem praenuntiat. Dicit ergo 'Bibite ex hoc omnes'; Cant. V, 1 '***Bibite et inebriamini, carissimi***'. Unde signatur quod Christiani possunt communicare loco et tempore.	Mt 26:28
177	*In Ioan.*, c. 2, lect. 1 (n° 347)	See [no. 167]	
178	*In Ioan.*, c. 21, lect. 2 (n° 2608)	Invitat autem ad convivium Christus interius inspirando per seipsum, dicens 'Venite, prandete', Matth. XI, 28 'Venite ad me omnes qui laboratis et onerati estis; et ego reficiam vos'; Cant. V, 1 '***Comedite, amici, bibite et inebriamini, carissimi***', et exterius docendo et exhortando per alios.	Jn 21:12
179	*In 1 ad Co.*, c. 11, lect. 4 (n° 630)	Hoc enim sacramentum, ut Augustinus dicit super Ioannem, est 'sacramentum unitatis et charitatis'. Et ideo non competit dissentientibus. Cant. c. V, 1 '***Comedite, amici, et bibite, et inebriamini, charissimi***'.	1 Cor 11:20 Augustine, *In Iohannis evangelium tractatus CXXIV*, XXVI, 13 (pp. 266–67)
180	*In 2 ad Co.*, c. 5, lect. 3 (n° 179)	Ps. CXV, 11 'Ego dixi in excessu meo'. Dionysius 'Est enim extasim faciens divinus amor', et cetera. 'Sive sobrii simus', id est commensuremus nos vobis, tradendo divina praecepta, hoc est vobis, id est ad utilitatem vestram. Sobrietas enim idem est, quod commensuratio. Bria enim in Graeco idem est quod mensura. Haec sobrietas non opponitur ebrietati, quae est de vino, quae ad bella trahit in terra, sed opponitur ebrietati quae est a Spiritu sancto, quae rapit hominem ad divina, de qua dicitur Cant. V, 1 '***Bibite, amici, et inebriamini, charissimi***'. Nam illa scilicet sobrietas est propter utilitatem proximi, sed haec ebrietas est propter amorem Dei	2 Cor 5:13 Dionysius, *De divinis nominibus* IV, 13 (PTS 33, pp. 158–59)
2		**ego dormio et cor meum vigilat.**	
181	*In Ps.* 4, 7 (p. 159)	Nota ergo, quod etiam in praesenti vita dicitur justus stare in bono, propter quatuor. [...] Tertio, quia sine solicitudine: unde, '*dormiam*'. Cant. 5, 2 '***Ego dormio***' et cetera.	Ps 4:9
182	*In Matth.*, c. 24, lect. 4 (n° 1994)	In tribus enim homo delinquit: quia vacant eius sensus, item quia vacat a motu, item iacet homo. Ideo 'Vigilate', ut sensus vestri eleventur per contemplationem; Cant. V, 2 '***Ego dormio, et cor meum vigilat***'.	Mt 24:42

183	*In Matth.*, c. 26, lect. 5 (n° 2244)	Secundum Augustinum, concedit eis, et supra negavit: sed alius est hic somnus, et supra. Quia est somnus aggravationis, et de hoc loquitur supra, unde dicitur 43: 'Erant oculi eorum gravati', somno, et hoc est increpandum. Hic autem somnus est somnus quietis; et iste permittitur. Item est somnus propter turbationem; et hic prohibetur. De isto dicitur ad Ephes. V, 14 'Surge qui dormis, et exurge a mortuis'. Aliquando enim est somnus propter quietem corporis, sed tamen anima vigilat ***'Ego dormio, et cor meum vigilat'***, Cant. V, 2. Item, quia laboraturi erant, ideo oportebat quod quiescerent.	Mt 26:45 Augustine: not identified
184	*In Ioan.*, c. 11, lect. 3 (n° 1495)	Sciendum est enim, quod somnus accipitur multis modis. Quandoque pro somno naturae [...]. Quandoque pro quiete contemplationis; Cant. V, 2 ***'Ego dormio, et cor meum vigilat'***. Quandoque pro quiete futurae gloriae; Ps. IV, 9 'In pace in idipsum dormiam, et requiescam'.	Jn 11:11
185	*In ad Ro.*, c. 13, lect. 3 (n° 1062)	Nec enim intelligendum est de somno gratiae, qui quandoque dicitur quies aeternae gloriae, secundum illud Ps. IV, 9 'In pace in idipsum', etc., quandoque autem est quies contemplationis etiam in hac vita. Cant. V, 2 ***'Ego dormio, et cor meum vigilat'***.	Rom 13:11
186	*In 1 ad Th.*, c. 4, lect. 2 (n° 93)	Unde signanter dicit 'de dormientibus'. Io. XI, 11 'Lazarus amicus noster dormit'. Dormiens enim tria facit. Cubat in spe surgendi. Ps. X 'Numquid qui dormit non adiiciet ut resurgat?' Sic et qui moritur in fide. Item in dormiente anima vigilat. Cant. c. V, 2 ***'Ego dormio, et cor meum vigilat'***, et cetera. Item postea homo resurget magis refectus et vegetus. Sic sancti resurgent incorruptibiles, I Cor. XV, 52.	1 Thes 4:12
		aperi mihi, soror mea, amica mea, columba mea, immaculata mea	
187	*In Matth.*, c. 3, lect. 2 (n° 300)	Apparuit autem [Spiritus sanctus] in specie columbae propter quatuor. Primo propter caritatem; columba enim est animal amorosum. Chrysostomus: 'Alia dona habet etiam servus diaboli in simulatione, quae habet servus Dei in veritate: solam caritatem sancti Spiritus non potest immundus spiritus imitari'. Cant. V, 2 ***'Aperi mihi, soror mea, amica mea, columba mea, immaculata mea'***.	Mt 3:16 John Chrysostom: not identified
* 187'	*Catena in Marcum* 1, 4	Hieronymus. In specie etiam columbae Spiritus sanctus descendit, quia in cantico de Ecclesia canitur: ***'Sponsa mea, amica mea, dilecta mea, columba mea'***. Sponsa in patriarchis, amica in prophetis, proxima in Ioseph, et mea dilecta in Ioanne Baptista, columba in Christo et apostolis, quibus dicitur: 'Estote prudentes sicut serpentes, et simplices sicut columbae'.	Mk 1:10

3		**lavi pedes meos, quomodo inquinabo illos ?**	
188	*In Ioan.*, c. 13, lect. 2 (n° 1762)	Quasi dicat: nescio an indigeam ablutione manus et capitis, 'nihil enim mihi conscius sum; sed non in hoc iustificatus sum': I Cor. V, 4, et ideo paratus sum lavare 'non tantum pedes', idest affectus inferiores, Cant. V, 3 '***Lavi pedes meos, quomodo inquinabo illos***', 'sed et manus', idest opera, Ps. XXV, 6 'Lavabo inter innocentes manus meas', 'et caput', idest rationem superiorem, Matth. VI, 17 'Faciem tuam lava'.	Jn 13:9 Cf. Augustine, *In Iohannis evangelium tractatus CXXIV*, LVI–LVII (pp. 467–72).
189	*In ad Ro.*, c. 6, lect. 1 (n° 471)	Et huius ratio est: 'Si enim mortui sumus peccato' per hoc scilicet quod peccatum est mortificatum in nobis, 'quomodo adhuc in illo vivemus?' Non enim naturalis ordo rerum habet, ut a morte redeatur ad vitam. Is. XXIV, 14 'Morientes non vivant', et cetera. Cant. V, 3 '***Lavi pedes meos, quomodo inquinabo illos?***'	Rom 6:2
4		**dilectus meus misit manum suam per foramen et venter meus intremuit ad tactum eius**	
190	*In Ier.*, c. 1, 5 (p. 581)	Item notandum, quod aliquos tangit dominus corripiendo. Job 19 'Miseremini mei, miseremini mei saltem vos amici mei, quia manus domini tetigit me'. A peccatis mundando. Matth. 8 'Et Jesus tetigit eum, dicens: volo mundare'. Gratiam infundendo. Cant. 5 '***Dilectus meus misit manum suam per foramen, et venter meus intremuit ad tactum ejus***'. In gratia confortando. Dan. 10 'Et ecce manus tetigit me, et erexit me super genua mea, et super articulos manuum mearum'. Fervorem excitando. Psal. 143 'Tange montes, et fumigabunt'.	Jer 1
5		**manus meae distillaverunt myrrham**	
191	*In Matth.*, c. 2, lect. 3 (n° 201)	[Ista tria munera] secundo possunt referri ad actionem nostram. Per aurum enim potest signari sapientia [...]. Per thus oratio devota [...]. Per myrrham mortificatio carnis: Col. III, 5 'Mortificate membra, quae sunt super terram'; Cant. V, 5 '***Manus meae distillaverunt myrrham***'.	Mt 2:11
192	*In Ioan.*, c. 19, lect. 6 (n° 2466)	Mystice autem datur per hoc intelligi quod Christum crucifixum debemus in corde nostro recondere cum amaritudine poenitentiae et passionis. Cant. V, 5 '***Manus meae distillaverunt myrrham***'.	Jn 19:39
		et digiti mei pleni myrrha probatissima	
193	*In Ps.* 44, 6 (p. 323)	Myrrha habet amaritudinem; et sic si referatur ad corpus Christi, signat amaritudinem passionis: Cant. 5 '***Digiti ejus***', scilicet confixi ligno, '***pleni myrrha probatissima***'. Si autem referatur ad sanctos, signat poenitentiam: Eccl. 24 'Sicut myrrha electa dedi suavitatem odoris'.	Ps 44:9

6		anima mea liquefacta est, ut [dilectus] locutus est	
194	*In* III *Sent.*, d. 27, q. 1, a. 1, arg. 4 (p. 854)	Praeterea, Dionysius 7 cap. *Cael. hier.*, inter proprietates amoris ponit acutum et fervidum; et etiam liquefactio amoris effectus ponitur. Cant. V, 6 '***Anima mea liquefacta est***'. Dionysius etiam 4 cap. De div. nom. ponit effectum amoris extasim, idest extra se positionem. Haec autem omnia ad divisionem pertinere videntur, quia acuti est penetrando dividere; fervidi vero per exhalationem resolvi; liquefactio autem divisio quaedam est congelationi opposita: quod est etiam extra se positum, a seipso dividitur. Ergo amor magis est vis divisiva quam unitiva.	"Quid sit amor?" Dionysius, *De coelesti hierarchia* VII, 1 (PTS 36, p. 27–28); Dionysius, *De divinis nominibus* IV, 13 (PTS 33, pp. 158–59)
195	*ST* Ia-IIae, q. 28, a. 5, arg. 2	Praeterea, liquefactio est quaedam resolutio. Sed amor est liquefactivus, dicitur enim Cant. V '***Anima mea liquefacta est, ut dilectus meus locutus est***'. Ergo amor est resolutivus. Est ergo corruptivus et laesivus.	"Utrum amor sit passio laesiva amantis?"
196	*In Ps.* 21, 11 (p. 221)	Vel dicendum quod liquefactio etiam est amoris. Cant. 5 '***Anima mea liquefacta est***'. Res antequam liquefiat, dura est et constricta in se; si liquescit, diffunditur et tendit a se in aliud. Timor etiam quandoque indurat, quando scilicet non est magnus: et sic est etiam de amore: quia quando supervenit amor, tunc homo tendit in aliud quod ante in se erat. Et de hac liquefactione potest exponi etiam de Christo secundum quod est caput: nam hoc liquefieri et est a Spiritu sancto, et est 'in medio ventris', idest affectus.	Ps 21:15
197	*In Matth.*, c. 13, lect. 1 (n° 1089)	Secundum est cordis duritia; Iob penult., 15 'Cor eius indurabitur quasi lapis, et stringetur quasi malleatoris incus'. Et hoc opponitur caritati, quia amoris est liquefacere; Cant. V, 6 '***Anima mea liquefacta est, ut dilectus locutus est***' et cetera. Durum enim est quod est in se constrictum, et propriis metis arctatum. Amor facit transferre amantem in amatum: unde diffunditur.	Mt 13:5
8		**ut nuntietis ei quia amore langueo.**	
198	*In Matth.*, c. 26, lect. 5 (n° 2237)	Sed notandum quod omnium caro est infirma, sed non omnium spiritus est promptus. In malis siquidem sicut caro est infirma, ita et spiritus: e contrario in bonis, quia spiritum habent promptum, et ideo in resurrectione spiritus redit corpus promptum. Vel potest esse duplex infirmitas. Una mala quae inclinat ad peccatum, secundum quod dicit apostolus ad Rom. VII, 18 'Non habitat in carne mea bonum'. Alia infirmitas bona, secundum quod carnalis deficit secundum promptitudinem, secundum quod dicitur in Cant. V, 8 '***Nunciate dilecto, quia amore langueo***'.	Mt 26:41

10		**dilectus meus candidus et rubicundus, electus ex milibus.**	
199	*In Ps.* 17, 15 (p. 201)	'Electus' autem potest dupliciter intelligi. Uno modo a Deo; hoc est commune omnibus sanctis: Ephes. 1 'Elegit nos Deus ante mundi constitutionem' et cetera. Alio modo dicitur electus qui habet excellentiam innocentiae et sanctitatis: Cant. 5 '***Dilectus meus candidus et rubicundus, electus ex millibus***'.	Ps 17:27
200	*In Is.*, c. 42, lines 14–23 [19] (p. 177)	Primo ostendit gratie plenitudinem quantum ad gratiam unionis: 'Suscipiam eum'; 'servus', secundum humanam naturam. Luce primo 'Suscepit Israel' etc.; quantum ad gratiam capitis: '***Electus***', ut sit capud Ecclesie, '***ex millibus***', Cant. v, Ps 'Beatus quem elegisti et assumpsisti' etc., 'complacuit', Mt iij 'Hic est filius meus' etc.; quantum ad gratiam habitualem, que fuit in ipso singularis, 'dedi spiritum meum'.	Is 42:1
201	*In Is.*, c. 63, lines 75–84 [81–82] (p. 245)	Nota super illo verbo, 'Iste formosus', quod Christus est formosus primo quia rutilans splendore divinitatis. Hebr. i 'Cum sit splendor glorie et figura substantie ejus'; secundo quia figuratus conformitate unionis, Ps. 'Speciosus forma pre filiis hominum'; tertio quia distinctus diverso colore virtutis. Cant. v '***Dilectus meus candidus et rubicundus***'; quarto quia vestitus honestate conversationis, Iob xl 'Esto gloriosus, et speciosis induere vestibus'.	Is 63:1
202	*In ad He.*, c. 9, lect. 4 (n° 457)	Miscetur autem 'cum aqua', quia baptismus a sanguine Christi efficaciam habet; aspergitur autem 'cum hyssopo', qui mundat pectus, per quod significatur fides. Act. c. XV, 9 'Fide purificans corda eorum'. Et 'lana coccinea', quae est rubei coloris, per quam significatur charitas. Cant. V, 10 '***Dilectus meus candidus et rubicundus***'. Quia per fidem et dilectionem passionis Christi mundatur populus.	Heb 9:19
11		**caput eius aurum optimum.**	
203	*In 1 ad Co.*, c. 3, lect. 2 (n° 156)	Et ideo opera quibus homo innititur rebus spiritualibus et divinis comparantur auro, argento et lapidi pretioso, quae sunt solida, clara et pretiosa. Ita tamen quod per aurum designentur ea quibus homo tendit in ipsum Deum per contemplationem et amorem; unde dicitur Cant. V, 11'***Caput eius aurum optimum***'. Caput enim Christi est Deus, ut dicitur I Cor. XI, 3. De quo auro dicitur Apoc. III, 18 'Suadeo tibi emere a me aurum ignitum', id est sapientiam cum charitate. Per argentum significantur actus, quibus homo adhaeret spiritualibus credendis, et amandis, et contemplandis; [...] Sed per lapides pretiosos designantur opera diversarum virtutum, quibus anima humana ornatur.	1 Cor 3:12

12		**oculi eius sicut columbae super rivulos aquarum, quae lacte sunt lotae, et resident iuxta fluenta plenissima.**	
204	*In Is.*, c. 25, lines 135–36 (p. 122)	See [no. 2]	
205	*In Is.*, c. 60, line 239 (p. 238)	See [no. 126]	
206	*In Ier.*, c. 4, 9 (p. 590)	Item notandum, quod lavatur cor aqua baptismatis [...]. Lacrymis compunctionis. [...]. Vino divini amoris [...]. Lacte divini sermonis. Cant. V '***Oculi ejus sicut columbae super rivulos aquarum, quae lacte sunt lotae***'.	Jer 4
207	*In Ioan.*, c. 1, lect. 14 (n° 272)	Quare autem potius in columba, quam in alia specie apparuit [Spiritus santus], multipliciter ratio assignatur. [...] Secundo, propter caritatis unitatem. Nam columba amore multum fervet; Cant. VI, 8 '***Una est columba mea***'. Ut ergo ostendat Ecclesiae unitatem, in specie columbae Spiritus sanctus apparet. Nec te moveat quod discipulis dispartitae linguae apparuerunt, quando sedit supra singulos eorum Spiritus sanctus, qui et dispartitus apparet, secundum diversa donorum officia, et tamen unit per caritatem; et sic propter primum apparuit in dispartitis linguis, ut dicitur I Cor. XII, 4: 'Divisiones gratiarum sunt', in columbae specie propter secundum. [...] Quinto, propter columbae cautelam. Sedet enim super rivos aquarum, in quibus respiciens, falconem volitantem conspicit, et sibi ab eo cavet; Cant. V, 12 '***Oculi tui sicut columbae***' et cetera. Unde, quia in baptismo est nostra tutela et defensio, congrue in specie columbae Spiritus sanctus apparuit.	Jn 1:32
208	*In 1 ad Co.*, c. 12, lect. 3 (n° 739)	Per membra ergo deservientia virtuti apprehensivae, designantur in Ecclesia illi qui student vitae contemplativae, inter quos sunt, sicut oculi, doctores, qui per seipsos veritatem inspiciunt. Unde dicitur Cant. V, 12 '***Oculi eius sicut columbae super rivos aquarum, quae resident iuxta fluenta plenissima***'. Per aures autem significantur discipuli, qui a magistris veritatem audiendo recipiunt.	1 Cor 12:16

14		**manus illius tornatiles, aureae, plenae hyacinthis.**	
209	*In 1 ad Co.*, c. 12, lect. 3 (n° 738)	Per membra autem deservientia motui, designantur in Ecclesia homines dediti vitae activae, ita quod pedes sunt subditi, de quibus dicitur Ez. I, 7 'Pedes eorum pedes recti'; per manus autem figurantur praelati, per quos alii disponuntur, unde et Cant. V, 14 dicitur '***Manus illius tornatiles aureae, plenae hyacinthis***'. Sunt autem in Ecclesia necessariae non solum manus, id est praelati, sed etiam pedes, id est subditi.	1 Cor 12:15
		venter eius eburneus, distinctus sapphiris	
210	*In Ps.* 44, 6 (p. 323)	Ex secundo dicit, 'a domibus eburneis'. [...] Domus signat fideles: 1 Pet. 2 'Et ipsi tamquam lapides vivi aedificamini in domos spirituales' et cetera. Eburneae, frigidae propter castitatem: Cant. 5 '***Venter illius eburneus***'. Item candidae propter puritatem, rubicundae propter castitatem: Thren. 4 'Rubicundiores ebore antiquo'.	Ps 44:9
15		**crura illius columnae marmoreae quae fundatae sunt super bases aureas.**	
211	*In ad Ga.*, c. 2, lect. 2 (n° 74)	'Qui videbantur columnae esse'. Metaphorice dicitur hoc, id est sustentatio totius Ecclesiae. Sicut enim totum aedificium sustentatur per columnas, ita per istos tota Ecclesia Iudaeorum sustentabatur et regebatur. Et de istis columnis dicitur in Ps. LXXIV, 4 'Ego confirmavi columnas eius', id est, apostolos Ecclesiae; Cant. V, 15 '***Crura illius columnae marmoreae, quae fundatae sunt super bases aureas***'.	Gal 2:9
		species eius ut Libani	
212	*In Ps.* 44, 3 (p. 321)	Tu Christe es potentissimus, 'specie tua', scilicet humanitatis, secundum quam etiam est maximus virtute: Cant. 5: '***Species ejus ut Libani***'. 'Et pulchritudine tua', scilicet divinitatis	Ps 44:5
16		**guttur illius suavissimum et totus desiderabilis**	
213	Sermo I, lines 215–21 [220–21] (p. 12)	[Erat enim homo] oppressus tyrannide intollerabili; sicut enim iniuriosus tradidit fuit inimicis, Osee viii 'Proiecit Israel bonum, inimicus persequitur eum'; Ysaie xiii 'Cum' liberatus fueris 'a servitute tua dura qua ante servisti'; et ideo desiderabat dulce dominum, Canticorum V: '***Species eius ut Libani***' et '***guttur***' eius suave '***et totus desiderabilis***'.	Hg 2:8: Veniet desideratus cunctis gentibus
17		**quo abiit dilectus tuus, o pulcherrima mulierum, quo declinavit dilectus tuus? et quaeremus eum tecum.**	
214	*In Ioan.*, c. 6, lect. 2 (n° 877)	Subtraxit autem Christus se tamdiu discipulis, primo quidem ut sentirent quid esset eius absentia; quod quidem experti sunt in tempestate maris. Ier. II, 19 'Scito, et vide quia malum et amarum est dereliquisse te dominum'. Secundo ut diligentius quaererent; Cant. V, 17 '***Quo abiit dilectus tuus, o pulcherrima mulierum? Et quaeremus eum tecum***'.	Jn 6:17

215	*In Ioan.*, c. 13, lect. 8 (n° 1841)	Et inde est quod etiam Christo dicente: 'Quo ego vado, vos non potestis venire', ipsum Petrus sequi volebat; et ideo interrogabat quo iret, quasi una de adolescentulis quaerentibus in Cant. V, 17 ***'Quo abiit dilectus tuus, o pulcherrima mulierum, quo abiit? Et quaeremus eum tecum'.*** [n° 1842] Dilatio autem huius desiderii est, quia ad praesens impeditur a sequendo; et hoc est quod dicit 'Quo ego vado non potes me modo sequi: sequeris autem postea'; quasi dicat: adhuc imperfectus es, et ideo non potes me modo sequi; postea autem, quando perfectus eris, sequeris me.	Jn 13:36

APPENDIX TABLE 6

1		**dilectus meus descendit in hortum suum ad areolam aromatum, ut pascatur in hortis, et lilia colligat.**	
216	Sermo VIII, lines 528–32 [537–38] (p. 111)	Primo dico: si vis proficere in conversatione humana, debes habere pietatem. Aliqui habent solum pietatem de se ipsis ut in pace vivant et in sapiencia proficiant sed aliis condescendere nolunt. Tales proficere possunt in 'gratia apud Deum', sed non 'apud homines'. Sed 'Iesus proficiebat in gracia et sapientia apud Deum et homines'. Illud significatur in descensu cum illis. 'Iesus' tempore suo 'mansit in Ierusalem', sed quando voluit 'descendit'. Unde in Cantico ***'Dilectus meus descendit in ortum suum'***, idest, in ortum deliciarum. Et in scala quam vidit Iacob, vidit angelos Dei ascendentes et descendentes; sic et nos debemus ascendere per spiritualem profectum et descendere per pietatem ad proximum.	
217	*In Is.*, c. 35, line 76 (p. 154) (Collatio 3)	See [no. 56]	
218	*In Ioan.*, c. 14, lect. 1 (n° 1861)	Et sic hoc quod dicit 'Iterum veniam, et accipiam vos ad meipsum', potest exponi de adventu spirituali, quo Christus semper visitat Ecclesiam fidelium, et quemlibet sanctorum vivificat in morte. Ut sit sensus: 'Iterum veniam', ad Ecclesiam spiritualiter continue, 'et accipiam vos ad meipsum': idest firmabo in fide et dilectione mea; Cant. VI, 1 ***'Dilectus meus ascendit ad areolam aromatum'***, idest ad congregationem sanctorum, ***'ut pascatur'***, idest delectetur in virtutibus, ***'et lilia colligat'***, idest, animas puras ad se trahat, cum vivificat sanctos in morte.	Jn 14:3

2		**ego dilecto meo, et dilectus meus mihi, qui pascitur inter lilia**	
219	*In Is.*, c. 65, lines 12–15 [14–15] (p. 250)	Et ponit promissionem: 'Dixi: ecce ego ad gentem', respondebo scilicet Iudeis, vel 'ad gentes' conversas convertar, Cant. viii '***Ego dilecto meo et dilectus meus michi***'.	Is 65:1
* 219'	*Catena in Matthaeum* 6, 19	See [no. 72']	
3		**pulchra es amica mea**	
220	*In Matth.*, c. 4, lect. 2 (n° 354)	Capharnaum enim interpretatur villa pulcherrima, et significat Ecclesiam; Cant. VI, 3 '***Pulchra es, amica mea***', et cetera. Capharnaum est maritima ad litteram, quia iuxta lacum quemdam dulcem. Iudaei enim omnem congregationem aquarum appellant mare: et mystice, quia Ecclesia posita est iuxta tribulationes mundi.	Mt 4:13
		terribilis ut castrorum acies ordinate	
221	*In Ioan.*, c. 21, lect. 2 (n° 2595)	Navigium significat Ecclesiam. Sap. XIV, 6 'Spes orbis terrarum ad ratem confugiens, remisit saeculo semen nativitatis'. Et per hanc signatur Ecclesia, ut habetur I Petr. III, 20. 'Alii vero navigio venerunt', idest protecti societate Ecclesiae, quae est '***Terribilis ut castrorum acies ordinata***'. Ps. XXX, 21 'Proteges eos in tabernaculo tuo a contradictione linguarum'.	Jn 21:8
222	*In 1 ad Co.*, c. 5, lect. 1 (n° 237)	Alio modo intelligi potest quod dicitur tradere huiusmodi Satanae, scilicet per excommunicationis sententiam, per quam aliquis separatur a communione fidelium, et a participatione sacramentorum, et privatur Ecclesiae suffragiis, quibus homo munitur contra impugnationem Satanae, propter quod de Ecclesia dicitur Cant. IV, 9 '***Terribilis ut castrorum acies ordinata***', scilicet daemonibus.	1 Cor 5:5
223	*In 1 ad Co.*, c. 12, lect. 3 (n° 743)	Ita si omnes in Ecclesia unius conditionis et gradus essent, tolleretur perfectio et decor Ecclesiae, quae in Ps. XLIV, 10 describitur 'circumamicta varietate'. Secundo asserit veritatem contrariam, dicens 'Nunc autem multa quidem sunt membra, sed unum corpus' quod ex omnibus integratur. Sic Ecclesia ex diversis ordinibus constituitur. Unde et Cant. VI, 9 describitur '***Terribilis ut castrorum acies ordinata***'.	1 Cor 12:20
224	*In ad Col.*, prol. (n° 2)	Et sic tanguntur duo in verbis propositis, scilicet Ecclesiae status, cum dicitur 'castra', et apostoli studium, ibi 'protexit'. In castris autem debet esse sollicitudo ad mala vitanda. Deut. XXIII, 14 'Ut sint castra tua sancta, et nihil in eis appareat foeditatis'. Item ordo ad ducem et ad se. Cant. c. VII, 1 '***Quid videbis in Sunamite, nisi choros castrorum ?***' Gen. XXXII, 2 'Castra Dei sunt haec'. Item terror ad hostes. Cant. VI, v. 3: '***Terribilis ut castrorum acies ordinata***'.	1 Mc 3:3 (theme of the Prologue)

8		una est columba mea, perfecta mea, una est matris suae electa genetricis suae	
225	*In IV Sent.*, d. 49, q. 4, a. 4, arg. 1 (p. 1229)	Videtur quod angeli habeant dotes. Quia super illud Cantic. 6: ‘***Una est columba mea***’, dicit Glossa: ‘Una est Ecclesia in hominibus et in angelis’. Sed Ecclesia est sponsa; et sic membris Ecclesiae convenit habere dotes. Ergo angeli dotes habent	“Utrum angeli habeant dotes?”
226	*SCG* IV, c. 78 (n° 4123)	Quia igitur per coniunctionem maris et feminae Christi et Ecclesiae coniunctio designatur, oportet quod figura significato respondeat. Coniunctio autem Christi et Ecclesiae est unius ad unam perpetuo habendam : est enim una Ecclesia, secundum illud Cant. 6, 8 ‘***Una est columba mea, perfecta mea***’; nec unquam Christus a sua Ecclesia separabitur,	“De sacramento matrimonii”
227	*ST* IIIa, q. 39, a. 6	Quarto, apparuit spiritus sanctus in specie columbae super dominum baptizatum, ad designandum communem effectum Baptismi, qui est constructio ecclesiasticae unitatis. Unde dicitur Ephes. V, quod ‘Christus tradidit semetipsum ut exhiberet sibi gloriosam Ecclesiam, non habentem maculam aut rugam aut aliquid huiusmodi, lavans eam lavacro aquae in verbo vitae’. Et ideo convenienter Spiritus sanctus in baptismo demonstratus est in specie columbae, quae est animal amicabile et gregale. Unde et Cantic. VI dicitur de Ecclesia, ‘***Una est columba mea***’.	“Utrum convenienter Spiritus Sanctus super Christum baptizatum dicatur in specie columbae descendisse?”
* 227’	*Catena in Ioannem* 1, 22	Augustinus: Unde ergo debuit demonstrari Spiritus sanctus unitatem quamdam designans, nisi per columbam, ut pacatae Ecclesiae diceretur: ‘***Una est columba mea***’?	Augustine, In *Iohannis evangelium tractatus CXXIV*, VI, 10 (pp. 58–59)
228	*Collationes in Symbolum apostolorum*, 9 (n° 973)	Licet diversi haeretici diversas sectas adinvenerint, non tamen pertinent ad Ecclesiam, quia sunt divisi in partes: sed Ecclesia est una. Cant. VI, 8 ‘***Una est columba mea, perfecta mea***’.	
229	*In Ps.* 21, 14 (p. 222)	Per haec vestimenta divisa signantur Ecclesiae sacramenta; sed per vestem quae non dividitur, signatur unitas Ecclesiae quam quilibet credit habere; sed non habet nisi unus, quia sola est unitas Ecclesiae: Cant. 6 ‘***Una est columba mea, perfecta mea***’.	Ps 21:19
230	*In Matth.*, c. 28 (n° 2421)	Sed non fuit sine mysterio, quod duae eiusdem nominis venerunt. [...] Item eiusdem nominis, quia per has unitas signatur Ecclesiae: primo enim una fuit ex gentibus, una ex Iudaeis, sed modo omnes sunt una Ecclesia; Cant. VI, 8 ‘***Una est columba mea***’.	Mt 28:1

231	*In Ioan.*, c. 1, lect. 14 (n° 272)	See [no. 207]	
232	*In ad Ep.*, c. 3, lect. 1 (n° 142)	Circa quod sciendum est quod Iudaei triplicem praerogativam habebant respectu gentilium [...]. Item per specialem a gentibus aliis distinctionem et electionem. Deut. VII, 6 'Te elegit dominus Deus tuus, ut sis ei populus peculiaris de cunctis populis qui sunt super terram'. Unde Ps. XCIX, 3 'Nos autem populus eius et oves pascuae eius'. Cant. VI, 8 '***Una est columba mea, perfecta mea***', et cetera [=***una est matris suae electa genetricis suae***]	Ep 3:6
233	*In 1 ad Tim.*, c. 3, lect. 1 (n° 96)	Sed quae est causa huius institutionis? Numquid non magis impeditur qui multas concubinas habet? Respondeo. Dicendum quod hoc fit non propter incontinentiam tantum, sed propter repraesentationem sacramenti, quia sponsus Ecclesiae est Christus, et una est Ecclesia. Cant. V '***Una est columba mea***'.	1 Tm 3:2
9	**Cf 6, 3**	**pulchra ut luna, electa ut sol, terribilis ut castrorum acies ordinata?**	
234	*In Ps.* 10, 1 (p. 178)	Alia littera habet 'in obscura luna'. Luna est Ecclesia: Cant. 6 '***Pulchra ut luna***', propter ejus claritatem, et propter ejus obscurationem. Claritas lunae est a sole; sic claritas Ecclesiae est a Christo: Jo. 1 'Erat lux vera quae illuminat' et cetera. Item medius lunae globus est clarus, et medius obscurus; sic in Ecclesia aliqui sunt clari, aliqui obscuri.	Ps 10:1
235	*In 1 ad Co.*, c. 15, lect. 6 (n° 978)	Et ad idem ulterius introducit diversam qualitatem caelestium corporum, cum dicit 'alia claritas solis', et cetera. Similiter inter stellas est differentia, 'stella enim differt', et cetera. Et potest intelligi per solem Christus, Mal. ult.: 'Orietur vobis timentibus nomen meum sol iustitiae', et cetera. Per lunam beata Virgo, de qua Cant. VI, 9 '***Pulchra ut luna***'. Per stellas ad invicem ordinatas, caeteri sancti. Iudic. V, 20: 'Stellae manentes in ordine suo', et cetera.	1 Cor 15:41
* 235'	*Catena in Matthaeum* 24, 7	Origenes in Matth. Vel Ecclesia est sol, luna et stellae, cui dictum est: '***Speciosa ut luna, electa ut sol***'.	Origen, *Commentaria in Evangelium secundum Matthaeum* (PG 13, col. 1672)
* 235''	*Catena in Lucam* 21, 6	Augustinus. Sed ne dominus, propinquante secundo adventu suo, ea pro magno praedixisse videatur quae huic mundo etiam ante primum eius adventum fieri consueverant, et rideamur ab eis qui plura in historia gentium et maiora legerunt, haec quae dicta sunt, melius in Ecclesia existimo intelligi. Ecclesia enim est sol, et luna, et stellae, cui dictum est: '***Pulchra ut luna, electa ut sol***'; quae tunc non apparebit, persecutoribus ultra modum saevientibus.	Augustine, "Epistula CXCIX," XI, 39 (CSEL 57, pp. 277–78)

10		**descendi ad ortum nucum [*meum*]** **ut viderem poma convallium**	
236	Sermo XVIII, lines 528–29 (p. 290)	See [no. 154]	"Ortum meum" is the liturgical version, cf. G. Dahan, "Recherches sur l'exégèse du Cantique au XIIIe siècle," 499–500.
237	*In Matth.*, c. 16, lec. 1 (n° 1353)	'Et venit in fines Magedan'. Magedan poma interpretatur et per hunc locum sacra Scriptura significatur, ubi poma simul cum aliis fructibus crescunt; Cant. VI, 10 '***Descendi ut viderem poma convallium***'.	Mt 16:1

APPENDIX TABLE 7

1		**quid videbis in Sunamite, nisi choros castrorum ?**	
238	*In ad Col.*, Prol. (n° 2)	See [no. 224].	
		quam pulchri sunt gressus [pedes] tui in calceamentis, filia principis	
239	*In ad Ro.*, c. 10, lect. 2 (n° 840)	'Quam pulchri supra montes pedes praedicantis et annuntiantis pacem, annuntiantis bonum'. Et similiter habetur Nahum I, 15 'Ecce super montes pedes evangelizantis et annuntiantis pacem'. In his autem verbis, primo, commendatur processus praedicatorum, cum dicit 'quam speciosi pedes', quod dupliciter potest intelligi. Uno modo ut per pedes intelligantur eorum processus, quia scilicet ordinate procedunt, non usurpantes sibi praedicationis officium. Cant. VII, 1 '***Quam pulchri sunt gressus tui in calceamentis, filia principis***'. Alio modo possunt intelligi per pedes affectus qui rectitudinem habent, dum non intentione laudis aut lucri verbum Dei annuntiant, sed propter hominum salutem et Dei gloriam. Ez. I, 7 'Pedes eorum, pedes recti'.	Rom 10:15

240	*In 1 ad Co.*, c. 12, lect. 3 (n° 748)	Cultus autem exterior membris adhibitus ad duo pertinet scilicet ad honorem, sicut ea quae apponuntur ad ornatum, ut monilia et inaures: et ad honestatem, sicut quae apponuntur ad tegumentum, ut brachae et alia huiusmodi. Quantum ergo ad primum cultum, dicit primo 'et quae putamus esse ignobiliora membra corporis, his circumdamus abundantiorem honorem', idest maiorem ornatum, sicut auribus alicubi suspenduntur inaures, oculis autem nihil apponitur, et pedibus apponuntur calceamenta depicta et gemmata, secundum illud Cant. VII, 1 '***Quam pulchri sunt gressus tui in calceamentis, filia principis***'. Manus autem nudae habentur	1 Cor 12:23
241	*In Is.*, c. 3, lines 361–73 [364–65] (p. 29)	Dicit ergo primo quantum ad pedes, 'ornamenta calceamentorum'; quaecumque, et specialiter 'lunulas', quasdam picturas factas in calceamentis de corio deaurato, Cant. vii: '***Quam pulcri sunt pedes tui in calciamentis, filia principis!***' [...] Tertio quantum ad pectus dicit, 'monilia', quaelibet ornamenta, sed specialiter fibulae, quibus munitur pectus, ne vestes aperiantur, Cant. vii : '***Iunctura femorum tuorum sicut monilia que fabricata sunt manu artificis***'.	Is 3:18–19
		junctura femorum tuorum sicut monilia quae fabricata sunt manu artificis	
242	*In Is.*, c. 3, lines 372–73, (p. 29)	See [no. 241]	
2		**Venter tuus sicut acervus tritici vallatus liliis**	
243	*In Is.*, c. 35, line 73 (p. 154) (Collatio 2)	See [no. 61]	
5		**comae capitis tui sicut purpura regis**	
244	*In 1 ad Co.*, c. 11, lect. 3 (n° 619)	See [no. 127]	
6		**quam pulchra es, et quam decora, carissima, in deliciis !**	
245	*In Is.*, c. 51, lines 78–90 [89–90] (p. 209)	Nota super illo verbo, 'ponet desertum ejus quasi delicias', quod sancti habent duplices delicias. Primas gloriae [...]. Secundas gratie, que consistunt primo in perceptione divini luminis [...]; secundo in proposito vel sollicitudine boni operis [...]; tertio in ornatu virtutum. Cant. vii: '***Quam pulcra est et quam decora in deliciis***'.	Is 51:3

8		**dixi : ascendam in palmam, et apprehendam fructus eius.**	
246	*In Is.*, c. 57 lines 158–70 [170] (p. 228)	Nota super illo verbo, 'Iustus perit et non est qui recogitet', quod in passione Christi homo debet recogitare primo dilectionem, ad reamandum. Cant. viii '***Pone me ut signaculum super cor tuum***'. [...] Quarto utilitatem, ad gratias agendum, Cant. vii '***Ascendam ad palmam, et accipiam fructus eius***'.	Is 57:1
247	*In Ioan.*, c. 7, lect. 3 (n° 1067)	Quia enim dixerat dominus 'quem vos nescitis', irati sunt Iudaei quasi simularent eum scire, et ideo iniqua proponebant, scilicet eum apprehendere, ad crucifigendum et occidendum, secundum illud Ps. LXX, 11 'Persequimini, et comprehendite eum'. Sunt autem aliqui qui Christum in se habentes, quaerunt tamen pie apprehendere; Cant. VII, 8 '***Ascendam in palmam, et apprehendam fructus eius***'. Unde et apostolus dicebat, Phil. III, 12 'Sequor, si quo modo apprehendam, in quo et comprehensus sum a Christo Iesu'.	Jn 7:30
248	*In Ioan.*, c. 7, lect. 5 (n° 1104)	'Voluerunt apprehendere eum', scilicet ex inimicitia ad occidendum; Ps. LXX, 11 'Persequimini et comprehendite'; Ex. XV, 9 'Dixit inimicus: persequar et comprehendam'. Sed tamen boni et fideles volunt Christum apprehendere, ut eo fruantur; Cant. VII, 8 '***Ascendam in palmam, et apprehendam fructus eius***'.	Jn 7:44
* 248'	*Catena in Matthaeum* 21, 7	See [no. 118']	
9		**guttur tuum sicut vinum optimum**	
249	*In Is.*, c. 5, line 147 (p. 39)	See [no. 105]	
10–12		**ego dilecto meo, ad me conversio eius. Veni, dilecte mi, egrediamur in agrum, commoremur in villis. Mane surgamus ad vineas**	
250	Sermo IX, lines 352–69 (p. 124–25)	See [no. 107]	
251	*In Matth.*, c. 7, lect. 1 (n° 642)	See [no. 111]	
252	*In Matth.*, c. 24, lect. 3 (n° 1992)	See [no. 53]	

253	*In Ioan.*, c. 21, lect. 1 (n° 2582)	Executio vero officii ponitur cum dicit 'exierunt et ascenderunt in navim, et illa nocte nihil prendiderunt'. Et tangit tria quae debent facere praedicatores. Primo quidem exire a peccatorum conversatione [...]. A carnalium affectione [...]. Et a quietis contemplatione; Cant. VII, 11 '***Egrediamur in agrum, commoremur in vineis: mane surgamus ad vineas***' et cetera.	Jn 21:3
13		**omnia poma nova et vetera, dilecte mi, servavi tibi.**	
254	Principium biblicum, *Hic est liber* (Marietti, n° 1203).	Tota sacra scriptura in duas partes principaliter dividitur, scilicet in vetus et novum testamentum; quae duo tanguntur Matth. xiii 'Omnis scriba doctus'... Et Cant. vii '***Omnia poma nova [et vetera, dilecte mi servavi tibi]***'.	
255	*In Matth.*, c. 13, lect. 4 (n° 1205)	Vel potest dici: simile est cuicumque alii patri, qui profert de scientia divinitus sibi data nova et vetera. Non sic Manichaei, quia non proferebant vetera. Cant. VII, 13 '***Omnia nova et vetera servavi tibi***'.	Mt 13:52
256	Sermo XVIII, lines 500–501 (p. 290)	See [no. 154]	

APPENDIX TABLE 8

1		**quis mihi det te fratrem meum sugentem ubera matris meae, ut inveniam te foris, et deosculer te?**	
257	*In Ps.* 48, 3 (p. 336)	'Frater non redimet' [...] Sed postquam frater non potest redimere quantumcumque sibi propinquum, numquid 'redimet homo'? Non, quia homo non potest aliquem eripere de manu Dei, sed solus Deus redimet eos. Et homo, scilicet Christus: homo, ut pretium, idest mors locum in eo habere possit, et Deus ut habeat virtutem redimendi, vel aliter, 'frater', idest Christus, qui est verus frater noster: Ps. 21 'Narrabo nomen tuum fratribus meis': Cant. 8 '***Quis mihi det te fratrem meum***' et cetera. Si non redimet iste, quis alius redimet? Quasi dicat, nullus.	Ps 48:8
258	*In Is.*, c. 7, lines 430–35 [433–35] (p. 59)	Notandum super illo verbo, 'Vocabitur nomen ejus Emmanuel', idest Nobiscum Deus, quod Christus est nobiscum multipliciter. Primo tamquam frater per nature consortium, Cant. viii '***Quis michi det te fratrem meum sugentem ubera matris mee, ut inveniam te foris et deosculer te?***'	Is 7:14

259	*In Is.*, c. 9, lines 172–75 [174–75] (p. 69)	Notandum super illo verbo, 'Datus est nobis', quod Christus datus est nobis primo in fratrem, Cant. viii '***Quis michi det te fratrem meum sugentem ubera matris mee?***'	Is 9:6
2		**apprehendam te, et ducam in domum matris meae, et in cubiculum genetricis meae**	
260	*In Is.*, c. 4, lines 179–85 [183–85] (p. 35)	'Apprehendent' per fidem, 'septem mulieres', septem Ecclesiae, de quibus Apoc. i 'Joannes septem Ecclesiis' etc., in quo omnes Ecclesiae secundum regulam Ticonii quintam; 'virum unum', idest Christum. Cant. ult. '***Apprehendam te, et ducam in domum matris mee, et in cubiculum genetricis mee***'.	Is 4:1
		ibi me docebis, et dabo tibi poculum ex vino condito, et mustum malorum granatorum meorum	
261	*In Is.*, c. 2, lines 74–85 [84–85] (p. 20–21)	'Venite'. Hic ponitur vocatio. Vocant autem ad tria [...]. Secundo ad doctrinam, cum dicit: 'Docebit nos vias suas', idest precepta quibus ad ipsum itur. Cant. viii '***Ibi me docebis, et dabo tibi poculum ex vino condito, et mustum malorum granatorum meorum***'.	Is 2:3
262	*In Is.*, c. 5, lines 156 (p. 39)	See [no. 105]	
263	*In Ier.*, c. 13, 2 (p. 612)	Nota, quod vinum mystice aliud est bonum, aliud malum. Est enim bonum vinum sapientiae contemplationis. Prov. 9 'Bibite vinum quod miscui vobis'. Divini amoris. Cant. 8 '***Dabo tibi poculum ex vino condito et mustum malorum granatorum meorum***'.	Jer 13:12
6		**pone me ut signaculum super cor tuum**	
264	*In Is.*, c. 57, lines 161–62 (p. 228)	See [no. 246]	
265	*In Ps.* 4, 5 (p. 159)	'Signatum est super nos lumen vultus tui, domine' et cetera [...]. Super hoc autem signamur signo spiritus. Eph. 4 'Nolite contristare spiritum sanctum in quo signati estis'. Et iterum signo crucis, cujus signaculum nobis impressum est in baptismo, et quotidie debemus imprimere. Cant. 8 '***Pone me ut signaculum super cor tuum***'.	Ps 4:7
266	*In Ioan.*, c. 3, lect. 6 (n° 539)	'Signavit', idest signum quoddam in corde suo ponere debet seu posuit, quod ipse Christus est Deus. [...] De isto signaculo dicitur Cant. VIII, 6 '***Pone me ut signaculum super cor tuum***'. Et II Tim. II, 19 'Firmum fundamentum Dei stat, habens signaculum' et cetera.	Jn 3:33

267	*In ad Ga.*, c. 3, lect. 1 (n° 118)	Dico vos fascinatos, quia 'ante quorum oculos', etc., id est proscriptio Christi, qui damnatus est in mortem, adeo vobis manifesta fuit, ac si ante oculos vestros fuisset, 'et in vobis crucifixus', id est, in intellectibus vestris erat crucifixio Iesu Christi, ita ut sciretis qualiter facta esset; unde si eam non videtis modo, nec obeditis, hoc contingit, quia estis ludificati et fascinati. Contra quod dicitur Cant. ult. '***Pone me ut signaculum super cor tuum***', et cetera.	Gal 3:1
		quia fortis est ut mors dilectio	
268	*Q. de virt.*, q. 2, a. 6, arg. 6	Praeterea, illud quod est fortissimum, non potest expelli a debilissimo. Sed caritas est fortissima '***Fortis***' enim '***est ut mors dilectio***', ut dicitur Cant. VIII, 6: peccatum autem est debilissimum, quia malum est infirmum et impotens, ut Dionysius dicit. Ergo peccatum mortale non expellit caritatem; et sic potest esse simul cum ea.	"Utrum caritas possit esse cum peccato mortali?"
269	*Q. de virt.*, q. 2, a. 12, arg. 11	Quarto modo deficit aliquod accidens per actionem contrarii agentis, sicut frigiditas aquae deficit per actionem caloris: sed nec hoc modo caritas deficere potest, cum sit fortior peccato, quod videtur in contrarium agere: secundum illud Cant. VIII, 6 '***Fortis est ut mors dilectio***'; et iterum: '***Aquae multae non possunt extinguere caritatem***'. Ergo caritas nullo modo potest deficere in habente eam	"Utrum caritas semel habita possit amitti?"
270	*In Ps.* 47, 6 (p. 334)	Quantum ad secundum dicit, 'Ponite corda vestra in virtute ejus'. Hieronymus, 'Ponite cor vestrum in manibus ejus'. Et haec est virtus Spiritus sancti, qui protegit hanc civitatem: Luc. ult. 'Sedete in civitate donec induamini virtute'. Haec virtus est dilectio: Cant. 8 '***Fortis est ut mors dilectio***'.	Ps 47:14
271	*In ad Ep.*, Prol. (n° 1)	Fideles enim Ecclesiae dicuntur columnae, quia debent esse recti, erecti, et fortes. Recti per fidem, erecti per spem, fortes per charitatem [...]. Fortes per charitatem, '***Fortis enim est ut mors dilectio***', ut dicitur Cant. VIII, 6; unde significatur per columnam ignis qui omnia consumit, de quo Sap. XVIII, 3 'Ignis ardentem columnam ducem habuerunt ignotae viae'.	Ps 74:4 (theme of the Prologue)
272	*In ad Ep.*, c. 3, lect. 4 (n° 172)	Et ideo subiungit 'habitare Christum per fidem', et hoc 'in cordibus vestris'. [...] Per quod ? Dico quod non solum per fidem, quae, ut donum est fortissima, sed etiam per charitatem quae est in sanctis. Et ideo subdit 'in charitate radicati et fundati'. I Cor. XIII, 7 'Omnia suffert, omnia credit, omnia sperat, omnia sustinet, charitas numquam excidit'. Cant. ult. '***Fortis est ut mors dilectio***'. Unde sicut arbor sine radice, et domus sine fundamento de facili ruit, ita spirituale aedificium, nisi sit in charitate fundatum et radicatum, durare non potest.	Eph 3:17

273	*In ad Ro.*, Prol. (n° 1)	Beatus autem Paulus, quia vas electionis nominatur in verbis propositis, quale vas fuerit, patet per id quod dicitur Eccli. l, 10 'Quasi vas auri solidum ornatum omni lapide pretioso'. [...] Solidum quidem fuit virtute charitatis, de qua dicitur Cant. ultimo '***Fortis est ut mors dilectio***'.	Acts 9:15 (theme of the Prologue)
274	*In ad Ro.*, c. 8, lect. 6 (n° 700)	Hoc autem apostolus se scire dicit ex persona sanctorum, dicens 'scimus'. Sap. X, 10 'Dedit illi scientiam sanctorum'. Procedit autem haec scientia tum ex experimento, tum etiam ex consideratione efficaciae charitatis, Cant. VIII, 6 '***Fortis est ut mors dilectio***', et etiam praedestinationis aeternae, Is. XLVI, 10 'Omnis voluntas mea implebitur, et omne consilium meum fiet.'	Rom 8:28
275	*In ad Ro.*, c. 8, lect. 7 (n° 730)	'Neque fortitudo', id est neque quaecumque creatura fortis, potest me separare a Christo, puta fortis ignis, aut fortis aqua: quia, ut Cant. VIII, 6 dicitur, '***Fortis est ut mors dilectio***'.	Rom 8:38
		lampades eius lampades ignis atque flammarum	
276	*ST* Ia-IIae, q. 28, a. 5, obj. 3	Praeterea, fervor designat quendam excessum in caliditate, qui quidem excessus corruptivus est. Sed fervor causatur ex amore, Dionysius enim, VII cap. Cael. Hier., inter ceteras proprietates ad amorem Seraphim pertinentes, ponit calidum et acutum et superfervens. Et Cant. VIII, dicitur de amore quod '***lampades eius sunt lampades ignis atque flammarum***'. Ergo amor est passio laesiva et corruptiva.	"Utrum amor sit passio laesiva amantis?" Dionysius, *De coelesti hierarchia* VII, 1 (PTS 36, pp. 27–28)
277	*ST* IIa-IIae, q. 24, a. 10, sc	Sed contra est quod caritas in Scriptura igni comparatur, secundum illud Cant. VIII, '***Lampades eius***', scilicet caritatis, '***lampades ignis atque flammarum***'. Sed ignis, quandiu manet, semper ascendit. Ergo caritas, quandiu manet, ascendere potest; sed descendere, idest diminui, non potest	"Utrum caritas possit diminui?"
278	*In Ps.* 18, 4 (p. 209)	Sol quando est in alto, omnes calefacit. Sic Christus ascendens misit spiritum sanctum discipulis; unde dicit. 'Nec est qui se abscondat a calore ejus'. Spiritus sanctus calefacit: Cant. 8 '***Lampades ejus lampades ignis***'.	Ps 18:7
279	*In Ps.* 26, 3 (p. 237)	[Desiderium] sollicitat, cum sit sicut stimulus et ignis, amor: Cant. 8 '***Lampades ejus lampades ignis***': 2 Cor. 9 'Charitas Dei urget nos'. Unde dicit, 'hanc requiram'.	Ps 26:4
280	*In Ps.* 44, 5 (p. 323)	Et dicitur Spiritus sanctus oleum. [...]. Tertio, quia oleum est diffusivum, sic Spiritus sanctus est communicativus: 2 Cor. ult. 'Communicatio sancti Spiritus sit semper cum omnibus vobis, amen': Rom. 5 'Charitas Dei diffusa est in cordibus vestris per spiritum sanctum'. Item oleum est fomentum ignis et caloris, et Spiritus sanctus fovet et nutrit amoris calorem in nobis: Cant. ult. '***Lampades ejus lampades ignis***'.	Ps 44:8

281	*In Iob*, c. 18, lines 68–71 [70–71] (p. 109)	'Nec splendebit flamma ignis eius ?'. Per ignem enim ardor amoris significari solet, secundum illud Cant. VIII, 6 '***Lampades eius, lampades ignis atque flammarum***'.	Jb 18:5
282	*In Ioan.* c. 4, lect. 2 (n° 577)	Et dicendum, quod per aquam intelligitur gratia Spiritus sancti: quae quidem quandoque dicitur ignis, quandoque aqua, ut ostendatur quod nec hoc, nec illud dicitur secundum substantiae proprietatem, sed secundum similitudinem actionis. Nam ignis dicitur, quia elevat cor per fervorem et calorem, Rom. XII, 11 'Spiritu ferventes' etc. et quia consumit peccata; Cant. VIII '***Lampades eius, lampades ignis atque flammarum***'.	Jn 4:10
283	*In Ioan.*, c. 5, lect. 6 (n° 812)	Ardor autem ignis significat dilectionem propter tria. Primo quidem, quia ignis inter omnia corpora est magis activus: sic et ardor caritatis, intantum quod nihil eius impetum ferre potest, secundum illud II Cor. V, 14 'Caritas Christi urget nos'. Secundo, quia sicut ignis per hoc quod est maxime sensitivus, facit multum aestuare, ita et caritas aestum causat quousque homo consequatur intentum; Cant. ult., 6 '***Lampades eius lampades ignis atque flammarum***'. Tertio sicut ignis est sursum ductivus, ita et caritas, intantum quod coniungit nos Deo	Jn 5:35
284	*In Ioan.*, c. 14, lect. 6 (n° 1942)	Intenditur autem in Deum per caritatem; et ideo caritas est quae nos servare mandata facit; II Cor. V, 14 'Caritas Christi urget nos'; Cant. VIII, 7 '***Lampades eius, lampades ignis***'.	Jn 14:23
285	*In Ioan.*, c. 20, lect. 1 (n° 2473)	Et ideo statim transacto sabbato ante lucem primae sabbati venit ad monumentum: nam nimius ardor amoris eam sollicitabat; Cant. VIII, 6 '***Lampades eius lampades ignis atque flammarum***', scilicet caritatis.	Jn 20:1
286	*In ad Ro.*, c. 12, lect. 3 (n° 1014)	'Hoc enim faciens, carbones ignis congeres super caput eius'. [...] Est exponendum in bonum, ut sit sensus 'hoc enim faciens' id est, in necessitate ei subveniens, 'carbones ignis', id est amorem charitatis de qua dicitur Cant. VIII, 6 '***Lampades eius, ut lampades ignis atque flammarum***' 'congeres', id est, congregabis, 'super caput', id est, super mentem 'eius'.	Rom 12:20
287	*In 2 ad Co.*, c. 5, lect. 3 (n° 181)	'Charitas Christi urget nos' ad hoc. Et dicit 'urget', quia urgere idem est quod stimulare; quasi dicat: charitas Christi, quasi stimulus, stimulat nos ad faciendum ea, quae charitas imperat, ut scilicet procuremus salutem proximorum. Hic est effectus charitatis. Rom. VIII, 14 'Qui spiritu Dei aguntur', id est agitantur, et cetera. Cant. VIII, 6 '***Lampades eius, ut lampades ignis***', et cetera.	2 Cor 5:14

288	*In ad Tit.*, c. 3, lect. 1 (n° 88)	Causa autem nostrae salutis est charitas Dei. Eph. II, 4: 'Deus autem, qui dives est in misericordia, propter nimiam charitatem suam, qua dilexit nos', et cetera. Hanc charitatem describit, primo quantum ad affectum; secundo quantum ad effectum. Interior charitatis affectus designatur in benignitate, quae dicitur bona igneitas. Ignis autem significat amorem. Cant. VIII, 6 '***Lampades eius, lampades ignis atque flammarum***'. Benignitas ergo est amor interior, profundens bona ad exteriora. Haec ab aeterno fuit in Deo, quia amor eius est causa omnium.	Titus 3:4
289	*In ad He.*, c. 1, lect. 3 (n° 58)	Item sunt ignis, inquantum ministri. Ignis autem, inter omnia elementa, est maxime activus et efficax ad agendum. Unde in Ps. CIII, 4 de angelis ubi dicuntur ministri eius, ibi additur 'et ministros tuos ignem urentem'. Item ignis calorem causat, per quod designatur charitas. Cant. VIII, 6 '***Lampades ignis atque flammarum***'. Unde describuntur in igne, et dicuntur Seraphim, Is. VI, 2.	Heb 1:7
7		**aquae multae non potuerunt extinguere charitatem, nec flumina obruent illam**	
290	*ST* Ia-IIae, q. 68, a. 1	Dixerunt quod virtutes ordinantur ad bene operandum, dona vero ad resistendum tentationibus. Sed nec ista distinctio sufficit. Quia etiam virtutes tentationibus resistunt, inducentibus ad peccata, quae contrariantur virtutibus, unumquodque enim resistit naturaliter suo contrario. Quod praecipue patet de caritate, de qua dicitur Cantic. VIII, '***Aquae multae non potuerunt extinguere caritatem***'.	"Utrum dono differant a virtutibus?"
291	*Q. de virt.*, q. 2, a. 12, arg. 11	See [no. 269]	
292	In orationem dominicam, p. 6 (n° 1100)	[Deus] regit autem hominem ne inducatur in tentationem per fervorem caritatis: quia quaelibet caritas quantumcumque parva, potest resistere cuilibet peccato. Cant. VIII, 7 '***Aquae multae non potuerunt extinguere caritatem***'.	
293	*De decem praeceptis*, IV (p. 72)	Manifestum est enim quod quando gravia pro eo quem vere diligimus, sustinemus, amor ipse non destruitur, immo crescit. Unde in Cant., '***Aque multe***', idest tribulationes et adversitates, '***non potuerunt extinguere caritatem***'. Et ideo sancti viri qui adversitates pro Deo sustinent magis in eius dilectione firmantur, sicut artifex illud artificiatum magis diligit in quo magis laborat.	

294	*In ad Ro.*, c. 8, lect. 7 (n° 722)	'Quis ergo nos separabit a charitate Christi?' Qua scilicet Christum diligimus et proximum, secundum quod ipse praecepit, Io. XIII, 34 'Mandatum novum do vobis', et cetera. Alio modo sic: dictum est, quod magna beneficia Deus sanctis suis confert, ex quorum consideratione adeo charitas Christi in cordibus nostris fervet, quod nihil eam extinguere potest. Cant. ult. '***Aquae multae non potuerunt extinguere charitatem***'.	Rom 8:35
295	*In 1 ad Co.*, c. 13, lect. 2 (n° 772)	Quantum ergo ad tolerantiam malorum, dicit 'Charitas patiens est', id est facit patienter tolerari mala. Cum enim homo diligit aliquem propter eius amorem, de facili tolerat quaecumque difficilia; et similiter qui diligit Deum, propter eius amorem patienter tolerat quaecumque adversa. Unde et Cant. VIII, 7 dicitur '***Aquae multae non poterunt extinguere charitatem, nec flumina obruent eam***'. Iac. I, 4 'Patientia opus perfectum.'	1 Cor 13:4
296	*In 2 ad Co.*, c. 2, lect. 1 (n° 49)	Et ratio quare noluit eos contristare est illa qua dominus noluit ieiunare discipulos suos, scilicet ad hoc, ut amore et non timore afficerentur ad Christum, et iungerentur sibi. Voluit enim eos dominus firmare et nutrire in fide, in omni dulcedine et desiderio cordis, et sic, firmati ex amore, non de facili avellerentur propter tribulationes, quia '***Aquae multae non potuerunt extinguere charitatem***', Cant. VIII, 7.	2 Cor 2:1
297	*In ad Ep.*, c. 3, lect. 5 (n° 179)	'Longitudo' autem eius attenditur quantum ad sui perseverantiam, quia numquam deficit, sed hic incipit et perficitur in gloria. I Cor. XIII, 8 'Charitas numquam excidit'. Cant. ult. '***Aquae multae non potuerunt extinguere charitatem***'.	Eph 3:18
298	*In 1 ad Th.*, Prol. (n° 1)	Secundo aqua extinguit ignem. Eccli. XXX: 'Ignem ardentem extinguit aqua'. Sic tribulationes extinguunt impetus concupiscentiarum, ne homines ad libitum eas sequantur, sed non extinguunt veram charitatem Ecclesiae. Cant. VIII, 7: '***Aquae multae non poterunt extinguere charitatem, nec flumina obruent illam***'.	Gen 7:17 (theme of the Prologue)
* 298'	*Catena in Matthaeum*, 17, 30	Rabanus. Mihi autem videtur, iuxta tropologiam, lunaticus esse qui per horarum momenta mutatur ad vitia; et nunc quidem in ignem fertur, quo adulterantium corda succensa sunt, nunc in aquas, scilicet voluptatum, vel cupiditatum, ***quae non valent extinguere caritatem***.	Mt 17:15–16 Cf. Jerome, *Commentariorum in Matheum libri IV*, III, 17, 16 (CCSL 77, pp. 151–52)

		si dederit homo omnem substantiam domus suae pro dilectione, quasi nihil eam despiciet	
299	*SCG* III, c. 130 (n° 3023)	Cum enim mens vehementer amore et desiderio alicuius rei afficitur, consequens est quod alia postponat. Ex hoc igitur quod mens hominis amore et desiderio ferventer in divina fertur, in quo perfectionem constare manifestum est, consequitur quod omnia quae ipsum possunt retardare quominus feratur in Deum, abiiciat: non solum rerum curam, et uxoris et prolis affectum, sed etiam sui ipsius. Et hoc significant verba Scripturae. Dicitur enim Cant. 8, 7 '***Si dederit homo omnem substantiam domus suae ad mercandam dilectionem, quasi nihil computabit eam***'. Et Matth. 13, 45 'Simile est regnum caelorum homini negotiatori quaerenti bonas margaritas: inventa autem una pretiosa margarita, abiit et vendidit omnia quae habuit, et comparavit eam'. Et Philipp. 3, 7 'Quae mihi aliquando fuerunt lucra, arbitratus sum ut stercora ut Christum lucrifacerem'.	"De consiliis quae dantur in lege divina"
300	*De perfectione spiritualis vitae*, c. 16, lines 11–20 [18–20] (p. B 88)	Sunt enim aliqui qui exteriora bona contemnunt propter proximorum dilectionem, dum vel ea particulariter proximis administrant, vel totaliter omnia necessitatibus erogant proximorum: quod videtur Apostolus tangere cum dicit, I ad Cor. XIII, 3 'Si tradidero in cibos pauperum omnes facultates meas'; et Cant. VIII dicitur '***Si dederit homo omnem substantiam domus suae pro dilectione, quasi nihil despiciet illam***'.	"Quod esse in statu perfectionis convenit episcopis et religiosis"
301	*In Matth.*, c. 13, lect. 4 (n° 1192)	Quando per fidem invenerit 'prae gaudio vadit', et incipit proficere 'et vendit omnia', idest contemnit, ut spiritualia habeat, 'et emit agrum illum'; hoc est vel bonam societatem sibi exquirit, vel emit sibi otium quod non habet, scilicet pacem spiritualem. Ad Phil. III, 8 'Omnia arbitratus sum ut stercora, ut Christum lucrifacerem'; Cant. VIII, 7 '***Si dederit homo omnem substantiam domus suae pro dilectione, quasi nihil despiciet eam***' et cetera.	Mt 13:46
302	*In ad Ro.*, c. 12, lect. 2 (n° 985)	Et primo quantum ad interiorem affectum, cum dicit 'Charitatem fraternitatis invicem diligentes'; ut scilicet non solum fratres diligamus per charitatem sed etiam diligamus ipsam charitatem, qua eos diligimus et ab eis diligimur. Sic enim si charam habemus charitatem, non de facili eam dissolvi faciemus. Hebr. ult. 'Charitas fraternitatis maneat in vobis'. Cant. ult. '***Si dederit homo omnem substantiam domus suae pro dilectione, tamquam nihil despiciet illam***'.	Rom 12:10

303	*In 1 ad Th.*, c. 1, lect. 1 (n° 16)	Et ideo dicit 'in tribulatione multa cum gaudio', id est, quamvis multa tribulatio immineret propter verbum, tamen illud accepistis cum gaudio. Iac. I, 2: 'Omne gaudium existimate, fratres mei, cum in tentationes varias incideritis', et cetera. Act. V, 41 'Ibant apostoli gaudentes a conspectu Concilii, quoniam digni habiti sunt pro nomine Iesu contumeliam pati'. 'Cum gaudio', inquam, 'Spiritus sancti', non alio quocumque, qui est amor Dei, qui facit gaudium patientibus propter Christum, quia amant eum. Cant. VIII, 7 '***Si dederit homo omnem substantiam domus suae pro dilectione, quasi nihil despiciet eam***'.	1 Thes 1:6
9		**si ostium est compingamus illud tabulis cedrinis.**	
304	*In Ioan.*, c. 10, lect. 2 (n° 1387)	Resumit autem quod dixit 'Ego sum ostium'. Cantic. ult., 9 '***Si est ostium, compingamus illud tabulis cedrinis***', idest attribuamus ei virtutem imputrescibilem.	Jn 10:9
10		**ego murus et ubera sicut turris**	
305	*In Ier.*, c. 1, 5 (p. 582)	See [no. 130]	
		ex quo facta sum coram eo quasi pacem reperiens	
306	*In ad Ga.*, c. 5, lect. 6 (n° 330)	'Gaudete in domino semper', et cetera. Gaudium autem istud debet esse perfectum. Et ad hoc duo requiruntur. Primo ut res amata sufficiens sit amanti propter suam perfectionem. Et quantum ad hoc dicit 'pax'. Tunc enim amans pacem habet, quando rem amatam sufficienter possidet. Cant. ult. '***Ex quo facta sum coram eo quasi pacem reperiens***', et cetera.	Gal 5:22
307	*In ad Ga.*, c. 6, lect. 5 (n° 376)	'Pax super illos', scilicet gloriantes quia nonnisi in Christo gloriantur. Pax, inquam, qua quietentur et perficiantur in bono. Pax enim est tranquillitas mentis. Cant. VIII, 10 '***Ex quo facta sum coram illo quasi pacem reperiens***'. Col. III, 15 'Pax Christi exultet in cordibus vestris, in qua', et cetera.	Gal 6:16
308	*In ad He.*, c. 12, lect. 4 (n° 706)	Ibi enim erit visio experimentalis pacis, quia nihil erit perturbans sive interius sive exterius. Unde dicitur civitas Dei, id est, civium unitas. Ps. CXXI, 3 'Ierusalem, quae aedificatur ut civitas'. Item CXLVII, 1 'Lauda, Ierusalem, dominum, lauda Deum tuum, Sion'. Sequitur: Qui posuit fines tuos pacem et adipe frumenti satiat te'. Gal. IV, 26 'Illa, quae sursum est, Ierusalem libera est'. Unde nihil ultra erit desiderandum. Cant. VIII, 10 '***Ex quo facta sum coram eo quasi pacem reperiens***'.	Heb 12:22
11		**vinea fuit pacifico in ea quae habet populos**	
309	*In Is.*, c. 5, line 141 (p. 39)	See [no. 105]	

12		vinea mea coram me est	
310	*In IV Sent.*, d. 49, q. 5, a. 3, qlc 3, s.c. 2 (p. 1238)	Praeterea, Cant. 8 super illud '***Vinea mea est coram me***', dicit Glossa: 'Ostendit quid singularis praemii doctoribus ejus disponit'. Ergo doctores habebunt singulare praemium; et hoc vocamus aureolam.	"Utrum doctoribus aureola debeatur?" *Glossa ordinaria in Canticum*, VIII, 107 (CCCM 170, p. 407)
311	*In Matth.*, c. 20, lect. 1 (n° 1623)	Primo quaeritur quae sit vinea, qui operarii, quare conducti. Quid sit vinea ista. Secundum Chrysostomum iustitia est, et quot virtutes producit, tot palmites emittit; Cant. VIII, 12 '***Vinea mea coram me est***'.	Mt 20:1 [pseudo] John Chrysostom, *Opus imperfectum in Matthaeum, Homelia XXXIV* (PG 56, col. 817)
13		**amici auscultant; fac me audire vocem tuam,**	
312	*In Ioan.*, c. 8, lect. 5 (n° 1238)	See [no. 100]	

313	Principium *Hic est liber* (Marietti, n° 1207)	Commendatur nobis sapientia, et hoc in libro sapientiae; vel sapientiae praecepta proponuntur, et hoc in tribus libris Salomonis: qui quidem distinguuntur secundum tres gradus virtutum quos Plotinus distinguit; quia praecepta sapientiae non nisi de actibus virtutum esse debent. In primo gradu, secundum eum, sunt virtutes politicae, quibus homo moderate rebus mundi utitur et inter homines conversatur; et secundum hoc est liber proverbiorum. In secundo gradu sunt virtutes purgatoriae, quibus homo se a rebus mundi exuit per contemptum; et secundum hoc est Ecclesiastes qui ad contemptum mundi ordinatur, ut patet per Hieronymum in prologo. In tertio gradu sunt virtutes purgati animi, quibus homo, saeculi curis penitus calcatis, in sola sapientiae contemplatione delectatur; ***et quantum ad hoc sunt cantica***.	
314	*In Is.*, In Prol. S. Iheronimi, lines 20–21 (p. 5)	'Metro ligari': metrum grece, mensura dicitur, unde illud dicitur metrice describi ubi servatur certa mensura pedum, sillabarum, et temporum; a qua lege prophete soluti sunt. 'Et aliquid habere de Psalmis', idest eis simile, 'vel operibus Salomonis', quantum ad finem Proverbiorum ***et in Canticis canticorum***.	See *Biblia sacra iuxta Latinam Vulgatam editionem*, p.1096

Appendix 2

Transcription of the Latin text of the Prologue of the *Postilla super Cantica canticorum* of Hugh of Saint-Cher

Deus in gradibus ejus, cognoscetur. Ita dicit alia editio, ubi nostra habet, Deus in domibus eius cognoscetur. Sunt autem tres illi gradus, scilicet, initiata Sapientia, provecta Sapientia, et consummata Sapientia. Hac autem triplici Sapentia, quasi tribus gradibus ascenditur ad Dei cognitionem. In primo gradu sunt incipientes; in secundo proficientes; in tertio perfecti. Primus gradus Sapientiae docet bene et licite mundo uti. Secundus, bene et utilius mundum contemnere et calcare. Tertius, in solis Sponsi amplexibus et osculis jucundari. Primum gradum ascendimus in Proverbiis. Secundum in Ecclesiaste. Tertium docemur ascendere in hoc libro. Juxta hunc igitur triplicem gradum Sapientiae, Salomon tres libros edidit. Proverbia, ubi docet et instruit parvulos et incipientes, qualiter in mundo pacifice conversentur, et a malo abstineant. Unde et ibi dicitur: 'Sapientia foris praedicat, dicens: Usquequo parvuli diligitis infantiam et stulti ea, quae sibi noxia sunt, cupient: et imprudentes odibunt scientiam? Convertimini ad correptionem meam etc' cap 1 c. Ecclesiasten, ubi instruit proficentes et grandjusculos de contemptu mundi. Unde incipit: 'Vanitas vanitatum, etc'. Cantica Canticorum, ubi maturos et perfectos de solo amore instrui. Unde ab osculo, quod est signum amoris, incipiens ait: 'Osculetur me osculo oris sui'. Et secundum hoc triplex opus, triplici censetur vocabulo Salomon, id est, pacificus, juxta Proverbia, ubi pacifice conversari in mundo hortatur. Ecclesiastes, id est, Concionator, juxta Ecclesiasten, ubi quasi in concione et consilio discordantes ad concordiam vocat. Idida, id est, dilectus Domini, juxta Cantica Canticorum, ubi affectiones et desideria caeteraeque amoris sequelae mutuaque amantium colloquia interscaliter exprimuntur.

Ex jam dictis patet, quis sit auctor hujus libri; quoniam Salomon. Restat ergo videre, quae sit eius intentio in hoc libro, quae materia, et quis finis, quis modus agendi, quis libri titulus, et cui parti Philosophiae supponatur.

Intentio igitur Salomonis in hoc libro est, exhortari Sponsam, id est, Ecclesiam ad amplexus et oscula Sponsi, quod est signum perfecti amoris. Quadruplex quidem est amor, scilicet, divinus, sive aethereus, vel coelestis, qui charitas appelatur; et hic in praecepto consistens, meritorius est in usu suo. Secundus venenosus, libidinosus, diabolicus, et hic in prohibitione consistens, damnabilis est. Tertius est carnalis, quo quis carnem propriam, vel parentes diligit. Et hic quidem si moderatus est, sub Deo est, et tolerabilis; si immoderatus, reprobabilis et damnosus. Quartus est mundanus: qui si moderatus sit, licitus est et concessus; si immoderatus, detestabilis et perniciosus. Unde Iacob. 4: 'Amicitia hujus mundi inimica est Deo'.

Materia hujus libri est Sponsus et Sponsa, quasi Christus et Ecclesia. Sunt autem quatuor personae, et sibi mutuo colloquentes inducuntur in hoc libro. Sponsus et sodales ejus, qui et paranymphi, sive amici Sponsi dicuntur, Sponsam commonentes et adjuvantes, ne cum alio fornicetur; sed soli Sponso cohaereat. 'Coangustatum est enim stratum, ita ut aliter decidat, et pallium breve utrumque operire non potest' (Is 28, 20). Sponsa et adolescentulae eius per quas signantur imperfecti, in fide teneri, qui Deum plene diligere, mundi mala aequanimiter sustinere nondum sciunt; tamen exhibent se humiles, ut Sponsam pro modulo suo imitentur. Congruum enim erat, ut in nuptiis esset cum Sponso juvenum turba, et cum Sponsa adolescentularum laudabilis multitudo. Sponsus Christus est; Sponsa vero Ecclesia, sodales sponsi Angeli, et omnes qui jam in virum perfectum pervenerunt; adolescentulae sunt incipientes. Sponsa etiam Ecclesia, vel quaelibet fidelis anima. Et notandum, quod sponsa semper in domo, vel in lecto, vel in aliquo interiori loco cum Sponso manere concupiscit quod bene mulieribus congruit. Sponsus vero sicut vir ad forinseca vinearum, vel aliqua hujusmodi opera Sponsam evocat. Nec est mirum, Ecclesia enim, si fieri possit, in tranquillitate pacis Domino sobolem educare desiderat. At ipse eam in praesenti crebris tentationibus et persecutionibus vult exerceri, quo mundior ad aeterna perveniat, et ne si omnia prospera contingerent, incolatu praesentis exilii delectata, minus ad coelestem patriam suspiraret.

Finis hujus libri est dilectio Dei, ad quam invitat Salomon. De qua in fine libri hujus dicitur : 'Fortis ut mors dilectio'.

Modus agendi talis est: paucus est in sermone, multos in sententia, procedens interscalariter, nunc Sponsum loquentem inducens, nunc Sponsam, nunc adolescentulas respondentes, nunc mutuo colloquentes.

Titulus talis est: Incipiunt Cantica Canticorum, sive Canticum canticorum, sic dictum per excellentiam dignitatis. Multa enim sunt Cantica: sed inter alia tria praecipua, duo Moysi, et tertium Salomonis. Primum canticum est de egressu vitiorum. Unde Moyses in exitu Israel de Aegypto, transito mari, Exod. 15 cecinit dicens: 'Cantemus Domino gloriose enim magnificatus est; equum, et ascensorem dejecit in mare'. Secundum Canticum est in progressu virtutum, et bonorum operum. Unde et Moyses in deserto vicinus terrae promissionis cecinit, dicens: 'Audite coeli, quae loquar, audiat terra verba oris mei' Deut. 32. Tertium Canticum est in consummatione virtutum. Unde et Salomon Epithalamium Sponsi et Sponsae amorose decantans, ait: 'Osculetur me osculo oris sui'. Vel certe ideo Canticum Canticorum dicitur, quia inter cantilenas, sive Cantica Salomonis, ultimum est. Tres enim libri Salomonis, quasi tres cantilenae, sive tria Cantica dicuntur, inter quae ultimum est Canticum illud. In primo canitur cantilena activis, in tertio contemplativis, in medio transeuntibus de activa ad contemplativam. In primo incipit Deus diligi quasi Pater. Unde crebro nomen filii exprimitur ibi. In secundo honorari, ut Medicus. In tertio desiderari, ut Sponsus. In Proverbiis enim Salomon fuit Ethicus, tractans de moribus, quasi pater filios instruens. In Ecclesiaste fuit Physicus, naturas rerum discernens id est Medicus aegrotum sanans, a mundanis nos prohibens. In Canticis Canticorum fuit Theologus, de divino amore pertractans. Unde et liber iste Canticum amoris dicitur a quibusdam. Et iste ternariusCanticorum signatus fuit in verbis Domini, quibus ait ad Moysen, Exod 19: 'Sanctifica populum hodie, et cras, et sint parati in diem tertium'. Duobus diebus jubebatur, sanctificari populus, ut tertia die dignus esset legem recipere, et videre gloriam Dei. Sanctificatione primae diei, sanctificantur illi, qui nondum mundo penitus abrenunciantes, Deum tamen omnibus, quae mundi sunt, praeponentes mundo licite utuntur, ut incipientes. Sanctificatione secundae diei, sanctificantur illi, qui mundum fugiunt, et contemnunt, ut proficientes. Sanctificatione tertiae diei sanctificantur illi, qui mundo penitus conculcatuo levant se supra se, ut perfecti, qui jam Deum quodammodo revelata facie speculantur.

Cui autem parti Philosophiae supponatur hic liber, jam patet; quoniam Theologiae totaliter.

Quia autem liber iste quandoque singulariter Canticum Canticorum, quandoque pluraliter Cantica Canticorum nominatur, inde est, quia et unum est, et multa. Unum propter unitatem cantus, quia quicquid hic canitur, amor est, qui est vinculum unionis. Multa propter diversitates personarum canentium, quae sunt quatuor, ut dictum est supra: Sponsus et Sponsa, sodales Sponsi et juvenculae vel adolescentulae Sponsae.

Salomon igitur luce Sapientiae et Spiritu prophetiae illustratus, adventum Christi in carnem praevidens, in persona antiquorum adventum istum desiderantium, et expectantium, et deprecantium ait: 'Osculetur, etc.'.

Works Cited

Association catholique française pour l'étude de la Bible. *Les nouvelles voies de l'exégèse: En lisant le Cantique des cantiques*. Paris: Cerf, 2002.

Aillet, Marc. *Lire la Bible avec S. Thomas, Le passage de la* littera *à la* res *dans la "Somme théologique"*. Fribourg: Editions universitaires, 1993.

Alan of Lille [Alanus de Insulis]. *Elucidatio in Cantica canticorum*. In *Opera Omnia*. PL 210. Edited by J.-P. Migne, col. 52–108. Paris, 1833.

Ambrose. *Expositio evangelii secundum Lucam. Fragmenta in Esaiam*. Edited by M. Adriaen and P.A. Ballerini. CCSL 14. Turnhout: Brepols, 1957.

Anselm of Canterbury. *Opera omnia*. Edited by Franciscus Salesius Schmitt. Edinburg: Thomam Nelson et filios, 1938–1951.

Apponius. *Commentaire sur le Cantique des cantiques*. Vol. 1, *Books I–III*. Edited by and translated by Bernard de Vregille, SJ, and Louis Neyrand, SJ. Sources Chrétiennes 420. Paris: Cerf, 1997.

———. *Commentaire sur le Cantique des cantiques*. Vol. 2, *Books IV–VIII*. Edited by and translated by Bernard de Vregille, SJ, and Louis Neyrand, SJ. Sources Chrétiennes 421. Paris: Cerf, 1997.

Aquinas, Thomas. *See* Thomas Aquinas.

Augustine. *The City of God*. Translated by Marcus Dods. New York: Modern Library, 1993.

———. *Epistulae. Pars IV, Ep. 185–270*. Edited by A. Goldbacher. CSEL 57. Vienna: F. Tempsky, 1911.

———. *Expositions on the Book of Psalms*. Translated by J. E. Tweed et al. Edited by A. Cleveland Coxe. Vol. 8 of Nicene and Post-Nicene Fathers (First Series). Peabody, Mass.: Hendrickson, 1995.

———. *Four Anti-Pelagian Writings: On Nature and Grace, On the Proceedings of Pelagius, On the Predestination of Saints, On the Gift of Perseverance*. Translated by John A. Mourant and William J. Collinge. Washington, D.C.: The Catholic University of America Press, 1992.

———. *Homilies on the Gospel of John 1–40*. Translated by Edmund Hill, OP. Edited by Allan D. Fitzgerald, OSA. Hyde Park, N.Y.: New City Press, 2009.

———. *Homélies sur l'évangile de Jean*. Edited by Marie-François Berrouard. Bibliothèque Augustinienne 74A. Turnhout: Brepols, 1993.

———. *Homilies on the Gospel of John*. Translated by John Gibb and James Innes. In *Augustin: Homilies on the Gospel of John, Homilies on the First Epistle of John, Soliloquies*, edited by Philip Schaff, 7–452. Vol. 7 of Nicene and Post-Nicene Fathers (first series). Peabody, Mass.: Hendrickson, 1995.

———. *In Iohannis evangelium tractatus CXXIV*. Edited by R. Willems. CCSL 36. Turnhout: Brepols, 1954.

———. *De peccatorum et remissione et de baptismo parvulorum ad Marcellinum libri tres ; De spiritu et littera liber unus ; De natura et gratia liber unus ; De natura et origine animae libri quattuor ; Contra duas epistulas pelagianorum libri quattuor.* Edited by Carolus F. Urba and Iosephus Zycha. CSEL 60. Vienna: F. Tempsky, 1913.

———. *Sancti Augustini sermones post Maurinos reperti: Probatae dumtaxat auctoritatis nunc primum disquisiti in unum collecti et codicum fide instaurati*. Edited by Germain Morin. Rome: Tipografia Poliglotta Vaticana, 1930.

———. *Sermons*. Vol. 4, *94A–147A, on the New Testament*. Translated by Edmund Hill, OP. Edited by John E. Rotelle, OSA. Brooklyn, N.Y.: New City Press, 1992.

———. *Sancti Aurelii Augustini Hipponensis Episcopi Opera Omnia. . . .* Vol. 5, *Sermonum classes quator, necnon sermones dubii*. Edited by J.-P. Migne. PL 38. Paris, 1841.

Auwers, Jean-Marie, ed. *Regards croisés sur le Cantique des cantiques*. Brussels: Lessius, 2005.

Bataillon, Louis-Jacques, OP, Gilbert Dahan, and Pierre-Marie Gy, OP, eds. *Hugues de Saint-Cher (1263), bibliste et théologien*. Turnhout: Brepols, 2004.

Bede the Venerable. *In Cantica canticorum*. In *Opera exegetica*, vol. 2B, *In Tobiam, In Proverbia, In Cantica Canticorum, In Habacuc*, edited by J. E. Hudson and D. Hurst, 166–375. CCSL 119B. Turnhout: Brepols, 1983.

Bell, David N. "Twelfth-Century Commentaries on the Song of Songs and the Nature of Monastic Spirituality: A Reassessment." In Guglielmetti, *Il Cantico dei cantici nel Medioevo*, 371–96.

Bellamah, Timothy F., OP. "The Interpretation of a Contemplative: Thomas' Commentary *Super Iohannem*." In Roszak and Vijgen, *Reading Sacred Scripture with Thomas Aquinas*, 229–55.

Benedict XVI. "General Audience on Rupert of Deutz," Wednesday, December 9, 2009. http://w2.vatican.va/content/benedict-xvi/en/audiences/2009/documents/hf_ben-xvi_aud_20091209.html.

Bernard of Clairvaux. *Opera omnia*. Edited byJ. Leclercq, C. H. Talbot, and H. M. Rochais. Rome: Editiones cistercienses, 1957–1977.

———. "Sermo De nativitate beatae Mariae." *Sermones II*. In *Opera omnia*, vol. 5. Rome, 1968.

———. *On the Song of Songs I*. Translated by Kilian Walsh, OCSO. Kalamazoo, Mich.: Cistercian Publications, 1971.

———. *On the Song of Songs III*. Translated by Kilian Walsh, OCSO, and Irene M. Edmonds. Kalamazoo, Mich.: Cistercian Publications, 1979.

Biblia sacra iuxta Latinam Vulgatam editionem. Stuttgart: Deutsche Bibelgesellschaft, 1994

Biffi, Inos. *I Misteri di Cristo in Tommaso d'Aquino: La Costruzione della teologia*. Vol. 1. Milan: Jaca Book, 1994.

Bonino, Serge-Thomas, OP. *Dieu, "Celui qui est"*. Paris: Parole et Silence, 2016.

———. "Les passions dans la théologie de saint Thomas d'Aquin: L'enseignement de la *Lectura super Ioannem*." In *Le emozioni secondo san Tommaso*, edited by S.-T. Bonino and G. Mazzotta. 7–25. Rome: Urbaniana University Press, 2019.

Crouzel, Henri, SJ. Introduction to Origen's *Commentaire sur la Cantique des Cantiques*. Sources Chrétiennes 375. Translated by Luc Brésard, OCSO, and Henri Crouzel, SJ, with the collaboration of M. Borret. Paris: Cerf, 1991.

Dahan, Gilbert. *L'Exégèse chrétienne de la Bible en Occident médiéval: XIIe–XIVe siècle*. Paris: Cerf, 1999.

———. "L'exégèse de Hugues: Méthode et herméneutique." In Bataillon et al., *Hugues de Saint-Cher (1263), bibliste et théologien*, 65–99.

———. "Introduction: Exégèse et théologie dans le commentaire de Thomas d'Aquin sur la Seconde Épître aux Corinthiens." In Thomas Aquinas, *Commentaire de la Deuxième Épître aux Corinthiens*, i–xli.

———. "Recherches sur l'exégèse du Cantique au XIIIe siècle." In Guglielmetti, *Il Cantico dei cantici nel Medioevo*, 493–536.

Dauphinais, Michael, and Matthew Levering, eds. *Reading John with St. Thomas Aquinas: Theological Exegesis and Speculative Theology*. Washington, D.C.: The Catholic University of America Press, 2005.

de Lubac, Henri, SJ. *Medieval Exegesis: The Four Senses of Scripture*. Vol. 1. Translated by Mark Sebanc. Grand Rapids, Mich.: Eerdmans, 1998.

Del Punta, Francesco, Silvia Donati and Concetta Luna. "Egidio Romano." In *Dizionario Biografico degli Italiani*, vol. 42, 319–41. Rome: Istituto dell'Enciclopedia Italiana, 1993.

Dezzuto, Carlo. "Il Cantico dei cantici nel XII secolo: Una presenza davvero significativa." *Studia monastica* 48 (2006): 59–99.

Dionysius. *Corpus Dionysiacum*. Vol. 1, *Pseudo-Dionysius Areopagita De divinis nominibus*. Edited by B. R. Suchla. Patristische Texte und Studien 33. Berlin: De Gruyter, 1990. Translated into English as *The Divine Names*, in Pseudo-Dionysius, *The Complete Works*, translated by Colm Luibheid with Paul Rorem, 47–131 (New York: Paulist Press, 1987).

———. *Corpus Dionysiacum*. Vol. 2, *Pseudo-Dionysius Areopagita De coelesti hierarchia, De ecclesiastica hierarchia, De mystica theologia, Epistulae*. Edited by G. Heil and A. M. Ritter. Patristische Texte und Studien 36. Berlin: De Gruyter, 1991.

Francis de Sales. *Treatise on the Love of God.* Translated by Henry Benedict Mackey, OSB. Rockford, Ill.: TAN Books, 1997.

Glossa ordinaria. Pars 22, In Canticum Canticorum. Edited by M. Dove. CCCM 170. Turnhout: Brepols, 1997.

The Glossa ordinaria on the Song of Songs. Translated by Mary Dove. Kalamazoo, Mich.: Medieval Institute Publications, 2004.

Gondreau, Paul. *The Passions of Christ's Soul in the Theology of St. Thomas Aquinas.* Münster: Aschendorff, 2002.

Gregory the Great. *Homélies sur Ezéchiel.* II. Sources Chrétiennes 360. Paris: Cerf, 1990.

———. *Homiliae in Hiezechielem prophetam.* Edited by M. Adriaen. CCSL 142. Turnhout: Brepols, 1971.

———. *Moral Reflections on the Book of Job.* Vols. 1–5. Translated by Brian Kerns, OCSO. Collegeville, Minn.: Liturgical Press, 2014–2019.

———. *Moralia in Iob, Libri I–X.* Edited by M. Adriaen. CCSL 143A. Turnhout: Brepols, 1979.

———. *On the Song of Songs.* Translated by Mark DelCogliano. Collegeville, Minn.: Liturgical Press, 2012.

Guglielmetti, Rossana E., ed. *La tradizione manoscritta dei commenti latini al Cantico dei cantici (origini–XII secolo): Repertorio dei codici contenenti testi inediti o editi solo nella "patrologia latina."* Florence: Sismel, 2006.

———. *Il Cantico dei cantici nel Medioevo.* Florence: Sismel, 2008.

Guillaume de Tocco. *Ystoria sancti Thome de Aquino.* Critical edition. Edited by Claire Le Brun–Gouvanic. Toronto: Pontifical Institute of Mediaeval Studies, 1996.

Hagedorn, Anselm C., ed. *Perspectives on the Song of Songs.* New York: De Gruyter, 2005.

Hugo de Sancto Charo [Hugh of Saint-Cher]. *Postillae in Bibliam.* Vol. 3, *In libros Proverbiorum, Ecclesiastae, Canticorum, Sapientiae, Ecclesiastici.* Venice: Pezzana, 1703.

Jerome [Hieronymus]. *Commentary on Ecclesiastes.* Translated by Richard Goodrich and David J. D. Miller. New York: Paulist Press, 2012.

———. *Commentariorum in Matheum libri IV.* Edited by D. Hurst and M. Adriaen. CCSL 77. Turnhout: Brepols, 1969.

———. *Epistola 66 ad Pammachium.* In *Epistulae 1–70,* edited by Isidorus Hilberg, 647–65. CSEL 54. Vienna: F. Tempsky, 1910.

———. *Tractatus in Marci Evangelium.* Edited by G. Morin. In *Tractatus sive homiliae in psalmos. In Marci evangelium. Alia varia argumenta,* edited by G. Morin, B. Capelle, and J. Fraipont. CCSL 78. Turnhout: Brepols, 1958.

John Chrysostom. *Homilies on the Gospel of John.* Translated by G. T. Stupart. In *Chrysostom: Homilies on the Gospel of Saint John and the Epistle to the Hebrews,* edited by Philip Schaff, 1–334. Vol. 14 of Nicene and Post-Nicene Fathers (First Series). Peabody, Mass.: Hendrickson, 1995.

John Chrysostom [pseudo]. *Opus imperfectum in Matthaeum*, Homelia XXXIV. Edited by J.-P. Migne. PG 56. Paris, 1865.

La Bonnardière, A.-M. "Le Cantique des cantiques dans l'œuvre de saint Augustin." *Revue d'Études augustiniennes et patristiques* 1 (1955): 225–37.

Labourdette, Marie-Michel, OP. *Cours de théologie morale: Les principes des actes humains (Ia-IIae, q. 49–70); Habitus et vertus*. Paris: Parole et Silence, 2017.

Laurent, Marie-Hyacinthe, OP, ed. *Fontes vitae S. Thomae Aquinatis, fasc. IV. Processus canonizationis S. Thomae Neapoli*. Saint-Maximin: Revue thomiste, 1937.

LaVere, Suzanne *Out of the Cloister: Monastic Exegesis of the Song of Songs 1100–1250*. Leiden: Brill, 2016.

Leanza, Sandro. "La classificazione dei libre salomonici e i suoi riflessi sulla questione dei rapporti tra Bibbia e scienze profane, da Origene agli scrittori medievali." *Augustinianum* 14, no. 3 (1974): 651–66.

Levering, Matthew. *Scripture and Metaphysics: Aquinas and the Renewal of Trinitarian Theology*. Oxford: Blackwell, 2004.

———. *Paul in the "Summa Theologiae"*. Washington, D.C.: The Catholic University of America Press, 2014.

———. "Mystagogy and Aquinas's *Commentary on Isaiah*: Initiating God's People into Christ." In *Initiation and Mystagogy in Thomas Aquinas: Scriptural, Systematic, Sacramental and Moral, and Pastoral Perspectives*, edited by Henk Schoot, Jacco Verburgt, and Jörgen Vijgen, 17–40. Leuven: Peeters, 2019.

Levering, Matthew, and Michael Dauphinais, eds. *Reading Romans with St. Thomas Aquinas*. Washington, D.C.: The Catholic University of America Press, 2012.

Levering, Matthew, Piotr Roszak, and Jörgen Vijgen. *Reading Job with St. Thomas Aquinas*. Washington, D.C.: The Catholic University of America Press, 2020.

Lobrichon, Guy. "Espaces de lecture du Cantique des cantiques dans l'Occident médiéval (IXe–XVe siècle)." In Association catholique française pour l'étude de la Bible, *Les nouvelles voies de l'exégèse*, 197–216.

Loiseau, Stéphane. *De l'écoute à la parole: La lecture biblique dans la doctrine sacrée selon Thomas d'Aquin*. Paris: Cerf, 2017.

Lombardo, Nicholas, OP. *The Logic of Desire: Aquinas on Emotions*. Washington, D.C.: The Catholic University of America Press, 2011.

Macrobius. *Commentaria in Somnium Scipionis*. Edited by F. Eyssenhardt. Leipzig: Teubner, 1868.

Matis, Hannah W. *The Song of Songs in the Early Middle Ages*. Leiden: Brill, 2019.

Matter, E. Ann. *The Voice of My Beloved: The Song of Songs in Western Medieval Christianity*. Philadelphia: University of Pennsylvania Press, 1990.

Miner, Robert. *Thomas Aquinas on the Passions: A Study of "Summa Theologiae," 1a2ae 22–48*. Cambridge: Cambridge University Press, 2009.

Morard, Martin. "Thomas d'Aquin, lecteur des conciles." *Archivum franciscanum historicum* 98 (2005): 211–365.

Murphy, Roland E., O.Carm. *The Song of Songs: A Commentary of the Book of Canticles or the Song of Songs*. Minneapolis, Minn.: Fortress, 1990.

Norris, Richard A., Jr., ed. *The Song of Songs: Interpreted by Early Christian and Medieval Commentators*. Translated by Richard A. Norris, Jr. Grand Rapids, Mich.: Eerdmans, 2003.

Origen. *The Song of Songs: Commentary and Homilies*. Translated by R. P. Lawson. New York: Paulist Press, 1988.

———. *Commentaria in Evangelium secundum Matthaeum*. Vol. 17, PG 13, col. 1515.

Pelletier, Anne-Marie. *Lectures du Cantique des cantiques: De l'énigme du sens aux figures du lecteur*. Rome: Gregorian University Press, 1989.

----. "Petit bilan herméneutique de l'histoire du Cantique." In Auwers, *Regards croisés sur le Cantique des cantiques*, 130–47.

Petrus Lombardus [Peter Lombard]. *Sententiae in IV libris distinctae*. Vol. 2, *Liber III et IV*. Edited by the Fathers of the Collegium S. Bonaventurae. Spicilegium bonaventurianum 5. Grottaferrata (Rome): Quaracchi, 1981.

Pétré, Hélène. "*Ordinata caritas*: Un enseignement d'Origène sur la charité." *Recherches de science religieuse* 42 (1954): 40–57.

Prügl, Thomas. "Thomas Aquinas as Interpreter of Scripture." In *The Theology of Thomas Aquinas*, edited by Rik Van Nieuwenhove and Joseph Wawrykow, 386–415. Notre Dame, Ind.: University of Notre Dame Press, 2005.

Rabanus Maurus. *Commentaria in Matthaeum*. PL 107.

Riedlinger, Helmut. *Die Makellosigkeit der Kirche in den lateinischen Hohelied-kommentaren des Mittelsalters*. Münster: Aschendorff, 1958.

Roszak, Piotr. "The Place and Function of Biblical Citations in Thomas Aquinas's Exegesis." In Roszak and Vijgen, *Reading Sacred Scripture with Thomas Aquinas*, 115–39.

Roszak, Piotr, and Jörgen Vijgen, eds. *Reading Sacred Scripture with Thomas Aquinas: Hermeneutical Tools, Theological Questions and New Perspectives*. Turnhout: Brepols, 2015.

Rupert of Deutz. *Commentaria in Canticum canticorum*. CCCM 26. Turnhout: Brepols, 1974.

Ryan, Thomas F. *Thomas Aquinas as Reader of the Psalms*. Notre Dame, Ind.: University of Notre Dame Press, 2000.

Sabra, George. *Thomas Aquinas' Vision of the Church: Fundamentals of an Ecumenical Ecclesiology*. Mainz: Matthias-Grünewald-Verlag, 1987.

Savigni, Raffaele "Il commentario di Aimone di Auxerre al Cantico dei cantici e le sue fonti." In Guglielmetti, *Il Cantico dei cantici nel Medioevo*, 189–225.

Schwienhorst-Schönberger, Ludger. "Das Hohelied." In *Einleitung in das Alte Testament*, 8th ed., edited by Erich Zenger, 474–83. Stuttgart: W. Kohlhammer GmbH, 2011.

Sixtus Senensis, OP. *Bibliotheca sancta ex praecipuis Catholicae Ecclesiae auctoribus*. Naples: Ex Typographia Mutiana, 1742.

Smith, Lesley. *The "Glossa ordinaria": The Making of a Medieval Bible Commentary.* Boston: Brill, 2009.

Swanson, Jenny. "The *Glossa ordinaria.*" In *The Medieval Theologians: An Introduction to Theology in the Medieval Period,* edited by G. R. Evans, 156–67. Oxford: Blackwell, 2001.

Thomas Aquinas. *The Academic Sermons.* Translated by Mark-Robin Hoogland, CP. Washington, D.C.: The Catholic University of America Press, 2010.

———. *The Catechetical Instructions of St. Thomas.* Translated by Joseph Burns Collins. New York: J. F. Wagner, 1939.

———. *In Canticum canticorum expositio altera.* In *Sancti Thomae Aquinatis doctoris angelici Ordinis Praedicatorum opera omnia,* vol. 14, 387–426. Parma: Typis P. Fiaccadori, 1863.

———. *Commentaire de la Deuxième Épître aux Corinthiens.* Translated by Jean-Éric Stroobant de Saint-Éloy, OSB. Paris: Cerf, 2005.

———. *Commentary on the Gospel of John: Chapters 13–21.* Translated by Fabian R. Larcher, OP, and James A. Weisheipl, OP. Edited by Daniel A. Keating and Matthew Levering. Washington, D.C.: The Catholic University of America Press, 2010.

———. *Commentary on the Gospel of Matthew.* Translated by J. Holmes and B. Mortenson. Lander, Wyo.: The Aquinas Institute for the Study of Sacred Doctrine, 2013.

———. *Commentary on Isaiah.* Translated by Joshua Madden as "Saint Thomas Aquinas's *Expositio super Isaiam*: Introduction, Translation, and Notes." PhD diss., Ave Maria University, 2017.

———. *Commentary on the Letters of Saint Paul to the Corinthians.* Translated by Fabian R. Larcher, OP. Lander, Wyo.: The Aquinas Institute for the Study of Sacred Doctrine, 2012.

———. *Commentary on the Letters of Saint Paul to the Galatians and Ephesians.* Translated by Fabian R. Larcher, OP. Lander, Wyo.: The Aquinas Institute for the Study of Sacred Doctrine, 2012.

———. *Commentary on the Letter of Saint Paul to the Hebrews.* Translated by Fabian R. Larcher, OP. Lander, Wyo.: The Aquinas Institute for the Study of Sacred Doctrine, 2012.

———. *Commentary on the Letters of Saint Paul to the Philippians, Colossians, Thessalonians, Timothy, Titus, and Philemon.* Translated by Fabian R. Larcher, OP. Lander, Wyo.: The Aquinas Institute for the Study of Sacred Doctrine, 2012.

———. *Expositio super Iob ad litteram.* Leonine edition. Vol. 26. Rome: Ad Sanctae Sabinae, 1965.

———. *Liber contra impugnantes Dei cultum et religionem.* Translated by John Procter, OP. London: Sands & Co., 1902.

———. *Light of Faith: The Compendium of Theology.* Translated by Cyril Vollert, SJ. Manchester, N.H.: Sophia Institute Press, 1993.

———. *Principium "Hic est liber mandatorum Dei."* Translated by Ralph McInerny under the title "Commendation of and Division of Sacred Scripture." In *Thomas Aquinas: Selected Writings,* edited by Ralph McInerny, 5–12. London: Penguin, 1998.

———. *Summa Contra Gentiles: Book Three: Providence Part II.* Translated by Vernon J. Bourke. Notre Dame, Ind.: University of Notre Dame Press, 1975.

———. *Summa Contra Gentiles: Book Four: Salvation.* Translated by Charles J. O'Neil. Notre Dame, Ind.: University of Notre Dame Press, 1975.

———. *Summa Theologica.* Translated by The Fathers of the English Dominican Province. Westminster, Md.: Christian Classics, 1981.

———. *The Three Greatest Prayers: Commentaries on the Lord's Prayer, the Hail Mary, and the Apostles' Creed.* Translated by Laurence Shapcote, OP. Manchester, N.H.: Sophia Institute Press, 1990.

———. *Tomus tertiusdecimus divi Thomae Aquinatis doctoris angelici complectens Expositionem in Iob, In primam Davidis quinquagenam, In Cantica canticorum, In Isaiam, In Ieremiam et in Threnos.* Rome: Apud Iulium Accoltum, 1570.

Torrell, Jean-Pierre, OP. "Quand saint Thomas méditait sur le prophète Isaïe." *Recherches thomasiennes,* 242–81. Paris: J. Vrin, 2000.

———. *Encyclopédie Jesus le Christ chez saint Thomas.* Paris: Cerf, 2008.

———. *Initiation à saint Thomas d'Aquin.* Vol. 1, *Sa personne et son œuvre.* 3rd ed. Paris: Cerf, 2015. Available in English as *Saint Thomas Aquinas.* Vol. 1, *The Person and His Work. 3rd ed.* Translated by Robert Royal and Matthew Minerd. Washington, D.C.: The Catholic University of America Press, 2022.

———. *Saint Thomas d'Aquin.* Vol. 2, *Maître spirituel.* 3rd ed. Paris: Cerf, 2017. Earlier edition available in English as *Saint Thomas Aquinas.* Vol. 2, *Spiritual Master.* 2nd ed. Translated by Robert Royal. Washington, D.C.: The Catholic University of America Press, 2003.

Valkenberg, Wilhelmus G. B. M. *Words of the Living God: Place and Function of Holy Scripture in the Theology of St Thomas Aquinas.* Leuven: Peeters, 2000.

van Lieshout, Henri. *La Théorie plotinienne de la vertu: Essai sur la genèse d'un article de la Somme théologique de Saint Thomas.* Fribourg: Studia Friburgensia, 1926.

Vrede, Wilhelm. *Die beiden dem hl. Thomas von Aquin zugeschrieben Kommentare zum Hohen Liede.* Berlin: Germania, 1903.

White, Kevin. "The Passions of the Soul (Ia IIae, qq. 22–48)." In *The Ethics of Aquinas,* edited by Stephen J. Pope, 103–15. Washington, D.C.: Georgetown University Press, 2002.

Index

ALSO IN THE

THOMISTIC RESSOURCEMENT SERIES

Series Editors: Matthew Levering
Thomas Joseph White, OP

Divine Speech in Human Words
Thomistic Engagements with Scripture
Emmanuel Durand
Edited by Matthew K. Minerd

Revelations of Humanity
Anthropological Dimensions of Theological Controversies
Richard Schenk

The Trinity
On the Nature and Mystery of the One God
Thomas Joseph White, OP

Catholic Dogmatic Theology, A Synthesis
Book I, On the Trinitarian Mystery of God
Jean-Hervé Nicolas, OP
Translated by Matthew K. Minerd

A Thomistic Christocentrism
Recovering the Carmelites of Salamanca on the Logic of the Incarnation
Dylan Schrader

Habits and Holiness
Ethics, Theology, and Biopsychology
Ezra Sullivan, OP

Reading the Song of Songs with St. Thomas Aquinas was designed and typeset in Arno by Kachergis Book Design of Pittsboro, North Carolina. It was printed on 60-pound Maple Eggshell Cream and bound by Maple Press of York, Pennsylvania.